Why Are
So Many
Minority Students
in
Special Education?

Why Are
So Many
Minority Students
in
Special Education?

Understanding Race & Disability in Schools

Beth Harry and Janette Klingner
Foreword by Lisa D. Delpit

Teachers College
Columbia University
New York and London

Published by Teachers College Press, 1234 Amsterdam Avenue, New York, NY 10027

Library of Congress Cataloging-in-Publication Data

Harry, Beth
    Why are so many minority students in special education? : understanding race and disability in schools / Beth Harry, Janette Klingner ; foreword by Lisa D. Delpit.
        p. cm.
    Includes bibliographical references and index.
    ISBN 0-8077-4625-8 (cloth : alk. paper) — ISBN 0-8077-4624-X (pbk. : alk. paper)
        1. Special education—United States—Evaluation.   2. Children with disabilities—Education—United States—Evaluation.   3. Discrimination in education—United States.   4. Minorities—Education—United States.
    5. Educational equalization—United States.   I. Klingner, Janette K.
    II. Title.

    LC3981.H36 2006
    371 .9'089—dc22

                                                                    2005048575

ISBN 0-8077-4624-X (paper)
ISBN 0-8077-4625-8 (cloth)

Printed on acid-free paper
Manufactured in the United States of America

13   12   11   10   09   08   07   06   8   7   6   5   4   3   2   1

Contents

Foreword by Lisa D. Delpit   ix

Preface   xiii

Acknowledgments   xv

1   Overview: Ethnic Disproportionality in Special Education   1

    Ethnic Disproportionality in Special Education Programs   2
    Constructing Disabilities in Schools   8
    Race and Disability: Parallel or Converging Discourses?   10
    The Paradox of the IDEA   12
    A Process Approach to Understanding
       Ethnic Disproportionality   15
    The School District of Hyphenated Identities   18
    Organization of the Book   21
    Our Premise   22

2   School Structure: Institutional Bias and Individual Agency   23

    School Leadership: Assignment of Principals to Schools   25
    Teacher Quality: Hiring and Retaining Good Teachers   26
    Discipline Policies   33
    Scheduling and Interruptions: "We're the Ones Who
       Make Them Hyper!"   36
    Conclusions   38

3   Cultural Consonance, Dissonance, and the Nuances of Racism   40

    Racism as a Structural Issue   41
    Documenting Behavior and Interpreting Racism   45
    Perceived Racial Bias in Classroom Arrangements and Referrals   48
    Ethnicity in Team Membership, Referrals, and Teaching Styles   49
    Crossing the Bias Barriers   53
    Conclusions   55

4   In the Classroom: Opportunity to Learn   56

    Contrasting Schools: Inequity in Opportunities to Learn   57
    Contrasting Classrooms: Students' Variable Behavior
        Across Settings   63
    Conclusions   67

5   The Construction of Family Identity:
    Stereotypes and Cultural Capital   70

    School Voices: "It Comes from the Home"   71
    Home Voices: "Doing the Best I Can"   77
    Stereotypes, Cultural Capital, and "Risk"   85
    Conclusions   89

6   At the Conference Table:
    The Discourse of Identity Construction   91

    The Rational Model   92
    Placement Patterns Across Schools   93
    The Culture of Referral   95
    Guidelines for Referrals   95
    The Teacher as Initiator; High and Low Referrers   97
    Alternative Strategies   102
    "Qualifying" for Special Education: A Rock or a Soft Place?   103
    Conclusions   111

7   Bilingual Issues and the Referral Process   113

    The Rational Model   113
    Inadequate Assessment   115
    Staff Confusion   115
    Differentiating Between English-Language Acquisition
        and Learning Disabilities   117
    Variable Referral Rates   118
    Parents' Role in the Process   119
    Conclusions   121

8   Constructing Educable Mental Retardation:
    Cracks and Redundancies   123

    "Falling Between the Cracks"   124
    Crossing the Border: From Delayed Development
        to Mental Retardation   125
    Conclusions   130

9   Constructing Learning Disabilities:
    Redundancies and Discrepancies   132

        Dilemmas of Definition and Assessment   133
        Crossing the Border: From Low Academic Achievement
            to Learning Disability   135
        Conclusions   144

10 Constructing Behavior Disorders:
    From Troubling to Troubled Behavior   146

        Matthew   147
        Kanita   148
        Robert   151
        Edith   154
        Conclusions   157

11 Into Special Education: Exile or Solution?   159

        Special Education Benefits: Ideal Versus Reality   159
        Variable Quality in EH Programs   167
        Restrictive Environments   168
        Low Rate of Exit from Special Education Programs   171
        Conclusions   171

12 Conclusion   173

        Findings and Recommendations   173
        In Conclusion: Attending to School-Based Risk   181

References   185

Index   195

About the Authors   207

Foreword

IN A RECENT speech, Renaissance scholar Asa Hilliard (2004) asked his audience to compare animals' strategies for educating their young to our own. Bears, for example, know what their cubs need to learn and proceed to teach them from birth. They continue teaching until their young learn what they need to know to survive in their world.

We, on the other hand, are consumed with issues of capacity and labeling. We first try to assess a child's capacity for learning in a variety of areas. We then determine whether the array of capacities each child exhibits fits into some predetermined category of capacity models. Teaching begins only after each child is sufficiently labeled as having low, medium, or high capacity, or as fitting into some "special" category of capacities. Imagine what would happen if bears followed our illustrious example. There would probably be so few bears who knew enough to survive that their continued presence in the world's ecological landscape would be greatly compromised. And yet we continue to believe that the system of assessment of capacity and labeling will assist our young in learning what they need to survive in our environment.

This book questions that premise. Would it not make more sense, the authors ask, to just teach children what they need to know, to provide them with the assistance they need to learn without concern about labeling and categorizing, and to keep teaching them until they have learned what they need to know?

This book also examines the assessment and labeling process itself. Is the system of special education systematically reproducing the racial and social inequities of our society instead of alleviating them? Are we burdening children of color with labels of "emotionally handicapped" and "mentally retarded" when the labels do not fit, and only serve to further marginalize them from the mainstream? Even when the labels are accurately applied, wouldn't it make more sense to avoid the stigma of labeling and, again, simply provide whatever assistance an individual child might need to maximize learning?

The issue of labeling brings to mind many young people's experiences. I had the opportunity to witness a group of dynamic African American high school students from my hometown of Baton Rouge, Louisiana, as they made a presentation at a national conference for educational researchers. The students, with the assistance of a local university professor, had conducted a carefully researched oral history project about their high school, one of the first high schools created after the Civil War for Black students in the South. Their research methodology and the data they had gathered were impressive and worthy of professional researchers. Their presentation, with the accompanying visuals and audio feed, was both engaging and thought provoking. As they concluded their findings, the audience gave them a standing ovation.

A question and answer period followed. An audience member asked about the current racial mix of the school, whether there were now White students enrolled, and if so, if any of them participated in the research project. One of the young people responded, "Oh yes, there are White kids at our school, but we don't ever work with them because they're all gifted." There was a rather stunned silence until one of the group's sponsors explained that their high school, located in what was still the heart of the Black community, was a magnet program for gifted students, and that all of the White students in the school were in the separately run "gifted" program, which shared no classes or resources with the all-Black "regular" program. As the implications of this revealing new information sank in, there was another hush in the room, until an audience member rose to her feet and spoke with great power and authority: "Young people, do not ever say that the word 'gifted' does not belong to you. You have proven through your work and your presentation that *you* are gifted. Someone else giving a label to others for political reasons has no relevance to you. *You* are gifted. Remember what you have done today and remember who and what you are. Thank you for your brilliance." The room was electrified with applause and shouts of approval. One could only ponder the messages that the "regular" program youngsters who did not attend the conference received on a daily basis from the very existence of a program in their midst in which only the White kids were gifted.

Race-linked labeling strongly reinforces the messages children of African ancestry get from the larger society. One young African American eighth grader asked his student teacher, "So, Ms. Summers, they made us the slaves because we're dumb, right?" How can we lead all children to their birthright of brilliance when we put them into settings where they are told covertly and overtly, that the labels ascribed to them indicate "less than"? I have received numerous telephone calls from distraught African American parents who have moved to the suburbs in search of quality education, only to have their sons or daughters (mostly sons), referred to special education classes.

The famous motivational speaker Les Brown spent most of his school years in special education classes. He tells the story of waiting for a high school friend outside the latter's "regular" classroom and having the teacher, Mr. Washington, call him, Brown, into the room to demonstrate a math problem on the blackboard. When Brown protested that he could not possibly come into the classroom, much less do a math problem, because he was "educable mentally retarded," Mr. Washington came from behind his desk, looked at him and said, "Don't ever say that again. Someone's opinion of you does not have to become your reality" (Brown, 1996). Brown credits this man's words, and subsequent mentoring support, with his completing high school and moving on to an extraordinary career. Rather than label and categorize, Mr. Washington simply taught.

I believe this is what the authors of this book call on us to do: just teach our children in whatever ways work best for them. They ask that we not concern ourselves with the kind of labeling and sorting that can serve to reinforce the negative stereotypes that this country's history has spawned. *We just need to teach them what they need to know.*

—Lisa D. Delpit
Eminent Scholar and Executive Director, Center for Urban
Education and Innovation, Florida International University

REFERENCES

Brown, L. (1996). "Mr. Washington." In J. Canfield & V. Hansen (Eds.), *A third serving of chicken soup for the soul.* Deerfield Beach, FL: Health Communications.
Hilliard, A. (2004, November). Keynote/Speech. *Urban Educational Expo*, Miami, FL.

Preface

THE SCHOOL DISTRICT in which we conducted our research has shown a strong concern regarding the issue of overrepresentation, as well as a commitment to working to improve its referral and decision-making process. Key special education administrators welcomed our request for research on this sensitive and controversial topic. They facilitated our access to schools and responded positively to even the most critical of our findings. They took the initiative in reaching out to their general-education colleagues in an effort to collaborate to improve the referral process. They also invited our opinions on their revisions of the Child Study Team, now known as the Student Support Team. New procedures require specific goals, target dates, and rigorous monitoring of progress for each child brought to the team. We are encouraged by these efforts. We thank our school-district colleagues for their support of our work and hope that this book will be received by the field as an effort to contribute to a more effective construction of special education.

This district can provide a model for others in terms of its collaboration with us as university researchers, as well as collaboration between general education and special education district administrators. It is through such partnerships that special education administrators can position themselves to play a role in developing effective intervention models designed to reduce inappropriate referrals to special education. Because the federal government now permits school districts to use discretion in deciding how to spend a percentage of IDEA funds, special education administrators have resources to "bring to the table" when meeting with their general-education colleagues. This enables leaders who in the past have worked separately, in what seemed to many like parallel universes, to come together to develop a shared vision and plan for assisting those students who show early signs of struggling in the general-education environment.

A note on terminology: Any terminology purporting to describe a group that has traditionally been oppressed or marginalized is potentially controversial. This is as true for people with disabilities as for ethnic groups. The reason is that the process of affirming identity includes discarding the negative stereotyping that has been imposed by others and creating language that reflects both group solidarity and individual realities. Any term may be interpreted as either too general or too exclusive.

Aware of the sensitivity of this process, we struggled to determine an appropriate umbrella term to use in our title. We settled on the term "minority students" after considering as alternatives "culturally and linguistically diverse (CLD) students" and "students of color." We decided on this term because it is more inclusive than the other two. We are aware that it is often criticized because it appears to diminish the importance of a group, while, in fact, such groups may be in the minority in one society but in the majority in others, even in the world. Nevertheless, the term is widely understood in the United States and internationally to imply issues of power that have resulted in the devaluing of racial, cultural, or linguistic features of a group. The concept of power is not implicit in the term "CLD." Nor does it necessarily include the concept of race, since ethnic groups may differ in their cultural and linguistic features, yet may share the same racial identity as the society's mainstream. Thus the term "CLD" does not necessarily include non-White groups. Conversely, "students of color," a term designed to target non-White identity, is limited in that it may be perceived as excluding Whites who identify with groups that have historically been oppressed within the society. We believe that "minority" allows for different configurations of these salient features.

Finally, a note on confidentiality: All names of schools and individuals are pseudonyms. In no case has the real identity of schools or individuals been revealed to school district administrators or to any other persons.

Acknowledgments

W E WISH TO thank our project coordinator, Keith Sturges, and our colleague, Robert Moore, for their extensive help in carrying out this research. Their assistance was invaluable. We would also like to express our gratitude for the essential contributions of our research assistants: Elizabeth Cramer, Juliet Hart, Cassaundra Wimes, Sherene McKesey, Patricia Stevens, Josefa Rascón, Thaissa Champagne, Heather Rutland, Aileen Angulo, Tony Ford, Christina Herrera, Tamara Celestin, and Jennifer Dorce. We could not have collected such an extensive amount of data without their tireless participation in the project. We also thank our consultants, Alfredo Artiles and Lisa Delpit, for their inspired insights and helpful feedback.

We dedicate this book to all culturally and linguistically diverse students who have experienced less than equitable educational opportunities in U.S. public schools, especially those who have been inappropriately identified as having disabilities. We thank the families who allowed their children to participate and are particularly grateful to those who, by welcoming us into their homes, provided us with a holistic view of their children. We also dedicate this book to the administrators, teachers, and other school personnel who so graciously opened their doors to us despite the sensitivity of the topic. We especially wish to thank Ron Felton and Joe Jackson, the "gatekeepers" whose support made this work possible.

We offer our heartfelt appreciation to our husbands, Bernard Telson and Don Klingner, and our children, Mark Teelucksingh, Heidi Warden, and Amy and John Klingner. We are deeply grateful for their love, encouragement, and patience over the years.

Finally, we wish to acknowledge the support of the U.S. Department of Education, Office of Special Education Programs, Grant #H324C980165-99C. We thank our project officers, Grace Zamora Durán and Bonnie Jones, for their unwavering support of our work.

CHAPTER 1

Overview: Ethnic Disproportionality in Special Education

IN MANY SCHOOLS across the United States, February is the month for honoring the history of the people who became American by virtue of forced emigration from Africa to the new world. It is the month for teaching about the accomplishments of African American heroes and martyrs, for learning that, because of their courage in the face of overwhelming oppression, the ideals of equality and freedom that once were a reality only for some, are now a reality for all. As part of this project, many children all over the country are introduced to Martin Luther King Jr.'s famous statement of his vision of racial equality and brotherhood, and many are required to write their own versions of Dr. King's dream.

Matthew was an African American second grader in a school where almost all the children of his ethnicity were bused from a low-income neighborhood "on the other side of the highway," into a school in a wealthy, predominantly White neighborhood where high academic achievement on the annual statewide tests earned the school an A in the governor's school-evaluation plan. The children in Matthew's class were given a dittoed sheet with a silhouette of Martin Luther King Jr. in the top right corner and six or seven lines on which to write their "dream." In a neat, slanted script, Matthew wrote:

> I have a dream that there will be no more wars. There will be no more fighting, throw away the drugs. I have a dream that one day there will be no more rich people poor people. We will all be equal. I have a dream that we will all wear helmets with our stoooters and bikes.

Matthew's identification of helmets as an indicator of social status in his community gave our research team a fascinating insight into the sensitivity of an 8-year-old. We believe that it tells us more about Matthew than did his label as a child with "emotional disturbance."

ETHNIC DISPROPORTIONALITY IN SPECIAL EDUCATION PROGRAMS

In the 1998–99 school year, Matthew was one of the 1,111,650 African American children served in special education programs across the United States. A National Academy of Sciences (NAS) study of ethnic representation in special education (Donovan & Cross, 2002) indicates that, in that year, across ethnic groups and disability categories, this number placed African American children at the highest risk of receiving a disability label—a risk index of 14.28% as contrasted with 13.10% for American Indians/Alaskan Natives, 12.10% for Whites, 11.34% for Hispanics, and 5.31% for Asians. These figures reflect a pattern that was first pointed out by Dunn (1968) and further elaborated on by Mercer (1973). Despite some variability by disability category, and a notable reduction in aggregated placement rates for Hispanics, the pattern has continued to be a thorn in the side of the education system. It has been so troubling that the Office for Civil Rights (OCR) has collected data on the problematic categories (to be explained below) ever since the early 1980s, and the National Academy of Sciences has twice been commissioned to study the issue (Heller, Holtzman, & Messick, 1982; Donovan & Cross, 2002).

Variability Across Place and Time

There are three crucial points about the figures cited above, all of which point to the tremendous variability across time and place in the pattern of ethnic disproportionality in special education. First, the figures are an aggregate of placement rates across 13 categories of disability. Second, they are an aggregate of placement rates across states. Third, behind these figures is the important history of changing rates of usage for what have come to be known as the "high incidence" categories. We will discuss each of these points in turn.

When these data are disaggregated by disability category, it becomes clear that the risk rates for African Americans and Native Americans are actually much higher in three of the "judgment" categories—those that depend on clinical judgment rather than on verifiable biological data. There are four such categories—Mental Retardation (MR), specifically Mild Mental Retardation (MMR),* also referred to as Educable Mental Retardation; Specific Learning

---

*Although only 17 states subcategorize MR according to level of severity (Muller & Markowitz, 2004), IQ scores at the higher end of this category represent the "high incidence" side of the MR spectrum.

Disability (SLD), also referred to as Learning Disability (LD); Emotional Disturbance (ED); and Speech and Language Impairments (SLI).* The OCR's focus has been on the first three of these, since the SLI category has evidenced only slight disproportionality and has not been seen as problematic by the OCR. These four categories are also referred to as high-incidence categories, since the vast majority of children served in special education are placed in these categories. By contrast, the other nine categories are referred to as "low incidence," since the numbers are small. These are Multiple Disabilities, Hearing Impairment, Orthopedic Impairment, Other Health Impairment, Visual Impairment, Autism, Traumatic Brain Injury, Deaf-Blind, and Developmental Delay. In these categories there is no evidence of systematic variation by ethnicity. As the NAS report (Donovan & Cross, 2002) noted:

> One of the reasons these [low-incidence] categories are not monitored by OCR is that for most of the disabilities represented, few would question the professional judgment or accuracy of a diagnosis in these cases. Moreover, the representation of racial/ethnic groups in these categories has not been at issue in the courts. (pp. 54–55)

As this statement suggests, many *have* questioned the accuracy of the professional judgments made in diagnosing EMR, LD, and ED. The most famous case was *Larry P. v. Riles* (1979/1984), in which the courts supported the plaintiffs' charge that the IQ tests being used to place children in the EMR category were biased against African American children. While the outcomes of litigation on this issue have varied, the range of cases points to the continuing contentious nature of ethnic disproportionality in categories based on clinical judgment (Donovan & Cross, 2002; Reschly, Kicklighter, & McGee, 1988).

The second crucial point to note is that these figures also represent an aggregate of placement rates across all states. When disaggregated by state, the picture becomes very complicated, defying adequate analysis (Donovan & Cross, 2002). The nationwide pattern for African Americans is of overrepresentation in EMR and ED categories though not in LD, but a closer look shows much variability in use of this category according to state. Similarly, while the national figures show no overrepresentation of Hispanics in any category, the picture is quite different in certain states. For example, according to Donovan and Cross:

> The nationally aggregated data have been interpreted to suggest no overrepresentation of either Black or Hispanic students in LD. But state-level data

---

*While disability terminology varies across states, in this book, we use those terms that are most commonly known.

tell a more complex story. For Black students, for example, the risk index ranges from 2.33 percent in Georgia to 12.19 percent in Delaware. For Hispanic students, the risk index ranges from 2.43 in Georgia to 8.93 in Delaware. Clearly there is overrepresentation for these two minorities in the LD category in some states. (p. 67)

In addition to this variability across ethnic groups and states, there have been marked changes in overall rates of usage of these categories over time, specifically, a reduction in the use of EMR, a dramatic increase in the use of LD, and a notable increase in the use of ED. The NAS report (Donovan & Cross, 2002) indicates that, from 1974 to 1998, the risk of any student (averaged across ethnic groups) being identified as EMR decreased from 1.58% to 1.37%. In LD, the increased usage was referred to as "epidemic" (p. 47), having gone from 1.21% in 1974 to 6.02% in 1998. For ED, the risk of identification increased from just over 1% in 1974 to just over 5% in 1998. This dramatic state-to-state variability and the changes over time caused Ysseldyke, Algozzine, & Thurlow (1992) to observe that the patterns look more like figures from the Dow Jones average than real disabilities among children.

What is to be made of such variability? Overall, most scholars agree that the variability and the changes over time and place are a sign of the instability and ambiguity of the categories themselves. Further, it seems evident that the direction of the MMR/LD shift reflects a response to social and political pressures. In order to understand this it is important to note the key difference between the mental retardation and learning disability designations: While EMR is used to refer to a significant delay or impairment in overall global development and functioning, LD indicates that the individual's overall development is within the normal range but that there is a specific area of learning (most frequently reading) in which the child falls significantly below the norm for his/her age. Thus, EMR is generally interpreted as a much more stigmatizing label than LD. It seems likely that perceptions of stigma, as well as sensitivity to interpretations of racism, contributed to the dramatic reduction in the use of the EMR category over the years, especially in the light of the *Larry P. v. Riles* (1979) ruling mentioned above. Conversely, the preference for the less stigmatizing LD category has led to the suggestion that this category is used inappropriately in school districts that want to avoid the charge of racial imbalance in EMR (MacMillan, Gresham, & Bocian, 1998).

Given the LD category's dependence on clinical judgment, we must ask why minority students were not, prior to the current period, overrepresented in this category. Several scholars have suggested a covert racial intent in the way LD was initially conceptualized. Collins and Camblin's (1983) succinct analysis explained that the definition itself effectively excluded many Black students through two mechanisms. First, the definition excluded learning difficulties that could have been caused by environmental factors (including poverty), and second, it required a discrepancy between the student's score on an IQ test and his or her score on a measure of academic performance. Collins and Camblin argued that cultural bias inherent in IQ tests makes it more difficult for Black students to attain a score high enough to contrast significantly with a low academic level.

Sleeter (1986), in a scathing analysis of the motivation behind this construction of the LD category, argued that LD came into being as a result of the 1960s concern with making the United States more competitive in the era of Sputnik. According to Sleeter, White middle-class families whose children were not proving competitive in that ethos sought the LD label as an alternative to the more generalized, more stigmatizing label of mental retardation. As Ferri (2004) observed, this process provided White middle-class students with greater access to the more privileged place within the hierarchy of special education categories, and "allowed racist notions of ability to remain in place . . . since White students might be failing but not for the same reasons as minority, poor, and immigrant students" (p. 511). Taking the argument further, Ferri questioned whether recent research focusing on dyslexia and other subgroups of LD may serve the purpose of further racial or class resegregation within the category.

The continuing debate over the validity of the discrepancy criterion for LD (Artiles, Trent, & Kuan, 1997; Fletcher & Morris, 1986; Fletcher et al., 1998; Stanovich, 1991), and the concern about the manipulation of eligibility criteria (MacMillan et al., 1998), indicate that the conceptualization of this disability is currently up for revision. Reid and Valle (2004) argued for a reconceptualization of LD "in terms of human variation rather than pathology" (p. 473). In the ED category, despite the presence of reliable rating scales, subjectivity continues to be evident in professional practice (Donovan & Cross, 2002). This is particularly so because, in many states, a determination of ED depends on projective testing, a process susceptible to the charge of subjectivity and unreliability (Gresham, 1993; Knoff, 1993; Motta, Little, & Tobin, 1993). The fact that the use of these tests varies widely across states (Hosp & Reschly, 2002) demonstrates that we cannot assume any equivalence among children designated ED from state to state. Moreover, according to a nationwide study by Muller and Markowitz (2004), differences in definitions and eligibility criteria for all the disability categories point out the lack of comparability across states.

From our point of view, the variability in patterns of disability designation over time and place simply underscores the main argument of this book—that the categories do not necessarily reflect real disabilities within children. Rather, their differential usage supports the perspective that the categories are reliant on definition and interpretation, which are influenced by social and political agendas of various states, groups, and individuals.

Coming Back to Matthew

Matthew's school, which we will call Sunnybrook, was a microcosm of the national picture on ethnic disproportionality in special education. African American children represented approximately 17% of the student population. They represented, however, approximately 35% of those served in special education classes for children with LD. Since Sunnybrook's special education program served only children designated as having LD, those designated as having ED or MR were transferred to a school that offered self-contained classes for children with these disabilities.

When Matthew was referred for evaluation, the decision on his disability designation seemed to have been a toss-up for either a learning disability or an emotional disturbance label. Although his reading and math skills were measured as being almost on grade level, and his composition and spelling were quite competent for an 8-year-old, Matthew's grades were generally at the bottom end of his high-achieving class. Further, his mood swings from emotional outbursts to silent withdrawal made him a difficult child to handle in a second-grade class of about 28 children. Knowing that Matthew had witnessed a death in the family, the school had provided counseling, which, according to the teacher, did not seem to help. When his African American classroom teacher initially referred him for evaluation, the referral papers cited "learning problems." However, the psychologist conducting the assessment reported no evidence of learning disability but found Matthew eligible for services under the category emotionally disturbed.

The school to which Matthew was transferred served a population with similar racial and socioeconomic demographics, but at least 80% of the students in the ED program were Black. Before the end of his third-grade year, Matthew had become "a star" in this structured, behavior modification program, almost always earning his full quota of behavior points and maintaining an academic level above those of most of his peers. His mother, who described Matthew as having a "bad temper," had accepted the placement but disliked the separateness it imposed on her son, and she wondered when the school would decide that he was doing well enough to go back to the regular class in his old school. When our research efforts ended in 2002, Matthew, then a fifth grader, was still doing very well in a self-contained class for children with emotional disturbance, and there was no talk of his return to the mainstream.

This brief summary presents only the kernel of Matthew's story, but it is sufficient to highlight the main purpose of this book. We will demonstrate that what has come to be known as the disproportionate representation of minorities in special education programs is the result of a series of social processes that, once set in motion, are interpreted as the inevitable outcomes of real conditions within children. These social processes do not occur by happenstance, or by the good or evil intentions of a few individuals. Rather, they reflect a set of societal beliefs and values, political agendas, and historical events that combine to construct identities that will become the official version of who these children are. In special education, the construct of disability has become the overriding metaphor by which differences in students' behavior and school achievement are explained. This metaphor comes to be taken for a reality, which, all too often, is treated as permanent. It should not be surprising that race has become intertwined with the construction of special education, since race has been an essential ingredient in the construction of all aspects of American life. Moreover, as Goffman (1963) argued, it is all too easy for categories that are understood as deficient to become associated with one another. But we will come to that theme later.

To those who would say that Matthew's placement was the natural outcome of his own learning and behavioral patterns, we suggest that had any of the circumstances of his situation been different, the outcome might have been different, and instead of being seen as a "disabled" child, Matthew might have been seen as a "normal" 8-year-old in need of continued counseling and an emotionally supportive school environment. We believe that Matthew's official identity was negatively affected by a combination of factors, including his status as a low-income, African American child in a wealthy, high-achieving, predominantly White elementary school; the competition between schools to earn a high rank in the state's testing system; the requirement of a specific deficit label in order for children to qualify for special education services; and the separateness of the general and special education programs.

This is not to say that Matthew had no problems. Rather, it is to say that, once the discourse of disability was set in motion, Matthew's problems came to be defined as a disability, and that disability as a fact. The concept of disability became reified—made into a "thing" that belonged to Matthew, a thing that would be very difficult to discard.

A common objection to this interpretation of events might be the question, But are you saying Matthew did not have a disability? Or, Is there no such thing as a disability? We would answer that there is an infinite range of abilities among individuals and that, while there are certainly individuals whose capacities are much more limited than the average, it is society's decisions related to such individuals that determines whether they will be called disabled. This is particularly true of the high-incidence, "judgment" categories for which Matthew was considered. We do not argue that there are no differences in performance and ability between children. Our concern is with what is made of these differences.

CONSTRUCTING DISABILITIES IN SCHOOLS

Our focus in this book is on the high-incidence disabilities, whose determination depends on clinical judgment rather than hard data. These categories stand on the "soft" side of science and that very "softness" provides the key to their analysis. Effective clinical judgment requires an understanding of the contexts in which children learn, the affective as well as the cognitive processes that influence their learning, and the cultural predispositions that prepare children for formal, academic education. In short, many intangibles that defy measurement and enumeration are essential ingredients of these "disabilities."

The "softness" of the high-incidence categories points also to the role of culture in how cognitive competence and incompetence are defined. As Cole (1996) noted, psychological theories of learning tend to assume that culture is irrelevant to the process of knowledge acquisition. This view ignores the considerable body of literature that demonstrates cross-cultural differences in the structuring of knowledge (Rogoff & Chavajay, 1995). Moreover, many studies have shown differential cultural interpretations of a wide range of impairments, including deafness, blindness, physical deformities, epilepsy, mild mental retardation, learning disabilities, and emotional disturbance (for a comprehensive review, see Kalyanpur & Harry, 1999). We mention this here to emphasize that the attack on the reification of disabilities has come from widely varying quarters and has targeted all but the most gross mental or physical impairments.

High-Incidence Disabilities as Points on the Continuum of Learning and Behavior

The National Academy of Sciences (NAS) has convened two panels to study disproportionality. The work of both these panels is very relevant to our study. The second NAS panel (Donovan & Cross, 2002) approached the issue by seeking data in all possible environments that could contribute to disproportionality. Despite recording a host of potential social, environmental, biological, and educational contributors, the report nonetheless emphasized that the high-incidence disabilities cannot be assumed to represent intrinsic deficits in children. We quote the report at length because it points to the essential ambiguity in what is generally interpreted as a firm set of categories:

The historical concept of a student with a disability or of a gifted student sug-gests that the characteristics of concern are within the child—an individual or fixed-trait model of ability—and that the student with a disability or a gift is qualitatively different from peers. However, for the high incidence disabilities with which we are concerned, as well as for giftedness, both of these proposi-tions are called into question. . . .

In terms of cognitive and behavioral competence, students fall along a continuum . . . there is no black and white distinction between those who have disabilities or gifts and those who do not. At the far ends of the continuum there is little dispute about a child's need for something different. . . . But as one moves away from the extremes, where the line should be drawn between students who do and do not require special supports is unclear. *A variety of forces push on the lines from opposing directions.* . . .

We have argued that where along the continuum of achievement the lines are drawn for specialized education is artificial and variable. Perhaps of greater concern, however, are *factors that affect where a student falls along the con-tinuum.* For students having difficulty in school who do not have a medically diagnosed disability, key aspects of the context of schooling itself, including administrative, curricular/instructional, and interpersonal factors, may contrib-ute to their identification as having a disability and may contribute to the dis-proportionately high or low placements of minorities. The complexity of issues of culture and context in schools makes it nearly impossible to tease out the precise variables that affect patterns of special education placement. (pp. 25–27; emphasis added)

This statement leads us directly to the main purpose of our book: To delineate the "factors that affect where a student falls along the continuum" of student achievement, and to elucidate the "variety of forces [that] push on the lines from opposing directions." We argue that the process of deter-mining children's eligibility for special education is anything but a science. Rather, it is the result of social forces that intertwine to construct an iden-tity of "disability" for children whom the regular-education system finds too difficult to serve.

The ambiguities inherent in converting a continuum into categorical sets are intensified by the social nature of the processes used to determine dis-abilities. Mehan, Hartwick, and Meihls's (1986) 5-year ethnographic study of decision making in special education demonstrated that decisions arrived at in special education conferences were essentially a "ratification of actions taken earlier" (p. 164). Acknowledging that schooling does "sort and stratify . . . students in such a way that differential educational opportunities are made available to them" (p. 171), Mehan et al. argued that this is not a simple process of reflecting students' measured abilities or their background char-acteristics. Rather, they emphasized that every act of evaluating a student, whether face to face or through committees' decisions and reports, constitutes a step in the creation of the student's "social identities" (p. 175). As each step builds on the next, the social identity of the student becomes reified and the evidence is perceived as more and more credible.

This book has a great deal in common with that of Mehan et al., and we acknowledge the influence of their work on ours. Our study cannot lay claim to the level of ethnographic intensity involved in that study, since we tended to take a broader rather than a deeper look at processes across 12 schools, and since our data collection did not include videotaping. Nevertheless, our goals and methods were similar but for one crucial concern: Mehan and his colleagues' study did not focus particularly on the role of race/ethnicity in special education decision making. This book does.

RACE AND DISABILITY: PARALLEL OR CONVERGING DISCOURSES?

Race has been an essential ingredient in the construction of American public education, and inevitably, of special education. With regard to both general and special education, the history of the second half of the 20th century was marked by the struggle for equity. Until the civil rights movement of the 1960s, ethnic minorities and children with disabilities were relegated to the margins of the educational system. Indeed, public schooling was explicitly concerned with containing and limiting the education of such groups (Tyack, 1993). The movement for universal schooling for children with handicapping conditions was fueled by the civil rights movement and deeply influenced by its rhetoric of equality and solidarity. Although these movements have been envisioned as parallel, we believe it is not far-fetched to say that they were actually on a collision course.

The pattern of exclusion introduced by the eugenics movement blended beliefs regarding the genetics of disabilities with beliefs regarding the racial inferiority of non-White peoples. Using the mental-testing movement as the main vehicle for applying the gospel of efficiency to education (Fass, 1991; Gould, 1981), American education became committed to the goal of sorting children. The construction of special education reflected and supported that goal, and by the middle of the century, special classes for "slow learners" were already showing high rates of placement (Gould, 1981). After the *Brown* desegregation decision (*Brown v. Board of Education of Topeka, Kansas*, 1954), special education classes became a vehicle for continued segregation, based on presumed learning deficits (Ferri & Connor, 2005). As these placements were challenged in the courts and in scholarly publications, the blending of special education and minority placements gradually came to public attention (e.g., *Diana v. State Board of Education*, 1970; Dunn, 1968; *Larry P. v. Riles*, 1979; Mercer, 1973).

Skrtic (1991) has offered an illuminating interpretation of the interplay between the needs of U.S. society and the construction of special education. Using the metaphor of a "machine bureaucracy," Skrtic described general education as having been charged with the responsibility of preparing the populace to function effectively in the bureaucratic structures of the society, and to do so by creating schools that were a microcosm of that system. As the mental-testing movement assisted schools in developing systems for sorting students into relatively homogeneous boxes, special education became the corner of the system that could contain those whose differences were perceived to be too extreme to serve in the mainstream. The challenge of an increasingly heterogeneous student population was met by institutionalizing the concept of individual deficit. Skrtic described special education as "the institutional practice that emerged in the 20th century to contain the failure of public education to realize its democratic ideals" (1991, p. 46).

Thus, sometime in the early 1970s, the special education movement and the desegregation movement officially collided. Those whom the society had rejected, and had excluded from its public schools, would meet in the special education system. The concept of deficit, by then an ingrained part of the educational belief system, would become the chief metaphor to encompass difference.

Special Education in a Standards-Based Environment

The current policy context of education in the United States adds to this history one more dimension of the sorting-and-classifying paradigm—the use of standardized, statewide testing to determine both teacher and school effectiveness. Through the drive for accountability, the movement seeks to ensure that students attain a predetermined standard of education. The recent restructuring of the Elementary and Secondary Education Act (ESEA), in the form of the No Child Left Behind Act (NCLB), mandates nationwide academic assessment of reading and mathematics achievement from the third to the eighth grade. The mandate includes testing of students in special education and allows for the application of appropriate accommodations according to children's individualized education plans (IEPs).

There are various ways in which the high-stakes environment is detrimental to minority students: Most noted up to this time is a teach-to-the-test syndrome that focuses on the lowest-level cognitive skills, such as formulaic writing, rote learning, how to bubble-in multiple-choice tests, and how to choose answers by a process of eliminating obviously incorrect items (Lomax, West, & Harmon, 1995; McNeil & Valenzuela, 2000; Sacks, 2000). McNeil and Valenzuela's 10-year longitudinal study of the impact of high-stakes testing in Texas showed that these effects were particularly evident in schools with a predominance of African American or Latino students or both.

In the state in which we conducted our research, as in many others, "accountability" is translated into a variety of rewards and punishments for teachers and schools. The "grading" of schools, based largely on the results of standardized testing, determines important outcomes such as the intrinsic rewards of being highly respected in the community, a variety of extrinsic rewards usually revolving around financial and material resources, and the negative sanction of provision of vouchers for students to transfer out of failing schools. But here's the rub: Although all students must take the state-wide exams, up until the time that this research ended in 2002, the scores of the students in special education did not "count" in the "grading" of schools. The implication is obvious, that it behooves a school aspiring only to a high grade to have as many potential culprits as possible placed in special education at the time of the testing. The fact that many of the lowest-achieving students are of ethnic minority status places these groups at increased risk of inappropriate special education placement. Shocking as this may sound, it was openly acknowledged by many school personnel in our study. Once more, the "machine bureaucracy" (Skrtic, 1991) works to the detriment of minorities.

THE PARADOX OF THE IDEA

An obvious challenge to the foregoing interpretation of special education's sorting process is that the Individuals with Disabilities Education Act (IDEA) and its predecessor, the Education for All Handicapped Children Act (EHA), represent a landmark achievement on behalf of the thousands of children for whom there had been no available schooling prior to 1975. There is no question that this powerful legislation represents the continuing commitment of U.S. society to its goal of equity. It therefore seems paradoxical that the provision of costly and specialized educational services should be interpreted as less than beneficial to children in need.

In addressing this question, Reschly, Kicklighter, and McGee (1988) proposed that the strong objections to special education overrepresentation arise from a reaction against the historical arguments of genetically based racial inferiority as well as from the perception that special education programs may not be beneficial. We agree with these arguments but would take them further. First, as contrasted with compensatory programs such as Head Start, which require only economic eligibility and are voluntarily chosen by parents, special education services can be obtained only through a child's being "proven" to be "disabled." Often, the recommendation is imposed by the school, not chosen by the parents. Further, the stigma that accompanies a disability label is seen as undesirable, particularly by people who are already stigmatized on grounds of ethnicity.

It is not just that members of minority groups, especially African Americans, construe their overrepresentation in disability categories as evidence of continuing racism, but that the labeling process, with the official sanction of the science of psychology, moves rapidly towards reification. In an ethos in which science rules, what else can such a pattern do but confirm historical stereotypes in the minds of those disposed to clinging to them? Thus, the stigma attached to cognitive or behavioral disabilities battles with the good intention of the provision of specialized services.

It is not surprising that the notion of intrinsic deficit has such sticking power. Labeling theorists (Becker, 1969; Bogdan & Knoll, 1988; Goffman, 1963) have long pointed out that when an official designation becomes "reified," it is interpreted as a definition of the person, and it overshadows, even excludes, the numerous other traits, abilities, and nuances of the individual. These classifications or labels become, as Goffman (1963) said, the "master status" by which the individual is defined. This process can be seen in the construction of various aspects of identity, including race, gender, and disability. While some classifications were developed with the specific intention of separating and isolating, as in the case of the construction of racial categories in the United States (Ferrante & Brown, 1998; Rosenblum & Travis, 2000), others have been conceptualized as means of identifying and serving people in need. This is the usual interpretation of the application of disability labels. The paradox arises when the classification system, instead of serving those in need, does them greater harm.

Besides the damage done to the individual by internalization of the label, there is also the possibility that the classification system can operate like a straitjacket, limiting the interpretation and insights of professionals. These negative effects are particularly likely in the practice of the mental health professions because of the overwhelming appeal of science as the basis of psychology and psychiatry, both of which have had a powerful influence on the conceptualization of special education. This conceptualization becomes doctrinal when endorsed by the *Diagnostic and Statistical Manual of Mental Disorders* (DSM) and accorded the "highest stamp of legitimate authority in the field" (Schwartz & Wiggins, 2002, p. 201).

Yet the scientific academy itself is divided on the extent to which we can put faith in the science of these fields. In a collection of essays titled *Prescriptions and Descriptions: Values, Mental Disorders, and the DSMs*, Sadler (2002) and his colleagues laid out the multifaceted debate around the development and validity of the DSM manuals. Sadler stated that the DSM-III, "through operationalizing diagnostic concepts into specific criteria," strove to "diminish ambiguities in psychiatric diagnostic concepts" (p. 5). He argued that, despite the advantages of this move toward greater accountability, ambiguities and value judgments are inherent in mental health practice, influencing "what is clinically relevant (what the clinician sees or doesn't see); what clinical evidence is salient, useful, or otherwise important; the criteria of pathology; the credibility of the diagnostic process, even the priorities in designing a classification" (p. 5).

To examine the other side of the paradox, we must ask what happens if it is decided that a child who is failing in school is not eligible for special services. Many professionals in our study were adamant on this point: This child would simply "fall between the cracks," and many do. As one psychologist put it, "No LD, no services." Thus, special education placement was often seen as the only alternative to school failure—a protective move in favor of a child; or, as the psychologist quoted above said, a move "to save their lives."

Such faith in the efficacy of special education is not borne out by research. Although the literature on special education interventions reports numerous studies of effective practices tested under research conditions, it appears that these practices are not widely disseminated or implemented (Donovan & Cross, 2002). Moreover, postschool outcomes are not encouraging: Data from the National Longitudinal Transition Study of Students in Special Education (SRI International, 1995), reporting on the postsecondary activities of former students who had been enrolled in LD programs, indicate that only 73% of these ex-students were working or studying, while only 50% of individuals who had been in ED programs were employed. Across these two categories, more than a third of the students did not graduate from high school. Thus, we believe that if the process of special education placement is, for some students, a matter of social decision making and questionable outcomes, the continuing pattern of certain minority groups being represented at disproportionately high rates must be treated as problematic.

The fact that there is a "crack" between general and special education speaks directly to one of the disadvantages of the *either*-"normal"-*or*-"disabled" construction of special education. If the continuum of achievement is, in fact, seamless, why should special education services not be tailored to whichever point on the continuum a child occupies, instead of the child having to be tailored to a set of arbitrarily determined categories?

In summary, there is no escaping the negative implications of minority overrepresentation in special education. Despite the NAS's acknowledgment that the high-incidence categories represent "artificial and variable" cutoff points on a continuum of ability, it may be only the academics on the academy's panel, and select school district administrators, who understand it in this way. For most teachers, a child so labeled most likely "has a disability," just as, according to one of our study participants, "some children have blue eyes." For the child who is labeled, and the family who must agree to the label and the placement, "to be labeled by mental deficit terminology is . . . to face a potential lifetime of self-doubt" (Gergen, 1994, p. 151). Moreover, the educational system's attempt at the categorization of children has resulted in dilemmas that force professionals to simplify findings, ignoring important contradictions and nuances of children's cognition and emotion. As Gergen (1994) argued, the discipline of psychology has produced a paradoxical situation in which the mental health professions' "prevailing vision of human betterment" has resulted in a "network of increasing entanglements for the culture at large" (p. 143). We concur, and we believe that this paradox and its "increasing entanglements" are well illustrated by the study we report in this book.

A PROCESS APPROACH TO UNDERSTANDING ETHNIC DISPROPORTIONALITY

In studying ethnic disproportionality we focused on the complex processes that led to special education placement. Our research was modeled on the recommendation of the NAS's first study of disproportionality (Heller et al., 1982). That report began by stating that one cannot assume that ethnic disproportionality in special education is a problem, since it could be that certain groups of students need special education in disproportionate amounts. Thus, the panel argued, to know whether or not the pattern is problematic, we must ascertain the adequacy and appropriateness of all phases of the placement process: early instruction, pre-referral activities, the decision to refer, and the process of assessment. Finally, we must know whether the outcome of the process—placement in a special education program—was beneficial to the child. If we find bias or inappropriate practice at any phase of this process, then we must treat disproportionality as a problem.

This approach begins its examination at the level of the school and asks two questions: first, whether the school provided adequate opportunities for children to progress and, second, whether it engaged in biased or discriminatory practices in making decisions about the evaluation and placement of children who were not progressing adequately. It does not ask whether the child came to school with a disability. It does not ask whether the child was predisposed, by virtue of prior exposure or experience, to have a disability. It simply asks whether the school did its job.

This is an important distinction for two reasons. First, in the deficit-oriented culture described by Gergen (1994), the presupposition of intrinsic deficit tends to trump all other reasoning. School personnel are heavily influenced by this thinking, if only because they operate under a legal framework that requires professionals to seek, find, and serve students with disabilities. Second, when deficit interpretations are being applied to members of a group that has historically been viewed through the lens of deficit, the deck is powerfully loaded. As critical race theorists have asserted, racism is "normal, not aberrant, in American society" (Delgado & Stefancic, 2000, p. xvi). For many people, blaming the victim is as natural as breathing.

"Risk" in Schooling

Studies of risk have focused on the long-term impact of early home experience. For example, Sameroff, Seifer, Baldwin, and Baldwin (1993) found that IQ scores are quite stable across time and are negatively affected when a child has been exposed to multiple risk factors in the home. Using a composite score that included 10 home-based risk factors, the studies found that the combination, rather than any one factor, accounted for depressed IQ scores at ages 4 and 13. Similarly, the research of Blair and Scott (2000) demonstrated strong correlations between pre- and perinatal risk factors and special education placement.

Strangely, these studies did not look at what happened at school during the years from age 4 to age 13. They did not ask how school experiences may have contributed to depressed IQ scores remaining depressed or to special education placement. This is particularly ironic when it is obvious that IQ tests are focused on the kinds of learning acquired in school. According to the NAS (Donovan & Cross, 2002), these should be considered "tests of general achievement, reflecting broad culturally rooted ways of thinking and problem solving" (p. 284). If much of the IQ test score reflects learning and experience, and school learning in particular (for example, vocabulary and analytic thinking), and if these children are exposed to poor schooling, then their ability to increase their scores on these tests will be further limited.

This gap in conceptualization of the problem is glaring, and Keogh (2000) has called for a better understanding of "risk and protective influences in schools" (p. 6) as well as in families. As we will show throughout this book, the presence of multiple family- and community-based risks tends to increase the likelihood of *school-based risk*, which appears in the form of poor teachers, overcrowded classrooms, negative social-class and ethnic biases, and a host of other detrimental influences. Thus, "risk" cannot be considered without attention to risks induced and exacerbated by poor schooling.

We acknowledge that it is extremely challenging to identify the school-based factors that affect where students fall along the continuum. Sophisticated models of statistical analysis have attempted the kind of teasing-out referred to in the NAS's statement cited earlier and have succeeded in pointing to important correlations, but they cannot explain the reasons or processes that cause these patterns to occur. For example, a line of work by Oswald, Coutinho, Best, and Singh (1999) displays the complex interplay between numerous key variables, such as size of ethnic group in a district and high- versus low-poverty conditions. Noting that Black and Hispanic students were more frequently labeled LD in high-poverty districts but more frequently labeled MR in low-poverty districts, the authors concluded that the MR label was inappropriately applied. Conversely, MacMillan et al. (1998), in a study of LD labeling, found that the LD label was inappropriately applied to Black students who had in fact qualified for MR. The NAS report (Donovan & Cross, 2002) argued that the latter trend could represent a competing hypothesis to explain the findings of Oswald and his team.

The foregoing debate points to the fact that, absent a qualitative investigation, we cannot know how bias in placements operates, whether through individual decision making; group pressure; or institutionalized forces built into the fabric of the education system, or even the society as a whole. As Mehan et al. (1986) observed, the creation of official student identities does not occur solely in face-to-face interactions. The same is true of racism or any type of bias. Bias is often inherent in social situations: in funding patterns, organizational arrangements, personnel hierarchies, and numerous other structural aspects of any social organization. There may be in an institution not one individual who professes or explicitly displays bias, yet all members may be, by virtue of uncritical participation in the system, purveyors of biased practice.

Special Education as a Support Rather Than an Alternative

As special educators, we are all too aware of the history of exclusion and oppression that brought special education services into existence. We believe that special education has a role to play in supporting and assisting children and youth whose needs make them more vulnerable to the competitive contexts of schooling and less receptive to run-of-the-mill, generic instruction in an education system whose mainstream caters to the middle. Therefore, we continue to believe that the individualization espoused by special education is desirable and necessary in education. We continue to believe that, for purposes of practicality, school systems will need to conform to specified guidelines regarding which children should be afforded the individualized supports of special education.

We do not believe, however, that it is necessary for guidelines for eligibility to be based on a belief system that constructs arbitrary borders between normalcy and disability. Like Artiles (2003), we believe that to continue to do so is to continue to stigmatize, alienate, and underestimate children, in particular, children whose families and communities are already underestimated and marginalized. A child should be able to obtain specialized services by virtue of his/her level of performance in the academic tasks of schooling, not on the basis of a decontextualized testing process designed to determine an underlying "deficit." We do not believe that it is necessary to conduct such testing in order to determine a child's educational needs.

This book points to the fallacies involved in relying on the disability construct for the provision of special education services. In exposing these fallacies we propose reforms that we believe are feasible and that would allow the field to avoid the negative outcomes too frequently associated with the reified views of cognitive and behavioral "disabilities." We conclude this chapter with a brief introduction to the way we approached our study of the processes involved in overrepresentation.

THE SCHOOL DISTRICT OF HYPHENATED IDENTITIES

The school district we studied, in the Southeast of the United States, presents a portrait of dynamic multiculturalism in a city that defies the country's centuries-old tradition of defining people by race. While the predominant ethnicities present in the public school system are officially classified as Black (33%), Hispanic (48%), White Non-Hispanic (17%), and Asian and "others" (2%), these labels have little meaning in the context of the tremendous cultural variability within all groups. People choosing the ethnicity "Hispanic" may appear to be either "White" or "Black," or any racial mixture. While the majority are from Cuba, other South and Central American nations are also well represented, such as Nicaragua, the Dominican Republic, Mexico, and Peru. Those choosing "Black" may speak Haitian Creole, French, Spanish, English, or any of the varieties of English spoken in Caribbean islands such as Jamaica or Trinidad and Tobago. The term *White* tends to be used mainly by people of Anglo American or Jewish origin. Asians and Native Americans represent a tiny minority.

Race, language, and socioeconomic status (SES) are the key variables that differentiate the county's public schools, since, as in many localities across the United States, ethnic minorities of low income tend to cluster in neighborhoods. However, this is modified by the presence of a desegregation order that was in place throughout the duration of the study, but has since been withdrawn. Matthew's school, described at the beginning of this chapter, still participated in the busing of African American students into an upper-income, predominantly White and Hispanic school.

Special Education Placement Patterns

Special education placement in this school district reflected the nationwide and state figures (Table 1.1). The figures show that Black students were overrepresented in the EMR and ED categories at all three levels. Hispanic students were overrepresented only in the LD category at the district level.

The Research Process

We refer those readers more interested in methodology and data analysis to a paper we have written on that topic (Harry, Sturges, & Klingner, 2005). We will explain here only those aspects of the research that are essential to understanding what we did and to ensuring its credibility.

We selected 12 schools that represented a range of ethnic populations, a range of socioeconomic levels, and differential rates of special education referral and placement. Envisioning children's school experiences as affected by a series of concentric circles (Strauss & Corbin, 1998), we designed the research as a funnel, beginning with the issue at its broadest level, including figures on nationwide, statewide, and districtwide patterns of ethnic distribution of students in special education. We then narrowed our focus to the school district and the rates of special education placement in various regions of the district, and then to the rates at particular schools. From there we moved into the center of the circle, investigating processes within the 12 schools, and, ultimately, to a focus on 12 individual children.

Table 1.2 shows the three types of ethnicity patterns and special education placement rates across the 12 schools we selected. Four of the schools were

Table 1.1. Students in Special Education Programs by Ethnic Group (percent)

	District			State			Nation		
	B	H	W	B	H	W	B	H	W
Total	34	51	15	25	15	59	17	13	66
EMR	60	35	6	48	11	40	31	8	58
ED	46	40	13	37	9	54	25	8	66
LD	33	54	13	25	13	62	17	13	67

Note. B = Black; H = Hispanic; W = White; EMR = Educable Mentally Retarded; ED = Emotionally Disturbed; LD = Learning Disabilities; Total = Percentage of ethnic group among the total population of students (with and without disabilities).

Table 1.2. School Demographics (percent)

School	Ethnicity of Students			Free or Reduced-Price Lunch	EMR	ED	LD
	W	B	H				
Bay Vista	8	1	90	68.7			6.6
Sunnybrook	55	17	23	18.5			4.1
Clearwater	3	92	3	70.1	0.2		4.1
Blue Heron	7	4	92	65.6		5.8	12.5
Green Acres	2	0	98	88.9			5.3
Centerville	0	99	1	97.1	7.0		9.8
Palm Grove	0	89	10	98.9	0.5		6.8
Creekside	0	92	8	97.2	0.1	0.01	3.5
Esperanza	6	11	82	89.6			4.2
Beecher Stowe	1	69	29	98.4	2.6		4.2
Mabel Oakes	2	56	42	99.0		0.1	4.4
South Park	2	79	19	98.3	0.5	0.3	5.8

Note. W = White; B = Black (African American as well as Haitian, Jamaican, and other Caribbean); H = Hispanic (various countries of origin); EMR = Educable Mentally Retarded; ED = Emotionally Disturbed; LD = Learning Disabilities.

predominantly African American, four were predominantly Hispanic, and four included mixtures of African American, Hispanic, and White. We also took account of SES, by including one school that served a high-SES White and Hispanic population with a minority of low-income African Americans bused to the school, and one that served a low- to middle-SES African American population (as contrasted with the schools that served African Americans of low-income to poverty levels). With regard to placement rates, we note that the absence of a percentage under the categories EMR and ED at some schools indicates that these programs were not offered at those sites.

We began by developing a broad picture of the 12 schools through interviews with school personnel, observations of all K-through-3 regular-education classrooms and of a sample of support and placement conferences. The research funnel narrowed further as we selected 2 classrooms in each school to observe intensively, focusing on those children about whom teachers were concerned and who might be referred to the special education process. We observed these children in various school settings and observed support and placement conferences and psychological evaluations, wherever possible. At the end of our intensive data collection in these 24 classrooms, we conducted a round of "exit" interviews with the teachers. In the 3rd year, we followed students into their postevaluation placements, whether in general or special education, and also observed in all the special education classrooms in their schools. Finally, we identified 12 students for whom we developed intensive case studies.

Overall, our data amounted to 272 audiotaped, open-ended or semi-structured individual interviews with students, parents, and school-based and district personnel; 84 informal conversations; observations of 627 classrooms; 42 child study team (CST) meetings; 5 psychological evaluations; 15 special education placement meetings; 14 other meetings; and observations in 15 home and community settings relevant to target students. Interview length ranged from 20 minutes to 2 hours, classroom observations ranged from 30 minutes to a full day, and CST and other meetings lasted from 5 minutes to more than an hour. The documents we examined included IEPs, students' work, psychological and other evaluations, school district guidelines and policies, and extant data on special education placement in the school district.

The main project lasted 3 years. In the 4th year we conducted quarterly visits to schools to monitor the progress of the 12 case study students. Additionally, the case studies of 3 students placed in ED programs were extended in a 5th year through the doctoral research of one of our students (Hart, 2003). We draw on all these sources in this book.

ORGANIZATION OF THE BOOK

We have organized our discussion to reflect the funnel-like process of our research, moving from broad to more individualized portraits of schools, school personnel, children and families. In Chapters 2 and 3 we describe the overall structural and administrative features, as well as personal and contextual biases, that operated in these settings. In Chapter 4, we explore the general climate of classroom instruction and the provision of opportunity to learn. In Chapter 5, we begin our close attention to individual cases by contrasting school personnel's constructions of families' identities with the voices of family members themselves. In Chapter 6, we describe the decision-making policies and contexts that determined special education eligibility, and in Chapter 7, we discuss how these applied to English-language learners. In Chapters 8, 9, and 10, we provide a close-up view of the process of disability assignment to individual children, and in Chapter 11 we address the question of whether special education placement provided beneficial outcomes. In Chapter 12, the final chapter, we offer solutions that we see as strong alternatives to the current special education model.

In view of the large body of research findings, we note here our concern with the challenge of selecting, for the purposes of this book, only the most salient exemplars of the broad-based issues we studied. We assure our readers that our findings are "grounded" in ethnographic data too extensive to be reported within the confines of one book (for further detail, see Harry, Sturges, & Klingner, 2005).

OUR PREMISE

We approached our very complex data with one guiding premise: We could only conclude that special education placement was appropriate if children had received adequate and appropriate opportunity to learn within supportive environments and had been placed through a fair and well-reasoned referral, assessment, and placement process. We found that this was by no means the case. The caveats to our conclusions are obvious: First, we could not study every case in the 12 schools; second, we did investigate some students whose placement process was appropriate and helpful.

To summarize here what we will explain in detail throughout the book, we found a host of explanations that competed with the belief that special education placement reflected genuine learning and behavioral deficits that required such placement. In many cases, there was simply no way of knowing how children would have fared in more effective educational circumstances in the regular classroom or with a more systematic and appropriate referral process.

There are many reasons that this conclusion is important. First, the belief that school-based disabilities reflect real impairments further fuels beliefs about the inferiority of any groups who seem to "have" these impairments in greater proportions than do other groups. On the symbolic level, there is no escaping that a label of disability carries a stigma; to add this to already existing historical prejudices against certain groups is to add insult to injury. The second reason to be concerned and to understand the social nature of disproportionality is that the benefits of special education placement continue to be questionable (Kavale, 1990; Reschly, 2000).

This book offers a unique view inside the assumptions, policies, and practices that characterized special education decision making in one of the nation's largest, most diverse school districts. The power of our findings lies in the voices and actions of school personnel, family members, and children. It lies also in the complex portrait of the social pressures and realities of schools operating under political mandates that sometimes work against children's best interests. By exposing the human and social processes at work in the designation of disability, we dispute the belief that the overrepresentation of minority groups in special education can be assumed to reflect real disabilities within children.

CHAPTER 2

School Structure: Institutional Bias and Individual Agency

So many principals! Each has worked an average of 3 years, and then they retire. One received a promotion, and then retired. The 12 years that I've been here, I've seen three principals retire. I think this one will be the fourth.

—School counselor

A T THE HEART of American democracy is the belief in social mobility. Schools have been envisioned as the main vehicle for ensuring a meritocracy based on individual ability and hard work. Social reproduction theory, however, as articulated by Bowles and Gintis (1976), argued that structural features of schools ensure that schooling tends to reproduce rather than change the societal status quo, by preparing children to function at the same societal level from which they came. Researchers such as Kozol (1991), Oakes (1985), and Anyon (1981) have provided portraits of schooling that demonstrate social reproduction in action through inequitable funding patterns, institutionalized low expectations resulting from tracking, and the provision of differential curricula according to the social-class level of students.

Structuralism suggests that many decisions and outcomes are somehow larger than the individual, operating through a force that seems designed more to serve bureaucratic and organizational ends than to advance individual ones. Yet it is individuals who make decisions, and critics have argued that the structural view inherent in social reproduction theory is too deterministic, ignoring the power of individual agency (Brantlinger, 2001). Lareau & Horvat (1999), arguing for a more nuanced understanding of the theory, proposed that it should be interpreted as a general trend that may be counteracted in individual cases by children's or families' acquisition of the cultural capital that allows upward mobility. As Lareau and Horvat noted, this acquisition is more likely if the family has the social capital, in the form of social networks, that allows such learning. Thus, certainly, some children will beat the odds. Nevertheless, the figures on the Black-White achievement gap indicate that the majority do not.

If social reproduction means that children from higher-SES contexts will get better schooling than those from low-SES contexts, our research certainly bore out the theory. We identified school quality in terms of administrative decisions regarding scheduling, instruction, discipline policies, and interactions with parents, as well as in terms of teacher quality, which we determined through classroom observations and objective criteria such as the percentage of teachers with advanced degrees. State ratings of the schools also provided a more global sense of achievement. The only exception to the social reproduction pattern was Green Acres, an excellent school serving a Hispanic population of whom 89% were on free or reduced-price lunch. Across the other 11 schools, higher SES was consistently associated with better school quality. At the lowest end of the pattern were those schools in which low-income Black children predominated. Social reproduction theory was chillingly reflected in the following statement of a special education teacher referring to a student at a school that served low-income Black and Hispanic students:

> She's lumped in with the dregs of society. . . . She doesn't understand what school is for. . . . We create blue-collar here at this school. If I could teach her social skills to get a job and not get fired, that's a goal—entering the labor force.

Despite the presence of social reproduction processes at work in these schools, our most important finding defied all simplistic assumptions about the overrepresentation of Black and Hispanic students in special education. We learned that special education placement showed no systematic relationship either to school quality or to children's own developmental or skill levels. Rather, it reflected a wide range of influences, including structural inequities, contextual biases, limited opportunity to learn, variability in referral and assessment processes, detrimental views of and interactions with families, and poor instruction and classroom management. Overarching all these was the power of each school's ideology regarding special education, which we came to refer to as the school's "culture of referral."

All of these contributing factors will be discussed as the book proceeds. In this chapter we describe the structural inequities we noted in children's schooling and grapple with the elusive line between structural and individual responsibility. We will be concerned with those aspects of school structure that seemed to be within the purview of the school and school district administrators. When a child entered a school building, what policies and practices would be in place to support his/her advancement? Who would be his principal? Who would teach him? Which peers would be in his classroom? What instructional programs would be used to assist him? How would he learn how to behave? What would happen if he misbehaved?

SCHOOL LEADERSHIP: ASSIGNMENT OF PRINCIPALS TO SCHOOLS

Beecher Stowe Elementary, located in the heart of the old city center, served a low-income, predominantly African American population. Besides the counselor quoted at the introduction to this chapter, who said that he had seen four principals assigned in 12 years, another teacher who had taught for 22 years at Beecher Stowe reported that he had worked under a total of eight principals during his time. This school, serving the neediest of children in the school district, had a pattern of constant change of leadership.

It was not only the inner-city schools that suffered from such discontinuity. The pattern was frequent across the 12 schools, and while teachers sometimes expressed dismay at the lack of continuity in leadership, principals' comments tended to be rather noncommittal, suggesting either acceptance of or resignation to a fact they saw as beyond their power. The principal at South Park, another inner-city school serving a mixture of African American and Hispanic students, was a 30-year veteran and had served as an assistant principal (AP) for 12 years "all over the district." In one year, she had been moved to temporary AP appointments six times. When asked about these moves, she replied:

> As an administrator, you have to be willing to serve in any capacity—wherever you're needed. . . . You know, tomorrow they might call and say, "I need you to report to the region office," and when you get there they would say, "Give me the keys to your building, because you are going over here." But I've had a very positive attitude about that.

Not only was the leadership of these two schools very changeable, but so were the faculty. The percentage of new teachers at Beecher Stowe and South Park in the 1999–2000 year was 17% and 25%, respectively. Such faculty instability has been cited as a key variable in school risk (Keogh, 2000).

At the other end of the spectrum was Green Acres, a school serving a population that was 99% Hispanic; 89% of these students received free and reduced-price lunch. This school ran exceedingly smoothly and efficiently under the leadership of a principal who had been there for 12 years and a new faculty of only 4%. In between these two extremes were variable leadership histories, but it seemed that most schools had had several changes. Frequent moves of APs were also common across the schools. At Mabel Oakes, which served a low-income Hispanic and African American population, there were three different APs during the 3 years of our research.

We do not know how these decisions were made. We learned only that, despite an apparently stringent screening process, the selection of applicants for administrative positions was influenced by unwritten policies such as asking the district superintendent whether he/she had anyone particular in mind for a position, and seeking ethnic and gender diversity among school administrators. Beyond these official guidelines, we had no way of knowing the inside details of the process or how any of the principals we met were selected.

What was clear, however, was that principals exerted tremendous influence over decisions at their schools, including hiring practices, discipline policies, student-retention procedures, class size and scheduling, visitor policies, tolerance of interruptions, resource allocation, and curricular decisions. Variability in all of these was evident across our 12 schools. We focus on the decisions that seemed to have the greatest direct impact on children—the hiring and assignment of teachers. We then discuss other variables prominent in our data: discipline policies, scheduling, and interruptions.

TEACHER QUALITY: HIRING AND RETAINING GOOD TEACHERS

Perhaps the most important responsibility of the principal is to hire teachers and assign them to classes. Yet finding and retaining qualified teachers is a challenge in urban schools (Ansell & McCabe, 2003, Darling-Hammond, 1995; Oakes, Franke, Quartz, & Rogers, 2002; Pflaum & Abramson, 1990), which typically have higher numbers of inexperienced, uncertified, temporary, and substitute teachers (Hardy, 1999). Whereas administrators in wealthier schools tell of having "stacks of résumés" to look through, principals in high-poverty urban schools relate how difficult it is to attract teachers to their schools—they must take whomever they can get (Krei, 1998). Retaining good teachers is equally challenging. Urban schools typically have high turnover rates as novice teachers gain experience and request transfers to schools they consider more desirable. Though a few districts have attempted to alleviate disparities in teacher quality by providing monetary incentives to keep teachers at urban sites, these efforts usually are insufficient (Ferguson, 1991; Jacobson, 1989; Krei, 1998). In some districts, issues of teacher quality are further complicated by principals in wealthier schools who transfer teachers deemed unsatisfactory to high-poverty urban schools rather than going through the process of dismissing them (Krei, 1998).

As noted by Krei (1998), "One of the most pervasive and important ways in which poor children are believed to be shortchanged in public schooling is in the quality of the teaching they receive" (p. 71). When students are placed in classrooms with less qualified teachers, their opportunity to learn is compromised and they are placed at greater risk for underachievement (Schneider, 1985), which, in turn, can result in referral to special education. It is our position that these hiring decisions are but one set out of a complex array of interrelated factors that affect the special education referral process and ultimately the disproportionate representation of culturally and linguistically diverse students in special education.

District Data on Teacher Qualifications

District data on teacher quality across our 12 schools indicated a clear bias against the higher-poverty schools, in particular, those serving Black populations. With advanced degrees (master's, specialist's, or doctoral) being employed as a measure of teacher quality (a commonly used indicator in federal reports), Table 2.1 shows two main patterns and one anomaly. Using free/reduced-price lunch (FRL) as an indicator of SES, we can divide the schools into two main groups—eight with more than 86% FRL, and four with 70% or less FRL. In the higher-income group (Group A) the percentage of teachers having master's degrees ranged from 39% to 47%. With the exception of Green Acres, which we refer to as the anomaly, the range in the lower-income group (Group B) is from 21% to 36%. At Green Acres, 54% of the faculty had master's degrees. This percentage was 18% higher than the highest of the other low-income schools, and 33% higher than the lowest school. It was also 7% higher than the percentage in the school serving the most affluent population. Green Acres was also different from other Group B schools in that 98% of the students were Hispanic, whereas the other low-income schools either had predominantly Black or mixed populations.

We observed all K–3 classrooms in the 12 schools and analyzed teacher behaviors in terms of three dimensions of teacher quality: instructional skills, classroom-management skills, and socioemotional behaviors. Our analysis, which preceded any checking of data on teachers' qualifications, was very much in line with the discrepant teacher quality outlined above. In the schools in Group A, and in Green Acres, teachers' instructional skills were consistently average to high, and it was rare to see a classroom where behavior was out of control or where instruction seemed haphazard, based on rote learning, or inappropriate to children's needs. By contrast, in Group B, teacher skills were very variable, with marked extremes of high and low as well as

Table 2.1. Student and Teacher Data

| | Students | | | | | | Teachers | | | | | | | |
| | Ethnicity (%) | | | | | | Ethnicity (%) | | | | | | | |
	White (Non-Hispanic)	Black (Non-Hispanic)	Hispanic	FRL (%)	LEP (%)	Mobility Index	White (Non-Hispanic)	Black (Non-Hispanic)	Hispanic	Master's Degree (%)	Specialist (%)	Doctorate (%)	New to School (%)	Average Years of Teaching Experience
Group A														
Bay Vista	8	1	90	68.7	27.2	21	5	22	73	44	5	0	10.3	10
Sunnybrook	55	17	23	18.5	5.8	10	36	31	33	47	7	2	12.0	11
Clearwater	3	92	3	70.1	2.0	22	38	41	21	43	14	0	15.2	15
Blue Heron	7	1	92	65.6	31.3	23	24	36	40	39	5	0	19.4	10
Anomaly														
Green Acres	2	0	98	88.9	50.0	22	12	25	63	54	9	0	4.5	12
Group B														
Centerville	0	99	1	97.1	0.5	47	44	36	20	36	10	0	17.1	11
Palm Grove	0	89	10	98.9	27.3	42	36	36	26	35	4	2	11.8	13
Creekside	0	92	8	97.2	43.2	41	36	34	25	35	6	0	8.5	9
Esperanza	6	11	6	86.6	46.2	26	9	28	63	27	3	0	16.7	8
B. Stowe	1	69	1	98.4	13.9	43	30	25	45	21	5	0	17.0	10
M. Oakes	2	56	2	99.0	26.1	50	38	23	39	32	9	0	16.9	8
South Park	2	79	2	98.3	8.3	44	18	30	53	21	2	0	25.0	8

Note. FRL = Free or reduced-price lunch; LEP = Limited English Proficient; Mobility Index = Rate of student mobility in school (turnover).

many in between. For example, in one such school, of 18 K–3 classrooms observed, we rated 5 very good, 6 average, and 7 very weak. In another, of 12 classrooms observed, we rated 5 very good, 2 average, and 5 very weak.

Since we have grouped the schools according to FRL, which is a feature of the children, not the teachers, a reasonable question to ask would be whether the children themselves, because of poor behavior or poor academic readiness, might account for the impression of classroom quality. Our observations indicated quite certainly that this was not the case. In subsequent chapters we will detail the tremendous variability in child behavior in response to the skills of teachers. As one excellent kindergarten teacher in one of the poorest neighborhoods stated, "When you close the classroom doors, the children in this neighborhood are no different."

Limitations to Principals' Selection of Faculty

Principals were not necessarily to blame for the patently unfair pattern of teacher quality. Although a senior district official told us that principals had "sole control" over the hiring of teachers who had satisfied the district-level screening, there were two exceptions to this: First, there was a desegregation requirement that between 24% and 36% of a faculty must be Black; second, it was mandated that district personnel decide where to assign "surplused" teachers (usually less experienced), who were released from a school when the student population had declined.

Regardless of policy, it seemed that some principals had more autonomy than others. When the principal at Green Acres was asked how she came to have such an excellent cadre of teachers, she confirmed that she was able to handpick her teachers, exclaiming, "I think I have pretty good eyes!" For the most part she listed the usual criteria one would expect, such as applicants' previous experience and behavior management strategies. However, one comment she made suggested that there may be more informal, more personalized aspects of the selection process: "I guess it has to do with the hiring of the people that I know in our community. We have a lot of children that do not speak English and you know [who can] do the best for those children." The phrase "our community" was not explicitly explained, but, since she followed it with a comment about English-language learners, we interpreted it as probably meaning that she sought teachers who would be compatible in terms of ethnicity and language—Hispanic teachers. However, it was not just an ethnic match that made this faculty look so good, since in the other schools we saw as many weak Hispanic teachers as we did weak teachers of any other ethnicity.

In contrast, other principals in high-need schools said they experienced many limitations in their ability to choose, including inadequate applicant pools. New teachers often avoided inner-city schools, not responding to phone calls from principals at schools they considered undesirable. Geographical location was another limitation. Most of the schools serving very low income populations were in the older parts of the inner city where few teachers lived. One principal explained that commuting was a source of stress that often resulted in teachers moving, as soon as an opportunity arose, nearer to their homes, leaving the principal to settle for teachers "who are not even mediocre [but] the bottom of the barrel!" These teachers then required a great deal of professional development and might still turn out to just "not have the capability."

Assignment of Teachers to Classes

Once teachers are hired, the next level of decision making is to determine which students will get the best teachers in the school. A central issue is whether to group children by ability, and if so, which teachers to assign to higher and lower levels. Some principals believed in ability grouping and others did not. In one school that had two pre-K classes, these children, thought to be more promising because of their pre-K experience, were kept together throughout kindergarten and into the first grade before they eventually were spread out. Many of them, reportedly, turned out to be the "top students." This school also grouped children according to ability in math and in writing. In two other inner-city schools, the principals told us they sorted classes by ability, since they believed that this allowed teachers to tailor their instruction appropriately, rather than losing children at either end of the spectrum.

The principal at Green Acres, however, reported not using ability grouping, with two exceptions. First, students in the lower ESOL (English for speakers of other languages) levels were grouped for self-contained classes. Second, students who had to be pulled out for special education classes were clustered into certain classrooms, no more than four in each room, so that the special education students would be "easy to pull and schedule." After placing these two groups of children, the principal then tried to "balance" the placement of children so that all the rest of the classes had "high and low" children. Our observations suggested that this process worked well: We saw no classrooms that had an overabundance of children with learning or behavioral difficulties. In another school with relatively high achievement, the presence of a magnet program meant that those children were grouped together, but, otherwise, grouping was heterogeneous. Our observations suggested that heterogeneous grouping was fairer to the lower-performing children, and, if the teacher had good organizational and instructional skills, better for all.

In decisions regarding which teachers were assigned to particular groups of children, again the policies varied. Several principals preferred to place teachers at the grade level at which they would be most comfortable. One principal explicitly stated that she tried to place her best teachers in the grades that were most affected by high-stakes testing. Some teachers believed that the principal used class assignment to reward or "punish" them. In one school, according to a teacher, her "punishment" was being assigned many ESOL students in her class even though she was not ESOL endorsed. For those who were ESOL endorsed, however, being assigned to a predominantly ESOL class was appreciated by teachers who perceived that the Hispanic children were easier to manage than were African American children.

In some schools, it was evident that the strongest teachers were assigned to the higher-achieving students. For example, in one inner-city, predominantly African American school, we noted that weak teachers tended to be placed in classes in which were clustered children with challenging behaviors, low academic achievement, or both. One such teacher was constantly moved over a period of 2 years—from her first-grade assignment, which she had had for many years, to a troublesome second-grade class, to an alternative-education class. When, in the following year, she was moved to a gifted class, the pattern had become incomprehensible to us. In the 3rd year, she enrolled in a graduate program in special education and was immediately assigned to a special education class. With regard to her second-grade class, the teacher told us that "almost half" the class had been referred for testing or were already receiving special education pullout services. She said that across the second grade, one teacher had the high-achieving children, one had half and half, and she had all the difficult children. She said that this arrangement, made by the principal, had overridden a more heterogeneous proposal from the teachers. She felt that there was favoritism and punishment involved in the decision. Our observations of the three classrooms confirmed that both the children and the teachers had been "tracked" by ability.

Firing

Terminating ineffective teachers was a complicated process. Within a probationary period of 97 days, a new teacher could be terminated by the principal, who was required to evaluate the new teacher during this period. According to a senior official, "all kinds of help were available" to support new teachers and, after the 97-day period, terminating a teacher took "a lot of process and documentation." This was evident in the number of weak teachers we saw who had been teaching for many years.

Generally, we could not tell whether principals did not know, did not care, or could not do anything about the many ineffective teachers we observed.

One inner-city principal, when asked what she could do about a teacher who was really struggling, offered some insights into the dilemmas she faced:

> [They've] got to go! . . . One teacher in particular I had to weigh the good with the bad. This person lacked the classroom management but she makes up for it with what she does with those children in the arts. And I had to make a decision, do you keep the teacher and try to deal with her classroom management in order to allow these children to experience something that they will not be able to experience? Or, do you immediately jump in there and then you don't have that particular teacher because there is a shortage because there is nobody else to take her place, or one who has the same problem? But, nevertheless, enough is enough and that person has been given notice. . . . You have to want to do it and you have to be willing to take the heat and get beat up and the whole bit.

Principals shared with us how constrained they felt in their ability to dismiss incompetent teachers. One principal explained:

> Many teachers just can't work in this [urban] environment. Then you have some teachers who have been here for 25 and 30 years. Some have been here for so long, when you go into their class [you see that] they know how to do just the minimum. So now I'm glad that we have this new observation [system] . . . that has certain standards. Even though I am not going to able to get rid of [teacher's name], this gives me ideas on how I will be able to work with her before we put her on prescription and then you have to go through that process. . . . You just keep plugging away and at the end of the year you do have the option of hiring a 3100 [a teacher on temporary assignment] to come in to replace them. But it is a year or 6 months that you have to go through.

This principal went on to say that there used to be a time when "if a teacher had a problem, and they really needed to get rid of them, then they put them in the inner-city schools where they had to suffer." We assumed that this policy was no longer in place.

These comments point to the difficulty of getting and retaining good faculty. As we will detail later, our observations showed that there were many teachers who simply should not have been in the classroom. On the other hand, teachers' most common complaint was lack of support from their administrators, particularly support for discipline problems.

DISCIPLINE POLICIES

The variability in discipline policies and in children's behavior across schools was staggering. Clearly, the question arises of whether the problem lay mainly in the children or in the schools' response to them.

The school we opened this chapter with, Beecher Stowe, located in the poorest of the inner-city neighborhoods, cited the most problems with discipline. In this area we had two schools, both of which we cited as having many leadership changes. School personnel who knew the neighborhood well offered the opinion that the children's circumstances were really getting worse. In one school, the counselor, an African American man who expressed great commitment to the community, noted: "The children have such anger. This anger and bad attitude are everywhere." Our observations in both these schools showed behavior problems in some classes, but not all. In a later section, we will detail our findings regarding classroom management, making the point that when we see, within one school, classrooms with dramatically different types of behavior, although the children are all coming from the same neighborhood, it seems more likely that the issue is management rather than the children themselves. Further, when we see a group of children actually change their behavior as they move from one teacher to another, we are even more certain of the importance of teachers' skills.

Regardless of whether individual classroom teachers are able to bring out the best in children, the policies of any school's administration are at the center of the issue. Some teachers placed the responsibility squarely in the hands of the administration. In the case of beginning teachers, this was particularly troubling, since new teachers' contracts required that they stay at their first appointed school for at least 3 years, in an attempt to encourage greater commitment to staying in inner-city schools. Lack of support from school administrators made this outcome unlikely. One new teacher in an inner-city school had a class of 30 children, 9 of whom she described as "EBD kids." She felt as though she had been thrown "into the lion's den," but she would not send children to the office, because "nothing happens." She exclaimed:

> I wasn't trained to deal with these kinds of problems. I never had any problems compared with this, even though I did some [field experience] in an inner-city school. . . . They just don't send you. I wanted to go [to the inner-city schools]. The first day was terrible. I left crying. I just hadn't understood the need, how there can be so much need here, and I'm from Peru, a third world country. Many of my parents [here] don't work. My kids who are behavioral problems are always here because it is the only way they eat. I want to help.

Something needs to be done. I have to give the students crayons and pencils because they don't have anything.

In an almost identical statement, a first-year teacher at another school said her primary need was

more administrative input. More support for beginning teachers. You need your back rubbed. If you've been called a White cracker bitch, you shouldn't see that child walking the hallways. At the beginning, I was fighting. I was not very popular. . . . These kids are all smart. They're not special ed. They are bright kids. They just need discipline.

The counselor in this school, an African American man, said that more needs to be done to retain new teachers such as the former speaker. He said:

Too many wait 2 years, then transfer. If they wait it out, it's gonna get better. What I learned in school [college], I had to throw it out! . . . Some years ago they used to give extra pay for working in this area . . . "combat pay."

Another teacher in this school felt she had very few options: "They told me not to put students in the corner, have them write lines, or send them out of the room. . . . And if we contact parents, when they go home, they get beaten." She said the school had started in-door suspension and after-school detention but, shaking her head, she added that a student in her class *liked* to go to after-school detention and deliberately pulled a fire alarm to get placed there. Another teacher told us, "What they really need to do is bring in someone from boot camp, and pay them a regular teacher's salary, and have them instill some discipline in the students." This school employed security guards who were called when students misbehaved, but they didn't always come to the classroom right away, and they didn't seem to be a deterrent to negative behavior. The view was that security needed to be stronger. One teacher described her administration as follows:

You go to the office with a complaint and they are like cockroaches. You know, when you first cut on a light, the cockroaches run everywhere. That's what the administration does when you come to them, they'll do nothing. They don't want to hear anything from you. I have never seen anything like this school and its administration. I'm not happy. I feel like I'm being wasted here. It's hard dealing with the disciplinary measures. I'm primarily isolated. We have to handle everything ourselves. "See no evil. Hear no evil. Speak no evil."

In the two inner-city schools frequently cited above, the most troubling aspect of the administrations' response to discipline was the excessive reliance on out-of-school suspension.

Out-of-School Suspension

Elaine, a mother who attempted to be an advocate for her children, exclaimed in frustration to the principal at her son's school, "Every little thing he does, you all throw him out." Table 2.2 shows the district's report of rates of suspension in our 12 schools. At South Park and Beecher Stowe, suspension was the discipline policy of choice, showing rates that were totally out of line with the norms for the other schools: 102 children suspended out of a total of 603 students, and 101 children out of a total of 806. This was particularly distressing because for these children, being out of school meant being in the very detrimental environments so derogated by school personnel.

Table 2.2. Suspensions by School

	Number of Students Suspended	Total Number of Students
Group A		
Bay Vista	1	1,379
Sunnybrook	8	828
Clearwater	12	658
Blue Heron	8	550
Group B		
Green Acres	9	1,160
Centerville	34	417
Palm Grove	2	820
Creekside	20	780
Esperanza	7	1,183
B. Stowe	101	806
M. Oakes	44	1,036
South Park	102	603

Many teachers were very vocal on this issue. Several felt that they had very few options for controlling behavior. One teacher said, "Some students get suspended all the time, but it doesn't work. How they handle discipline doesn't work." Another teacher said she tried to handle discipline problems on her own and not send students to the office. Although three of her students were out on suspension, she had not suspended them—other teachers or administrators had. She explained that she did not suspend kids, because "they just go home and get into more trouble. It is not a punishment for these kids."

SCHEDULING AND INTERRUPTIONS: "WE'RE THE ONES WHO MAKE THEM HYPER!"

The proliferation of programs at some schools was a matter of great prominence in our observations. With the best of intentions, several of the schools serving the neediest children were detrimentally affected by this problem. In some cases the programs that contributed to an impression of overall curricular fragmentation were, in themselves, excellent programs or represented some very convincing educational philosophy. The difficulty, it seemed, was in the implementation and coordination with other potentially good programs.

Four of the inner-city schools were using Success for All (SFA) as their reading program. This program requires that children receive reading instruction in small groups of peers at their own level. For approximately 2 hours every morning, therefore, the children went from their homerooms to another classroom for this instruction. While some teachers liked SFA and some did not, we noted that the more "special" programs there were in a school, the greater the frustration that was expressed, even by many who liked SFA. Other "special" programs included physical education (PE), music, and art. Also, in three of these schools, children had to go to different rooms for language programs, including ESOL, Curriculum Content in the Home Language (CCHL), or Home Language Arts (HLA). One teacher exclaimed:

> I've never had such a bad schedule. I don't have time to teach. I have them for less than 30 minutes, then they go to PE. Just when they have settled down and are working well, it's time for them to leave again. Then they come back for 10 minutes, then they go to lunch. Then they come back and go to Spanish (for an hour on Mondays and Fridays, and half an hour on Wednesdays). Then they come back at 2:00. We're the ones that make them hyper!

Our observations absolutely corroborated the statement that constant movement contributed to the children being "hyper." In schools with a high population of recently arrived immigrant children it seemed to us that what they needed most was stability—a teacher who would get to know them well so that they could become socially and linguistically confident and able to focus on their work. It was obvious that homeroom teachers had little opportunity to get to know students personally or even to be sure of their academic levels. In one first-grade classroom we had direct evidence that a child's reading and math levels were quite unclear to the teacher. The researcher gave a child initial prompts with the first set of sums on a test sheet, then sat and watched him do all the rest correctly. The teacher expressed surprise at the level of his work, saying that the teacher for the HLA program (using Haitian Creole) did most of his math with him. In the third-grade classroom of an otherwise excellent teacher, we saw her giving a child manipulatives to add and subtract, while, in the HLA classroom, taught by the same Haitian Creole speaker, we observed the same child doing complex multiplication on the blackboard and getting all the answers correct.

It was ironic that this type of "hyper" scheduling occurred most often in the neediest schools. It seems that principals were trying to find a "magic bullet" for their children but, in so doing, failed to note the lack of coherence that resulted from "overdosing." In contrast, we once more cite Green Acres, where SFA was not included, but the high ESOL population was also served by an array of language programs. However, the scheduling was done so that the teachers, rather than the children, did most of the moving. In this school there was a much greater sense of stability and continuity, although the ESOL teachers were sometimes noticeably weaker than the classroom teachers.

Another contributor to a hyper feeling in some schools was the high tolerance for interruptions, whether from intercom announcements at any time of the day, people stopping by to chat, or students switching classes. As with all other features, this varied widely from school to school. At several schools, interruptions to instructional time seemed to be pervasive, perpetuated by administrators, and accepted by many at the school as normal practice. These disruptions reduced instructional time. Most problematic seemed to be students going to and returning from special education classes. For instance:

> Students continue to come in. One boy shouts loudly, "Hey, Elton!"
> The teacher asks, "Why are you late?" Then she asks, "Why did she keep Robby?" Another student responds, "She didn't keep Robby." As it turned out, Robby wasn't there because he was wandering the school grounds, mad about something that had happened in the previous class.

Another program that proved quite disruptive showed the irony of too many uncoordinated efforts to boost the performance of children in inner-city schools. This was an individualized computer-curriculum program that required children to do half an hour a day working on the computer at his/her own level. The individualization required by this program, however, was effective only in the hands of very organized teachers, since they were required to monitor students on the computers at the same time that they were trying to teach. Students cycling on and off the computers seemed to give the message that the teacher's instruction was not important. Many teachers were unsuccessful in catching students up or in structuring the flow smoothly.

There was much coming and going to and from classrooms in many schools. Teachers were called out of the room for CST meetings or placement conferences, sometimes without prior notice. People entering classrooms during lessons included, for example, the counselor, security guards, parent volunteers, parents, paraprofessionals, other teachers, other school support staff, other students, and computer repair people. Some of these interruptions were to pick up children for various reasons, or to borrow materials, but at other times the visitor simply had a comment or question, such as, "Did anyone in here go to the Girl Scout meeting on Wednesday?"

Other than during SFA, when there seemed to be an effort not to interrupt instruction, intercom announcements were common and occurred at varied times. At some schools we noticed a policy that instruction could only be interrupted over the intercom at set times, such as at the end of the day, but this did not appear to be the case at several inner-city schools. Overall, in the better schools, there was less of a tendency to use the intercom for unnecessary announcements and much less coming and going. This was clearly a matter of administrative policy, since it varied from school to school even in the inner-city schools.

CONCLUSIONS

The line between individual agency and structural discrimination is blurred by the variability in the decision-making process. We did not note any particular pattern in the skills of principals. Some of the least effective schools had principals who were energetic and imaginative. However, it was evident that some of these schools experienced the highest turnover in administrators. Certainly, in those schools that served predominantly poor, Black populations, the most vulnerable children were placed at increased risk by virtue of inequitable hiring practices, assignment of weak teachers to weak students, retention of extremely weak teachers, homogeneous classroom groupings, unsupportive discipline policies, and poorly coordinated curricular programming. All of these factors were to some extent within the realm of individual principals' agency.

There is no underestimating the importance of school leadership. It has long been demonstrated that strong leadership is a key element of effective urban schools (Edmonds & Frederickson, 1978; Jackson, Logsdon, & Taylor, 1983; Scheurich, 1998; Weber, 1971). The principal's beliefs, values, educational philosophies, and interpersonal as well as management skills have a great influence on the climate and culture of a school. Yet the principal operates within the larger culture of the school district, which, in turn, responds to state and federal mandates and policies (Bridgeland & Duane, 1987).

At Green Acres, individual agency was evident. With a strong principal, high-quality teaching, and positive personal interaction with parents, the children of low-income, immigrant families did well, special education placement rates were moderate, and the school consistently earned a B or A on the state grading system. At another school with a similarly high percentage of non-English speaking, immigrant children, Haitian rather than Hispanic, we saw a high-energy, enthusiastic African American principal struggling to increase educational outcomes in the midst of a faculty of whom perhaps one third were effective. This principal told us she could not choose her faculty, while the principal at Green Acres did.

This discrepancy seemed to reflect different policies across the school district's administrative regions, differential treatment of administrators, or both. What accounts for this? Is it a matter of social capital in terms of who knows whom in the school district? Is it ethnic prejudice so deeply embedded in the thinking of educators as to be unrecognized? Is it just the way things are, with established patterns being too hard to break even by those who are aware of the inequities? Brantlinger (2001) has challenged this last type of interpretation, stating that structural theories make it appear that external forces are in control, while "agency and deliberate intention remain invisible. Yet, if there are no intentions, there is no responsibility and no possibility for change" (p. 12).

In concluding our discussion of how school structures affected children, we reiterate that there was no clear-cut connection between structural issues and special education placement. The fact that poor Black children received the least adequate schooling did not mean that they were necessarily at greater risk of special education placement, since placement rates in these schools ranged from 3.5% to 9.8%. Nevertheless, the structural issues outlined in this chapter point to an accumulation of detrimental policies that combined to limit children's achievement. In some cases, this pressure pushed children at the border further toward the special education end of the performance spectrum. However, whether or not children would be placed depended more on the context of each school than on the child's own performance. In the following chapter we consider the roles of race and culture in these children's educational contexts.

CHAPTER 3

Cultural Consonance, Dissonance, and the Nuances of Racism

I guess you're looking for racial bias in referrals. But all the students here are Black!

—School administrator

TO SAY THAT discrimination is systemic or "institutional" is not to say that individuals bear no responsibility for it. In the case of schools, it is in the privacy of the classroom that each individual teacher bears the responsibility of being the mediator of the larger ecology. In this chapter we ask, How does institutional racism play out in the classroom?

One of the first reactions we received from school personnel in many schools was exemplified by the quotation that introduces this chapter. Many school personnel believed that the concept of overrepresentation was not relevant in schools where Black or Hispanic students predominated. In answer to this comment, we pointed out that although ethnic disproportionality in special education referrals will not exist *within* a school that has all Black or all Hispanic students, a high rate of referral from that school contributes to the overall pattern of disproportionality within the school district and the state.

Reflecting on the above quotation, however, brings us to a deeper understanding of the complexity of racism. The commonsense notion behind school personnel's view was that racially discriminatory practice cannot be found within a racially homogenous population. Certainly, in the absence of a second ethnic group it is not possible to say that one child was referred over another because of race. However, it is still possible that professionals' views of a child may be influenced by aspects of the child's racial identity that become interwoven with historical stereotypes of low intelligence, stigmatized behaviors, poverty, or detrimental family circumstances. In such a situ-

ation, a high rate of referral to special education may be related to prejudices based on combined racism, classism, or cultural hegemony. Further,
the possibility of racism becoming internalized by its victims has also been
noted (K. B. Clark, 1965; Delgado & Stefancic, 2000), with the implication
that individuals may engage in race-based discriminatory practice against
members of their own group.

Our findings were not identical in all schools. In some schools we saw
clear-cut examples, even patterns, of educational practice that seemed to be
affected by racist or classist preconceptions. However, in most schools the
findings were ambiguous, even contradictory, as we observed across and
within classrooms. Thus, as we discuss various aspects of this theme, we will
offer vignettes illustrating different findings, but only in rare cases will we
argue that any one of these represented a general pattern.

RACISM AS A STRUCTURAL ISSUE

Despite our nation's official ideology of equity, data on inequity in public
services, including education (Darling-Hammond & Post, 2000; U.S. Department of Education, 2001) and health (National Academy of Sciences, 2002),
indicate the ongoing impact of the legacy of racist beliefs on the social, political, and economic structures of the society. How does this legacy become perpetuated?

Most scholars addressing racism currently describe it in terms of an
insidious ideology whose presence is so pervasive as to be invisibly present
in the lives of most people (e.g., Tatum, 1992). Essed (1991), arguing that
the distinction between individual and institutional racism is a false dichotomy
that obscures the role of individual agency, proposed the term "everyday
racism," as the intersection of micro- and macrosociological dimensions of
racism. Practices and meanings that have developed as a result of "social-
ized racist notions" (p. 52) become normative within our daily routines and
appear as the "common sense . . . rules for perceiving and dealing with the
other" (Bonilla-Silva, 1996, p. 474).

The idea that racist practice may be so interwoven into the affective
landscape of classrooms as to be hard to isolate and document gives rise to
several questions: Exactly how do racist attitudes infiltrate the classroom?
Is there an important difference between personally held prejudice and discriminatory practice? If a teacher holds racist beliefs, will it be evident in the
kinds of decisions she makes about children? Will it be evident to the children themselves? Will it affect their performance? Irvine (1990) answers these
questions in the affirmative, stating:

Part of the puzzle of black non-achievement has to be related to this predicament: Some teachers are in classrooms with black and low-income students whom they prefer not to teach and, even worse, do not like as individuals. (p. 48)

There have been many approaches to explaining how negative attitudes affect students. The "self-fulfilling prophecy" (Merton, 1948; Rosenthal & Jacobson, 1968) argues that children respond to teacher's expectations of them. Ogbu (1987), Fordham (1988), and others have interpreted low achievement of Black students as a form of resistance and withdrawal by the students themselves. Spencer (1995) has argued that student resistance must be viewed in terms of normal responses of youth at different developmental periods, and Steele's (1997) research has demonstrated that perceived "stereotype threat" can depress Black students' academic functioning and test scores. A study by Jussim, Eccles, and Madon (1996) goes further, suggesting that Black students' academic performance is actually more vulnerable to negative teacher perceptions than is the performance of their White peers. In a well-controlled study of 1,664 sixth graders, these researchers found that teacher perceptions had a negative impact three times greater on the test scores and grades of Black students than that on those of White students.

Beyond personal interactions and perceptions, a large body of literature has focused on culture and cultural hegemony as the mediators of discriminatory practices. Thus, Gay (2000) makes a subtle distinction between attitudes to race and to culture, arguing that "while most teachers are not blatant racists, many probably are cultural hegemonists. They expect all students to behave according to the school's cultural standards of normality" (p. 46). Gay proposes that the goal should be "culturally responsive caring" by teachers who are at the same time "academic task-masters" (p. 75).

As we searched for examples and counterexamples of biased practice, we treated issues of cultural hegemony in curriculum content as beyond our scope. We focused instead on the cultural contexts of schools, interpersonal communications, and referral practices.

Cultural Hegemony as a Contextual Bias

The concept of cultural hegemony (Gramsci, 1929–1935/1971) means that the cultural style, beliefs, and practices of the mainstream of a society infiltrate the values and behaviors of all sectors of the society and are valued and privileged above all others. Thus, public contexts explicitly and implicitly favor the dominant culture, which, in the case of the United States, is derived from what Spindler and Spindler (1990) have called the referent ethniclass—or White, middle-class Americans. This is certainly the case in schools. We refer to these biases as contextual to distinguish them from the specific actions of individual faculty and staff.

The hegemony of this group means that a bias in its favor is built into most public situations, resulting in a sense of cultural consonance for some and dissonance for others. Let us consider the meaning of *cultural consonance* for a moment. We could define it as a comfort level that does not require one to change one's accent, one's language, one's tone of voice, or one's laughter, or as an environment where language preference, customs, and interaction style are shared and implicitly valued by all. It is natural for most of us to prefer such a setting, although members of many minority groups, through necessity, develop skills in becoming "border crossers" (Giroux & McLaren, 1994). As the notion of "White privilege" suggests (McIntosh, 1989), the opposite is not necessarily true, in that most White middle-class Americans can choose not to cross over into minority cultures.

Although we noted nuances of cultural difference in the public areas of schools in which Hispanic or African American students predominated, it was clear that middle-class Anglo American culture was the normal currency of classrooms. It was also clear that students most familiar with this culture were at an advantage affectively, if not cognitively. Arising from this fact is the question, Is cultural consonance between teachers and students a requirement for success in schools? Our answer is no, since we saw effective and ineffective teachers of all ethnicities. The counselor in one of the predominantly Black, inner-city schools was adamant on this point, exclaiming:

> The best-qualified teacher should be the teacher for the job. There's a teacher who's been called all kind of White names, but she was good. . . . If you care enough about the kids, you're gonna do the job. . . . But a workshop isn't really going to do it. It has to be your heart. It has to be strong.

We do believe, though, that cultural consonance was a plus, once the basic requirements of good teaching were met.

Understanding across cultures can be hard to accomplish in the face of the U.S. history of racial oppression. An African American community involvement specialist at the same school as the counselor cited above felt strongly that there needed to be more African American teachers at the school, because other teachers could not understand the community as well. She said:

> I think that basically it is because they are different. I mean if they were to just study Black culture, maybe they would understand. And there again, I came up during the time of Dr. Martin Luther King. I know what it is to be segregated. I know what it is to be looked

down upon because of my race. I remember when I first started, when the Whites didn't want us there but they had to because of the law. . . . If they could truly, truly, truly know and get down with our culture and understand what poverty really is, what kind of fights there are for you. And we shouldn't have to fight, I was born here. They just get more things just given to them and we have to fight. And don't get me started there!

The last sentence underscores the fact that racial tensions in this study ran in many directions. A notion of "people of color" as a generalized group, distinct from Anglo American Whites, does not work in this community, since many Hispanics in the region generally do not see themselves, and are not seen as, "people of color." This teacher's reference to a privileged "they" (who, implicitly, were not "born here") represented a theme of resentment common among African Americans in this city—a belief that immigrants, particularly from Hispanic countries, tend to get preferential treatment and allowances that are not available to African Americans. Also, because many Hispanics in the area have a combination of Caucasian features, relative wealth and status, or both, they tend to be accorded a higher place in the community's ethnic ranking. This was explicitly stated by a Black faculty member in a predominantly Hispanic school, who spoke of the difficulties experienced by students who were not Hispanic, such as an African American girl who was suffering from low self-esteem because she "does not look like" the rest of her classmates. This teacher spoke also of racial bias among her colleagues. She said:

> Here they make sure that you understand the distinction, you're Black. And this is a White person, a Hispanic, and I feel we need to get away from that. And when I came in one day in that class, one adult told me, "I'm having a problem, this Black kid has been disrespectful," and I was very upset. And, I cannot hide my feelings when I'm upset and I said, "I'm sorry but, this Black kid has a name." Let's call him by his first name. So, already you can see, if the person is talking to me as an adult and using that, what happens when I'm not around in that room?

Although we saw many Hispanic and other teachers who related very well to African American children, information from several schools indicated that many teachers had a preference for the "ESOL" group. The comparison between African American and Hispanic children was not only offered by non-Black personnel, however. An African American faculty member who had been moved to a predominantly Hispanic school described her fifth graders as being "super innocent . . . like babies . . . with their Barbies and their . . . Pokémon cards." By contrast, she said, second graders in the African American neighborhood "knew about drugs . . . about sex . . . about guns."

Teaching the Culture of Power

While the negative aspects of inner-city communities are clearly detrimental to many children, our observations of strong teachers in the inner-city schools showed that children being "street smart" or "too grown" did not mean they could not be taught the behavioral and academic skills needed for school success. In the face of much discussion over the extent to which success in school requires that students meet the expectations of the dominant culture (e.g., Fordham, 1988; O'Connor, 1997; Ogbu, 1987), we concur with Delpit (1988), who argued that explicit inculcation of the "culture of power" is needed, along with strong support of the children's home cultures and languages. Thus, the children are given the cultural capital that will contribute to their success in the mainstream. In the following chapter we will offer an exemplar of this process—a strong African American teacher in a predominantly African American school who argued that teaching the culture of power was exactly her purpose in explicitly teaching acceptable school behaviors to her kindergartners.

DOCUMENTING BEHAVIOR AND INTERPRETING RACISM

While there was ample evidence that race and culture were inextricably woven into the fabric of the school contexts we observed, personal racial bias in classroom practice was not easy to document. Perhaps it was the tightness of the weave that made it difficult for us to isolate racism from all the other "isms" that pervaded our interviews and observations. In our research we looked for bias in terms of negative or positive preconceptions or preferences expressed by teachers as well as in terms of negative or positive relationships with students. We sought examples of behaviors that appeared to reflect these essentially intangible aspects of classroom interactions.

We found that relationships were easy to document, whether positive or negative. Positive relationships could be seen in the physical affection between a child and teacher; smiles or laughter that produced a good feeling in the classroom; or a teacher who would take an angry or sad child aside and counsel her gently, out of earshot of the other children. Negative relationships were evident when a teacher insulted children and their families to their face or in front of the entire class, and in the angry or defiant expressions on children's faces when that teacher addressed them. In all schools, both positive and negative relationships were evidenced between teachers and children of their own ethnicity, as well as across ethnicities. However, it was much harder to determine whether racial or social-class bias motivated these relationships. We will use one classroom as an example of how difficult it can be to determine the presence of bias, despite teachers' explicit statements and researchers' nagging intuitions. The story is also an example of the possibility of a teacher being able to practice professionalism despite the presence of personal biases.

AN EXEMPLAR: "VERY GOOD, MAH MAN!"

Ms. Q, a White, Hispanic teacher in an inner-city school, was potentially a strong teacher. However, a tendency to be unduly harsh undermined this impression. She described the African American children and their community in extremely derogatory terms, stating, for example, that her first graders did not know "how to walk, how to sit in a chair." Concluding her list of deficiencies, she exclaimed: "It's cultural!"

We observed Ms. Q's classroom twice toward the end of our first (academic) year of research. Seeing her getting inches away from a child's face and reprimanding her in an extremely loud and harsh voice for some minor infraction, we had to assume that her negative attitude to this child and others had been building throughout the year. On the second occasion a few weeks later, a visitor joined our observation and expressed shock at Ms. Q's harsh manner with the children, noting that she seemed either to not like teaching or not like the students. Ms. Q seemed unhappy and angry.

In the fall of the following year, Ms. Q was a changed person. She greeted us with smiles, exclaiming delightedly that she was happy that she had been assigned "the ESOL [infusion] class." The class included approximately one third Hispanic students, whom she described as "generally calmer and better behaved." Certainly, in our eight observations of this classroom, we saw that Ms. Q's relationships with the group as a whole were much better than with the previous year's class, and we noted her strong instructional skills. Indeed, both the children and the teacher were "calmer and better behaved."

Despite Ms. Q's characterization of the superior behavior of the Hispanic children, our observations showed that the troublesome children were as often Hispanic as African American. Two Hispanic boys, Juan and Francisco, though reasonably compliant under Ms. Q's firm hand, would literally run wild in the less structured setting of the music class, tormenting the teacher and instigating others to do the same. One or two other children stood out, such as Jimmy, an African American boy whose family problems were severe and who would act out occasionally, and Tomás, a Hispanic boy who tended to be a bit hyperactive when he was bored. Andre was an African

American boy about whom the teacher complained consistently. This was a puzzle to us, since in four out of five observations where he was a target focus (unknown to him), we found him very attentive and eager, shooting his hand up to answer, but seldom being called on by the teacher.

Ms. Q's greater empathy for the Hispanic children was evident in the way she interpreted their difficulties. For example, after describing Juan as "a very angry child" and Francisco as having behavior problems but "very manageable," she said she "feels bad" for these two, because they may have a learning problem and the bad behavior may be a result of frustration. She did not express such feelings of sympathy for any of the African American children with behavior and academic problems, although they were all lower academically than Juan and Francisco, yet generally better behaved. In fact, Juan's Scholastic Aptitude Test (SAT) scores were above those of the group generally—at the 62nd percentile in math and 25th in reading; Francisco's scores were at the 21st percentile in math and 17th in reading. Andre and Jimmy, whom Ms. Q described as having behavior problems, had much lower scores—both around the 2nd percentile in reading and the 10th in math, indicating that their learning needs were greater than those of both the Hispanic boys.

Despite this evident ethnic preference, Ms. Q's feelings did not seem to affect her referrals. This teacher was one of the three-highest-referring teachers across the 12 schools; the other two were Anglo American teachers, also in predominantly Black schools. However, we noted that Ms. Q used the CST process as a supportive as well as an evaluative mechanism. That year, she referred 18 students of varying ethnicities, about half of whom were found eligible for special education services. At the CST conferences, with the exception of negative interactions with Andre's mother, Ms. Q treated the parents with respect and seemed to use the committee for the benefit of the children, often by seeking parents' cooperation through daily or weekly home-school contracts. One such case was Jimmy, about whom Ms. Q was concerned because of his mother's alcoholism, but whom she did not feel needed special education placement. We concluded that, while we did note ethnic bias in Ms. Q's interactions with the children, she did engage in an equitable and helpful referral process.

Despite this teacher's strengths, however, in our classroom observations we noted a steady undertone of cultural bias. Our final illustration of this is of a particularly subtle form, whereby the teacher's attitude seemed to be condescending toward the child's ethnicity. In the example we give here, this might not be evident to anyone who has not experienced such condescension, but we believe it would be understood by people who have. Ms. Q, who normally spoke in Standard English to her class, became effusive when an African American boy who seldom participated gave a surprisingly good answer. She exclaimed: "Good! Very good, mah man!" The switch to an approximation of African American vernacular was out of place and made the two researchers present feel distinctly uncomfortable. Both researchers were Black and their immediate exchange of glances confirmed that their gut reactions had been identical.

To be clear on this example, the impression of condescension did not come merely from the fact of a Hispanic teacher's using a Black vernacular phrase. It was that this was so unusual for Ms. Q, so out of character, that it came across as contrived. By contrast, in a classroom in another similar school, we noted an excellent Hispanic kindergarten teacher whose regular repertoire of interaction included terms of endearment commonly used by African American teachers, such as *baby* and *honey*. These expressions seemed natural to the teacher in the context of affectionate and caring relationships with her students. We believe that these two groups of children would know the difference.

PERCEIVED RACIAL BIAS IN CLASSROOM ARRANGEMENTS AND REFERRALS

Our sense of "easy to spot but hard to prove" bias was frequently triggered in schools in which African American students were in the minority, whether among Anglo American or Hispanic peers. In such classrooms, it was common to see an African American, usually male, student seated separately in the classroom, often at the teacher's desk or at the back of the room. This child might be the only, or one of a couple of, African American children in the room, so this seating arrangement was very noticeable. We were not always aware of what behaviors had earned the children this distinction, but we did see some classrooms where the children so seated did, indeed, display behaviors that the teacher found troubling. Occasionally, though not usually, the teachers in these rooms were African Americans.

The best exemplar of this pattern was Sunnybrook, the school that Matthew attended. African American students from a relatively low-income neighborhood were bused into this affluent, predominantly Anglo American neighborhood and constituted approximately 17% of the student population. The distinction between the two groups was marked by common references to students being from either "east or west of the highway." As we will detail later in the book, the high achievement of the majority of students made that of the African American students seem lower than it would have seemed at low-income schools. The same was true of their behaviors, which were perceived by school personnel as less compliant and more troublesome. The principal of this school commented on the fact that such judgments are relative to local norms and expectations.

The teachers whom we observed intensively in this school were both very strong, one an African American and one an Anglo American. In observing their classrooms, we detected no differential behavior toward the children based on ethnicity. However, all of the six referrals from the latter teacher's class were for African American children. Three of these were found eligible for special education—one as EMR and two as LD. Unfortunately, we were not able to gain permission to examine the level of these students' work. The other three did not go to testing—one because the parents did not sign consent, another because it was agreed to get the child into tutoring and monitor her progress, and for the third we do not know the outcome. The African American teacher referred two children, Austin and Matthew, both also African American, who were found eligible for LD and EH respectively. We will report on these cases in detail in our later discussion of the construction of these disabilities.

Despite an initial welcome from this school's administration, as our research progressed we had considerable difficulty obtaining access to detailed records of placement rates. All indications were that this was a school where much more intensive research was needed to ascertain the reasons for the disproportionately high rate of placement of Black students. Indeed, we noted an approximately equal distribution of White students and Black students in the school's LD classrooms. This balance led one of the special education teachers to say that the numbers were not disproportionate, since they were equal. Clearly this teacher had not reflected on the meaning of the term, for Black students represented 17% of the school's population, but approximately 50% of her class. In reflecting on our findings, we felt frustrated at our inability to adequately probe the processes in this school. Not only was the pattern similar to the findings of Oswald, Coutinho, Best, and Singh (1999) that Black overrepresentation was evident in high-income districts that were predominantly White, but, we believe, the presence of court-ordered school desegregation was also salient. Eitle (2002), in an analysis of survey data on 1,203 school districts nationwide, found that Black overrepresentation in special education programs increased in districts that were operating under court-ordered desegregation. Eitle concluded that the pattern reflected "alternative forms of segregation" (p. 599) being practiced by school or school district administrators. Whether or not the discriminatory effect was intentional in this school, we believe that the context of a forced racial mixture had many disadvantages for Black students, one of which could have been increased likelihood of special education placement.

ETHNICITY IN TEAM MEMBERSHIP, REFERRALS, AND TEACHING STYLES

In most schools, faculty membership on CST teams was ethnically diverse, revealing an attempt to reflect the mixture of the student population. However, since district policy required that membership include an administrator and a counselor, ethnicity could not be a criterion for these two key positions. Additional members were usually a general education teacher, the referring teacher, and other ad hoc members according to the case being considered. Some schools included the psychologist as a regular team member.

In one inner-city school serving a student population that was 99% African American, three issues related to teacher ethnicity came to our attention. One was the complaint of an irate parent that the CST team comprised only White members. The administration explained that this was coincidental, since the requirement is that the AP, counselor, and psychologist serve on the CST. All three happened to be White. The fourth team member had to be a teacher, and the teacher thought most appropriate by the administration was a reading specialist who also happened to be White. After the parent's challenge, however, the administration changed the CST composition to include an African American teacher who was much respected in the school as an excellent teacher.

The second issue related to ethnicity at this school was the fact that most special education referrals came from White teachers. Some personnel believed that this reflected Black teachers' lack of confidence in the special education system, while others argued that it might be related to a third issue—differential behavior management styles.

The question of behavior management was particularly interesting because it reflected the notion of cultural fit with African American students' behavioral styles (Gay, 2000). An African American professional associated with this school believed that the expressive verbal and physical interaction style displayed by many African American children tended to intimidate some Anglo American teachers and that the children, perceiving this, acted out as a result. She was speaking in general, not just regarding this school. However, our observations of 11 of the 16 general-education classrooms in this small school did reveal differential classroom-management styles that, to some extent, seemed to relate to teacher ethnicity. Specifically, what we refer to as the "passive" style was displayed only by Anglo American teachers.

Authoritarian Style

There were three teachers, one African American, one Hispanic, and one White, whose management styles were characterized by a stern authoritarianism. The White teacher ran a calm, very structured classroom in which students typically scored well, although we noted a great deal of negative ignoring of a child who was working well but whose grooming left much to be desired. The Hispanic teacher's class was generally chaotic. She made sporadic efforts to use positive reinforcers such as stickers, but mostly resorted to yelling and threats. The African American teacher used an overly rigid structure and constant yelling. The researcher commented in her notes that, while in this room, she felt as though she was in "boot camp."

Authoritative, but Friendly

Five teachers (four African American and one Hispanic) displayed this approach, four very effectively and one moderately so. While none were effusive in their manner, all used a lot of verbal praise and enforced clear standards for behavior. Their instructional approaches varied, but all included explicit instruction, consistent monitoring of seat work, and relevance to children's lives and interests. Overall, these teachers were effortless in their reinforcement of behavior and their quietly authoritative handling of their students. The children had no doubt about who was in charge. Two African American teachers in this group had the reputation of being excellent teachers and both demonstrated what Ladson-Billings (1994) has referred to as a key feature of effective teachers of inner-city children—an explicit affiliation with the community, even the neighborhood of their students. One of these teachers told us that she works in this school to "give something back to the community," while the other spoke of her willingness to go directly to students' homes to talk with parents when issues arose, a strategy which, she said, "the White teachers won't do!"

Passive Style

Teachers exhibiting this style made little effort to impose authority on the class. All three teachers who fitted this pattern were Anglo American. At the most extreme end was a music teacher, whose total neglect of classroom management resulted in chaos, which will be described in the following chapter. The behavior in the classrooms of the other two "passive"-style teachers was not as extreme, but the teachers' management styles were characterized by minimal or no intervention related to troubling behavior. One of these began her lesson with a creative approach—using a puppet that initially gained the children's attention and enthusiasm—but her ignoring of two disruptive individuals gradually led to total inattention and finally a chaotic environment. At the end of the lesson, the teacher, who had started with a friendly and relaxed style, was visibly angry. The other "passive"-style teacher was Ms. E, whom we observed twice, once in a first-grade class in the spring and then in the subsequent fall when she was assigned to a second-grade class. In both classrooms, this teacher showed a low-key, friendly manner toward the children but made no effort whatever to curtail the early signs of disruptive behavior. Rather, she ignored these signs, allowed the behavior to escalate and spread to other members of the class, and then demonstrated an expression of resignation and frustration that she had been assigned a class with all the troublesome children. A brief excerpt from the second-grade observation will illustrate:

> The children work quietly for about 10 minutes, moving from one worksheet to the next, while the teacher circulates looking at work. Larry enters the room. He never really settles down. Within minutes he starts playing with his chair, rocking and balancing it. Next, he goes over to a girl who is standing next to her chair, and he whisks her chair away, grinning. The girl responds with a show of annoyance but is smiling. The teacher is standing quite close to them but with her back to them as she looks at a child's work. She does not turn around or show any awareness of Larry's behavior. A boy in a green shirt gets up and starts to walk around. He goes and sits on the high stool at the blackboard in the front of the room and looks around the room with a grin. Soon he gets down from the stool and starts a slow chase after Larry. They make it through a couple of rows of desks and then the teacher looks up and says the boy's name softly. He sits down for a few minutes. Larry is still walking around . . . the noise level is gradually rising. . . . The boy in the green shirt gets up and starts to chase after Larry until he gets to the row where the teacher is standing and she reaches out and stops him by putting an arm gently on his shoulder. She tells him to go and copy his homework from the board. He goes to his desk and, standing, copies the work neatly into his notebook. . . . By now all the children in the room are talking to each other, moving around, and the general sense of disorder is escalating steadily. . . . When the children leave for their Spanish class, the teacher turns to us with a resigned expression and says, "You see what I mean?"

Ms. E's tone of resignation indicated a pervasive sense of low expectation for her students. As one of the highest-referring teachers in the school, she had, in the previous year, referred almost half her class. She told our team that she did not believe in the "cooperative consultation" (pre-referral) process, because she believed in handling the children's problems by herself until she was sure they really needed to be evaluated. She believed that the children in the school were becoming steadily "worse" because of their detrimental home and community settings. Thus, she felt that the team should "trust" her judgment and that her referrals should go forward to evaluation.

From these observations, we cannot come to any conclusions about typologies of behavior management according to teacher ethnicity. However, this limited, but in-depth, view offers examples of concerns frequently expressed in the field about low expectations and about cultural mismatch in behavioral management, particularly in reference to the difficulties of some Anglo American teachers in handling behavior issues with African American children. We are not suggesting that teachers' ethnicity needs to be matched to that of their students. Rather, we concur with scholars such as Gay (2000), Cartledge and Milburn (1996), and Ballenger (1992), who argue that caring, responsive teachers can become aware of different cultural patterns in children's behavior and can learn strategies and approaches that may work better with either individuals or groups.

Most important to this discussion is the role of poorly managed classrooms in referrals to special education. As we will note at length in our chapter on decision making at the conference table, Ms. E's total lack of behavior management was never mentioned when her referrals were brought to the CST conference. One of her students was Kanita, a child found to "qualify" for emotional disturbance, whose case we will describe in detail in later chapters.

CROSSING THE BIAS BARRIERS

To what extent did the various kinds of bias we have noted show up in most classroom interactions? We cannot generalize across classrooms or schools. We saw examples of them all. However, we also saw examples of many teachers who successfully crossed the barriers of bias. There was no single route to this success, since these teachers represented a range of teaching and personality styles. Perhaps the only common thread we could feel sure of was that these teachers expected the children to work and to succeed, yet they were capable also of a light touch that reached out to the children as people worthy of respect. They seemed to illustrate Gay's (2000) model of "culturally responsive, academic task-masters." The following examples will illustrate.

In one classroom in a predominantly Haitian American school, a veteran Anglo American teacher was simply a very good teacher, despite the fact that she was a very high referrer. She was strict, but she tried to be fair. Laughing at herself as an old dinosaur who couldn't understand the children's complicated schedules, she would give the children the responsibility of telling her when they had to go to some special program. She was humorous and entertaining while also being very serious about the children's learning. She cared if the children did well and they knew it. Despite the complaints of many teachers that the SFA materials were boring and repetitive, this teacher made wonderful use of them, and she adapted some of the SFA strategies to the skill levels and interests of her students (for more detail on this, see Klingner, Cramer, & Harry, in press). For example, she explained that the SFA "jump in reading" is supposed to have children "jump in" spontaneously to read aloud. Her children, she felt, were not ready for that, so she modified the activity by moving quickly around the room touching children on their shoulders to indicate their turn to read. As she chose the children, she would put on a comical facial expression and wiggle her legs to indicate her own excitement at deciding which child to call on. The children giggled and became very excited waiting for their turns. Every child was called on.

A Cuban American teacher in a predominantly African American school used humor and her own natural spontaneity to build wonderful relationships with her students. For example:

> She encourages them to think of a special day in their life. She breaks out singing the song "Unforgettable." Then she goes around the classroom brainstorming with the class. The students give examples of special days in their life. She encourages everyone to volunteer an answer, reminding them that it won't be wrong—she just wants them to think.

In a school that served a very low income community of African American and Hispanic students, negative comments from faculty often suggested biases against the former group. In the class of one of our selected teachers, a lively Anglo American New Yorker, we saw no sign of negative interactions with any children. Her natural humor and strong relationships with the children made behavior management seem easy, as in the following example:

> While they worked on their assignment, the students spoke freely, but quietly. (They seemed to know the limitations for acceptable activity). A few students who had questions about their assignments or who sought approval for their work went to the teacher while she helped an African American girl whose hair was braided and beaded. . . . Other students followed suit and, after a few minutes, seven students surrounded her. She said to the class in a direct but soft voice, "Now listen. How many teachers and how many students are there here?" "One and thirty-two," called out most of the students in unison. Then, she asked the class, "Can I talk with each of you at the same time?" All, almost all, said, "No." One boy, Osvaldo, however, said, "Yes." The teacher heard him and responded, "Well, Osvaldo, it may seem like that to you, since I'm always talking to you." The whole class roared with laughter, especially the teacher and Osvaldo.

In a predominantly African American inner-city school, where negative stereotypes of children's families were openly expressed by faculty of all ethnicities, the researcher sometimes sought refuge in the class of an outstanding African American teacher who addressed her boys and girls with the titles *Mr.* and *Ms.* Halfway through an excellent math lesson, we could feel the sense of solidarity occasioned by the teacher's spontaneous shift from Standard English into an African American tone and accent as she exhorted her class to keep their attention focused: "Y'all wit me?" she challenged, to which the students chorused a rousing, "Yeah!"

CONCLUSIONS

Our classroom observations do not give us clear-cut answers to the question of whether racial bias against particular groups contributed to ethnic disproportionality in special education. The subtleties of racism are difficult to document, and though we could detect it in various "moments of exclusion" (Lareau & Horvat, 1999) that we observed in schools, we had no direct evidence of its contribution to disproportionality, since there was no clear pattern, across schools, of referrals by teacher ethnicity.

Yet we could see clearly that racial bias was present in the nuances of teachers' tone and manner toward children. It was present in the built-in hegemony that creates a "goodness of fit" (Keogh, 2000) between a school and some of its students, but not others. It was present in some teachers' discomfort with, even fear of, the behavioral styles of their students and in the low expectations that accompanied this discomfort. We suspect that the more vulnerable children were affected by these biases in ways that our research was not able to substantiate. In contrast, bias was countered by professionals whose authenticity allowed them to develop the skills of a border-crosser (Giroux & McLaren, 1994).

While teacher bias can most often only be inferred, teachers' behaviors are readily evident. In the following chapter we will paint a broad picture of the types of instruction and behavior management we observed across the 12 schools. We argue that the institutional bias against schools serving the poorest, Black populations resulted in an imbalance of teacher quality that limited these students' opportunity to learn. This placed the most vulnerable students at increased risk of school failure and special education placement.

CHAPTER 4

In the Classroom: Opportunity to Learn

We ask whether the school experience itself contributes to racial dispro-
portion in academic outcomes and behavioral problems that lead to placement in special and gifted education . . . our answer is "yes."
        —M. Suzanne Donovan & Christopher T. Cross,
        Minority Students in Special and Gifted Education

SIX HUNDRED and seventy nine observations over three years revealed
a clear trend in which the weakest classrooms were in schools serving
the lowest-income Black populations. This reflected the pattern noted earlier of a discrepancy in teacher qualifications according to the economic level
of the student body. In these schools, the quality of teacher instruction and
classroom management was extremely variable, ranging from excellent to
absolutely unacceptable. In most other schools, teacher quality was much
more even, with no teachers exhibiting the extremely weak skills observed
in the low-income, predominantly Black schools.

What do we mean by "extremely weak" teaching? We mean classrooms
in which teachers were often distraught or angry; where rough reprimands,
idle threats, and personal insults were common; and where teachers' attempts
to curb out-of-seat and off-task behavior were either sporadic and ineffective
or unduly harsh. In these classrooms, instruction was frequently offered with
no context, no attempt to connect to children's previous learning or personal
experience. Here, rote instruction took the place of meaningful explanation
and dialogue. Often, poorly planned lessons were at the heart of the problem.

In the previous chapter we offered an example of an excellent Anglo
American teacher, in a predominantly Haitian school, who effectively crossed
"the bias barriers" in her instruction. This teacher was one of a handful of
excellent teachers in the school. In a classroom just below hers, a second-
grade teacher, trying to use group work, had not thought through the details
or timing of the tasks. When the children became inattentive or disruptive,

the teacher would give up on the activity and introduce another poorly structured task. Another very weak second-grade teacher tried to recapture children's attention by suddenly requiring them all to raise their hands or put their hands on their heads for a few moments. Across the hallway, a third-grade teacher continually threatened punishments that he never implemented and finally resorted to a threat to keep the children from going to lunch, which, of course, he could not do. Upstairs, another third-grade teacher would repeatedly insult and physically threaten children.

We contend that this discrepant teacher quality limited poor Black children's opportunity to learn. While not the only factor, this was a key feature that pushed vulnerable children toward the failing end of the continuum. We present examples from two contrasting schools: In the first there were only a few teachers whom we rated as highly effective, and in the second there were only a few we considered weak.

CONTRASTING SCHOOLS: INEQUITY IN OPPORTUNITIES TO LEARN

Creekside Elementary: Few Effective Teachers

We conducted 33 observations across 18 general-education K–3 classrooms at this predominantly Black school, where 97% of the students were on free or reduced-price lunch. Our overall evaluation was that three teachers were very effective, seven were average, and eight were weak. As in many of the schools serving low-income, predominantly Black students, we witnessed a great deal of yelling and many teachers who really seemed frazzled, frustrated, and uncertain about how to manage their students. In many classrooms, students seemed out of control, with very little teaching or learning taking place. When we did see instruction, much of it was uninspired, to say the least (for example, of the rote or "do the exercises in the book" variety), as in our first example below.

The following brief excerpt is from our field notes of an observation in a third-grade classroom, taught by an Anglo American teacher with several years' experience. We considered this teacher to have adequate control of the class, but to be weak in instruction. This teacher's failure to engage students in meaningful learning activities was typical of the instruction we saw in many classrooms in inner-city schools and is of great concern because it compromises students' opportunity to learn. The excerpt focuses on the lack of context for the lesson as well as on the teachers' low expectations for students' performance:

It's time for social studies. The teacher hastily explains that
students are to copy a sentence from the board: "There are seven

continents: . . ." She emphasizes, "To get an A, you must write neatly on the lines and include your name and the date."

[Observer's Comments: There was no look at a map, or identification of the continents, or linking with prior knowledge, or questioning, or checking for understanding. The teacher read the sentence to the students very quickly and told them to copy it. That was it. What struck me most was the low level of the work—no thinking involved whatsoever that I could tell. And I doubt much learning took place, either, except that Ms. A really likes for writing to be on the lines. And this is a third-grade class!]

The next example is from a lesson on the five senses that was so poorly conceptualized as to make little sense to first graders in a self-contained ESOL class for students at a beginning level of English proficiency. The teacher, who was Anglo American, and relatively new, was very verbal and rarely used the visual cues and other ESOL strategies that might have facilitated both her work and her students' learning. The example demonstrates ineffective ESOL instruction as well as poor classroom management:

The class was learning about the five senses. . . . The teacher said, "The last sense is the sense of touch. That means you feel." The teacher directed students to feel the floor with their elbows. "Can you feel it?"

[Observer's Comments: I noted that kids couldn't follow this, didn't understand what to do.]

The teacher yelled, "Some of you are being extremely rude. You are moving all around." Then she asked more calmly, "So you did feel the floor with your elbows, but do you normally feel with your elbow?" A few students responded, "No." The teacher asked, "What am I using to pick this up?" Next she yelled again, "You just finished telling me you were listening, Ezekiel. Were you lying to me? I'm only going to call on the people who are listening." Then she asked, "What am I using?" A girl said that she was using her hands and the teacher responded, "Excellent." Then she said, "Jefferson, touch my leg." "Go ahead. . . . what are you going to use to touch my leg?" Jefferson responded, "I use my hand." The teacher next snapped her fingers. . . . She turned to a boy standing in the corner (being disciplined): "I'm very unhappy with you. Turn around." To everyone else, she asked, "If I wanted to eat cake, what sense would I use?" . . .

The teacher said, "My point is that you use your sense of taste to decide if you like it." She yelled, "Pay attention to me, not his shoes! His shoes aren't going to give you a grade. I will." "If one more person touches shoes, I'm going to throw it in the garbage. It's important to make sure your shoes are tied, but not while I'm teaching."

[Observer's Comments: The students weren't really following this, or "getting it." There are so many ways to teach the senses! I'm not sure how much they understood, but these are ESOL 1s and 2s and she did not use visuals or other ESOL techniques—she just talked.]

We observed in this class seven times and found that the preceding example was typical. Although this was a school where the CST process was underused and very few referrals were made, this teacher referred seven of her students, including Ezekiel. She was very verbal, yelled a lot, and rarely used visual cues and other ESOL strategies. Yet at a CST meeting for Ezekiel, the teacher told the committee that she frequently used "visuals, manipulatives," and other ESOL techniques, "but he doesn't retain it. He can't transfer it to do it on his own." Our observations suggest, however, that Ezekiel and his classmates did not retain what was being taught because information had not been presented in comprehensible ways in the first place. This and the previous example illustrate a lack of planning and preparation for what potentially could have been rich topics of instruction. The standard of instruction in this and other, similar schools was clearly lower than that observed in schools in higher-income neighborhoods.

The following example is from a different first-grade class, from an observation of a science lesson taught by a Hispanic teacher who, like the previous teacher, was in her first few years of teaching. It is similar to the preceding example in that it also illustrates weak classroom management and instruction, as well as a lack of planning.

While asking about plants and animals, she is passing around Unifix cubes for the math lesson that will follow. Jamal throws his at his neighbor. The teachers tells him, "Jamal, go to time-out for a couple of minutes." She then continues with the lesson: "Trendon is going to tell us one of the differences between plants and animals." A student says, "Plants can't walk." The teacher interrupts, "Jamal, would you please put your shoes on and turn around and put your nose in the corner." Kids are playing with their Unifix cubes. . . .
    More and more students are playing with their cubes. The teacher's voice rises. "If I hear another block rolling across the table,

I'm going to take them away from you." She says something else about plants and animals and how animals can communicate, but then yells, "Leave them still [the blocks]!! Didn't I say not to use them yet? I don't want to see you pulling them apart." Students are still playing with blocks. (She previously had said that she would take them away, but doesn't). Now a student holds up his cubes with his pencil stuck on top. The teacher says sternly, "Darian, take your pencil off of there." "Michael, don't sit on your desk. You can only sit on a desk when you've finished college."

If only the teacher had waited to pass around the Unifix cubes! This teacher's good intention of using manipulatives for the teaching of math concepts was defeated by the critical mistake of distributing the cubes before the appropriate time. Having introduced this inevitable distraction, the teacher followed her mistake with empty threats that continually undermined her attempts to conduct the science lesson. It seems that the natural result of such a tactical error would be evident to any adult, yet such errors were frequent in classrooms such as this. Principals in inner-city schools lamented that they were stuck with "the bottom of the barrel" when selecting new hires. As illustrated by this example, however, we often had the impression that we were watching well-meaning teachers who were not adequately prepared for their assignments. It was clear that these teachers needed extensive professional development and support, yet we saw very little of this provided.

The next example is from a third-grade class taught by an experienced Black teacher who was known for being an advocate for her students. Eight students were sitting at computers working on math. Their computer screens showed pictures of ones, tens, and hundreds blocks. The teacher was instructing the rest of the class.

The teacher is at the front of the room. She asks students to take out their math books. Most students do so. The teacher says, "Johnson, you need to get out your math book. We are on page 149." A boy by me at the computers is shouting something in a loud voice, in Haitian Creole. The teacher adds, "Get out a piece of paper." Mike and Zachary are talking loudly, fooling around and laughing. Zachary now takes out a piece of paper and writes his name. Mike does not.

The boy at the computers is still talking. I hear, "Dr. Poo Poo." Another boy at the computers says, apparently to me, "Dr., he's cursing." Then to the teacher he says, "Ms. _____, he's talking about her mama [apparently mine]." The teacher says to the boy in question, "Why are you acting like this?" Another boy at the computers says to his neighbor, "Did you hear him talking about her mama?" The boy who had been shouting now calls out, "I didn't say her mama's stupid!" The teacher says, "Edgar, get off [the computer]." He does not.

Now the teacher turns her attention to the class. She says, "Take out a sheet of paper. We are going to do math." In a sarcastic tone, she adds "I love the way you waste your time." "You are going to look at problems and tell me what the thermometer says. I'm going to put the problems on the board and you are going to tell me if it's cold, warm, or hot." Perhaps three students are paying attention, while the others are watching the kids who are fooling around at the computers or at their seats, talking with their neighbors. One is playing with pencils in his pencil box.

This vignette illustrates how challenging it was for teachers to try to conduct a lesson while simultaneously managing students on computers. This difficulty was evident in many of the classrooms in the inner-city schools in which this computer program had been adopted. It was certainly typical in this classroom. Further, the teacher seemed at a loss to know how to respond to some of the boys' impolite behavior and really had no control over the flow of interactions among her students. Yet, in one notable exception, we learned that these same students were capable of focused, productive engagement in a well-structured and motivating task: We observed them taking a practice test in preparation for the upcoming mandatory statewide testing, and we were struck by how engaged they were, both while taking the test and while going over the answers, enthusiastically exclaiming, "Yes!" when an answer was correct. In contrast to other "lessons," this clearly was a meaningful activity for them, in that everyone was focused on the same activity and there were no interruptions. This contrast revealed that it was not the students who were lacking, but their teacher. Their motivation to do well on the test underscores the sad conclusion that excellent minds were being wasted in this school.

Some children, of course, were fortunate to be in the classrooms of the three strong general-education teachers we observed. These teachers, two African Americans and one Hispanic, had succeeded in establishing a positive rapport with their students and were effective at management and instruction. Lessons were appropriate, engaging, and well paced and students seemed excited about learning. High expectations were evident.

Bay Vista Elementary: Few Weak Teachers

Bay Vista was the antithesis of Creekside. At this predominantly Hispanic school, in which 68% of the students were on free or reduced-price lunch, we observed 34 K–3 general-education teachers. We considered 24 of these teachers to be strong, 9 to be adequate, and 1 to be weak. Overall, teachers seemed enthusiastic, well prepared for lessons, skilled in presentation and engagement, and "connected" with their students. We noted many examples of stimulating instruction and effective classroom management. The coordination across classrooms and within grade levels was impressive. The positive thinking among teachers, their belief that they were "doing it right" and truly helping their students, seemed palpable, a feature lacking in schools such as Creekside. As we walked into classrooms, we were struck with the impression that teachers really were *teaching*, not just sitting at their desks or giving assignments.

The two examples that follow indicate the rapport that was evident between teachers and their students as well as highlight effective instruction. Teachers used praise frequently and criticism rarely. This first example, from a bilingual first-grade class, represents the imaginative nature of many lessons as well as context and relevance:

> The teacher was walking around the room with a plastic board that had green glitter on it. She asked the students to place their hands on the glitter and then shake hands with the student next to them. When she had finished asking all the students to do this, she explained that, like the glitter, germs are easily transferred from one person to another. She explained that the germs could not be seen like the glitter could be, and that germs could only be removed with soap and water. The teacher explained that this is why it is important to take showers and wash our hands. She asked the students what they could do to stay healthy. Students raised their hands and waited to be called on before responding. Next the teacher explained the assignment. She told them they were to write two ways of staying healthy. She wrote the following on the board: "*Para ser saludable debo* _____. *También debo* _____." (To stay healthy I should _____. I should also _____.) The teacher handed out white notebook paper to the students. She asked them if they had any questions. No students raised their hands. The students began to work on their assignment. They were quiet, focused, and on task.

This next is from a bilingual kindergarten class:

> The teacher told them that now they were going to do something special, that she had a magic word. She said, with great suspense, "*Científicos.*" (Scientists.) She asked what it meant. A student said, "*Locos.*" (Crazy.) The teacher shook her head and said no. Another

student asked, "*Mágicos?*" (Magicians?) "No." Other students guessed, but their guesses weren't close. The teacher said that she was going to tell them. "*Son personas importantes que hacen experimentos.*" (They are important people who do experiments.) She said the last word with emphasis, and then, after a slight pause, building suspense, went on, "like discovering medicine." "They were the ones who observed that plants need water and sun to grow." The students were listening, enraptured. The teacher told them they were going to become scientists. She had them put on their thinking caps, special glasses, special gloves, and lab coats (all in pantomine). A student said, "*Y los pantolones!*" (And pants!) The teacher said that they didn't need pants because they had their lab coats. Now they were going to say the magic words and they would become scientists, "*Uno, dos, tres, cachachumbre.*" She shook all over while saying this. Then she said, "There are many intelligent and special scientists in this class." She put two glasses on each table. A student said (while she was doing this), "*Yo quiero mi mamá.*" ("I want my mother.") The teacher responded, "*Yo tambièn.*" (Me, too.) The students laughed. The teacher told them not to touch the glasses or they would get contaminated. She asked if they knew what that meant, and explained it meant "dirty." Then she let some students bring one of the cups from their table and go with her to get water.

These examples contrast noticeably with those from Creekside. Lessons were carefully planned and well prepared, and appropriate props were used. Instruction was motivating and exciting, at an appropriate level for students, with support so that they could be successful. Notably, these examples were not rare exceptions, but the norm. We were confident that, in contrast to students in some of our other schools, students at Bay Vista were receiving an adequate opportunity to learn.

CONTRASTING CLASSROOMS: STUDENTS' VARIABLE BEHAVIOR ACROSS SETTINGS

Besides revealing the pattern of variability across schools, our observations led us to a second clear-cut conclusion: Children's classroom behavior could not be assessed without reference to the skills of the teacher. We saw the same children behave very differently with an effective teacher as compared to an ineffective teacher, and we saw two classrooms side by side that were like night and day despite the fact that the children were from the same neighborhood and had the same racial and socioeconomic characteristics. We must note that the excellent teachers we saw in these schools proved absolutely that most of the children were malleable and responsive to their school environments.

In the better schools, where teacher skills were more consistent, the range of children's behavior across settings was noticeable but not extreme. In schools with wide teacher variability, contrasting behavior across settings could be dramatic. Below, two examples of the behavior of a group of kindergartners in a school serving a low-income African American population illustrate how the variability in teachers' skills resulted in totally different child behavior.

AN EXEMPLAR: FROM "I AM SPECIAL" TO CHAOS

Ms. L was an African American kindergarten teacher who told us that she saw her 16 years of teaching in this neighborhood as an opportunity to "give something back." She explained that because many of her students come from homes where they are given a great deal of responsibility for taking care of themselves, they have to be explicitly taught to comply with the behaviors expected in school. She said that this takes no longer than the first half of the fall semester. Our first observation in her room was toward the end of the school year, and on that occasion we observed 22 kindergartners filing into their classrooms from lunch with their fingers on their lips to remind themselves to be quiet. Six children went directly to the computer and the others to their desks without having to be told where to go. In the subsequent fall we had the opportunity to see the beginnings of Ms. L's program, as noted in the following excerpt from an observation in the last week of August—the 2nd day of the new school year:

> Ms. L leads her children in very quietly and tells them it's story time so they should sit on the mat. The kids go quickly over to the mat and sit. There are about 15 kids, all Black, half boys and half girls. All the children are dressed very neatly, most in school uniforms but a couple of girls are in very pretty dresses. Most of the girls have their hair braided neatly, some with dozens of beads.
>
> Ms. L stands in front of them, next to a small white board on which a few words are written. She begins by showing them the cover of the book and reminding them that they started reading it yesterday. [The story is "I Am Special."] She has a pleasant expression on her face and smiles frequently, speaking in a soft voice. Soon after beginning, she says quietly to a child, "Leroy, I've had enough, I've spoken to you three times. Now come and stand by me and I'll help you control your body, since you can't." Leroy comes over to her and stands at her side. . . .

She begins questioning to elicit the title of the story. . . . She encourages tangential discussions about several points, such as Leo being a sloppy eater. She points to the white board, where three words are already written—*late, bloomer,* and *sloppy.* . . . Throughout the story the children are attentive and participate well. At the end of the story the children clap spontaneously. She smiles and says, "When we like something, we don't have to clap. Let's learn how to rate the stories by a sign." She demonstrates thumbs up, thumbs down, and a shake of the fingers for "so-so." She asks them to rate the story and most give a thumbs up; one or two indicate so-so.

She goes on, "What was a special thing that Leo learned? Think! When you have an answer, hands up." The children raise hands and one says, "He can skate." She looks at him quizzically and smiles, shaking her head "no." Several children are calling out excitedly and she pauses, telling them that all they need to do is raise their hands and that she won't call on those who are yelling, "Me, me." She says, "You have to follow the rules."

. . . Then Ms. L leads them in Simon Says, but tricks them by doing something different from what she's telling them to do (puts her hands on head while saying, "Shoulders"). The children have a hard time following the spoken direction and most tend to imitate what they see her doing. She keeps at this, pointing out to them that she's "tricking" them and they need to listen to what she says no matter what she's doing. The children are all smiling, trying to beat her trick. She does body parts, and as she asks them to name the parts they shout excitedly. She tells them, "I like it when you talk soft." And she models a soft voice. The children begin to imitate her soft voice and their tone is much lower for the rest of the exercise.

Then she tells them it's time to go out to PE and says, "Yesterday when we did our tour, I showed you how to go to PE." . . . As she's reminding them, a girl standing in front of her is trying to scratch her back and Ms. L reaches over gently and scratches it for her without stopping what she's saying. She then tells the "young ladies" to walk to the door, then the "young men." The children follow her instructions quietly and form a line at the door.

After several such observations, our researcher was shocked one day, some months later, as she followed Ms. L's students from their homeroom to the music class. This teacher was one who, in our discussion of teacher styles, exemplified the profile of what we called the "passive" teacher. The excerpt is an abridged version of two full pages of field notes:

The students walk quietly, then line up against the wall outside the music room. The teacher opens the door. . . . She is an older White woman in her forties or fifties. She appears to be soft-spoken and easygoing. The students run into the classroom. . . . Some are crawling on the floor . . . most have taken off their shoes. . . . Matthew does flips across the classroom. He stands on a stack of books. He and Tom chase each other around the room. It is total chaos. The children are sliding across the floor in their socks . . . the teacher turns to the class and counts for quiet: "One, two, three." They quiet down but continue to run and play. Quintana is crying because she fell while running and the other children laughed at her. . . . The teacher says, "I don't think that's nice." She is holding on to Brenda. All but two boys are running and sliding. The teacher says, "Can we sing a nice song?" Brenda yells, "No!" The boys are play fighting and Brenda joins in. . . .

The teacher has absolutely no control of the class. . . . Some students are sitting on the guitar and other instruments. . . . Tom is on top of the piano. . . . Dequon is hitting Leroy. Now Leroy is crying like a baby, and so is Ben. All the other boys join in. . . . The boys are scattered across the classroom, on the floor, throwing fits and crying like babies. . . . The girls are running and sliding. Quintana falls again and begins to cry. The teacher is trying to get the boys to stop. The more she pleads, the louder they get. . . . Finally, the teacher mentions treats. The students quiet down immediately. They straighten up long enough to get a treat. . . .

[At the end of the period] the homeroom teacher arrives to pick up the children. As I leave, the music teacher says to me: "This is exactly the same thing that follows them [these students] through the grades. If you can find some way to change it, God bless you!"

The students line up for their homeroom teacher. She says, "How do we carry books?" because the children were dragging their books. The children hold their books in front of them. They follow their teacher quietly to the homeroom.

The music teacher's comment at the end was typical of the comments we heard from the weakest teachers, who usually showed no awareness of their role in children's behavior. This classroom was an extreme example but was not the only chaotic room we observed. It contrasts sharply with the careful, caring, effective instruction we saw in the students' homeroom.

We believe that the differences between these teachers reflect both teacher skill and teacher expectations. Clearly, Ms. L had a repertoire of skillful instructional techniques, while the music teacher did not. More important,

Ms. L understood that the children possessed skills that were helpful to them in their homes and communities; she understood also that their success in school would be contingent on their learning the behaviors and skills valued in this new setting. She was confident that her students would learn what she taught them, and her confidence in them and in herself was evident to the children. Further, she treated them with respect and expected no less in return. She was teaching them "the culture of power," and they learned it willingly.

We found it troubling that, despite this obvious variability in classroom contexts, the environment of the regular class was seldom taken into account when children were referred to a CST, so the question of how these children might have performed in more effective classrooms was never raised. In the exception that proves the rule, we note that there was only one school CST team in which we sometimes saw a recommendation that the child be changed to another class as an "alternative strategy," to see if a different teacher could better meet the child's needs.

CONCLUSIONS

In describing teacher influences on student achievement, Brophy (1986) noted, "The most consistently replicated findings link student achievement to their *opportunity to learn* the material, in particular to the degree to which teachers carry the content to them personally through active instruction and move them through the curriculum at a brisk pace" (p. 1069; emphasis added). Similarly, Lee (1982) conducted classroom observations and interviews in 55 schools serving low-income, culturally and linguistically diverse students and found that more time on instruction, greater correspondence between tests and curriculum material covered in class, and increased on-task behavior raised student achievement. Others have viewed opportunity to learn as an equity issue. Murphy (1988) discusses educational equity in terms of access to learning, to resources, and to school, especially among students who are tracked in low-ability groups.

This concept of adequate opportunity to learn is also a fundamental aspect of the definition of learning disabilities as part of its exclusionary clause—when a child has not had sufficient opportunity to learn, the determination cannot be made that she has a learning disability. Unfortunately, the classroom context is seldom taken into account as a source of children's learning and behavioral difficulties (Keogh & Speece, 1996) and is readily forgotten as soon as the search for intrinsic disability begins. As we consider why students from certain ethnic groups are overrepresented in high-incidence special education programs, this is a critical issue.

Our observations left no doubt that, overall, the schools serving the poorest Black neighborhoods had the most extremes in quality of instruction and classroom management. Although we saw some pockets of excellence in all schools, we emphasize that extremely unacceptable quality was seen only in those schools. In one sense, SES seemed to be very important, since it seemed to make the difference between fairly even and very uneven teacher quality. Thus, in the one higher-SES Black school, the overall level of instruction was far more even than in the poorer schools, and we saw nothing there to compare with the worst classrooms in the poorest schools. Based on this comparison, it would be tempting to conclude that SES was the determining factor regarding teacher quality.

Ethnicity, however, seemed to be a key factor within the low-income populations, with the highest-poverty Black schools tending to be worse off than the highest-poverty Hispanic schools. When this observation was broached in our interviews with school personnel, a common reaction was to blame the children, with the statement that the Hispanic children are more compliant and more focused on school than are Black children. Some personnel distinguished between African American and Haitian children, saying that the latter are generally very compliant, while the former are hard to handle. These features were attributed to more positive parental attitudes and child-rearing practices among the Hispanic and Haitian populations, although school personnel also commented that immigrant parents' support of education was limited by their demanding work schedules and low educational levels. Interviewees who made these comments tended to see African American parents in the low-income areas as simply not caring about their children's schooling.

In light of our evidence of successful instruction and classroom management by teachers such as Ms. L, who easily taught her African American kindergartners the behaviors and social interaction styles that are valued in school, we find it impossible to blame the children and their families for disorderly schools and classrooms. Throughout this book, we argue that school practices, such as limited opportunity to learn, present a powerful explanation for many children's educational outcomes. This explanation competes with the assumption of intrinsic or school-induced cognitive deficits. Students in predominantly Black schools were more likely to experience ineffective teachers than were the children in schools that were of higher SES or not predominantly Black. When added to our previous arguments regarding ineffective administrative practices and pervasive, though often covert, racism, evidence of diminished opportunity to learn is but one more factor contributing to the pattern of institutional discrimination that works against children in the poorest, Black neighborhoods of this school district. When applied to the question of special education placement, the variable quality of instruction and the evidence of diminished opportunity to learn indicate that we have no way of knowing how referred children would have fared in more appropriate educational settings.

The variability in school contexts described in this chapter provided the most vulnerable children with considerable "school risk" (Keogh, 2000). In the following chapter we address an aspect of risk that seemed self-evident to school personnel—the family and community contexts from which children came. It was ironic that school personnel indicated great concern for family contexts but showed little awareness of the role of context in school-based risk.

CHAPTER 5

The Construction of Family Identity: Stereotypes and Cultural Capital

Imagine that you are a parent and I say to you, talk to me a little bit about Kaura. Who kept Kaura before she started at school? . . . I am sure you will tell me it was one of your relatives, it was your church nursery . . . somewhere that you were comfortable with because you believed in those people. So we [the school] didn't touch Kaura until she was already 4, 5, 6 years old and these beliefs were already in her. . . . So you can't come in here and say that if Kaura is not reading and writing and can't pay attention and always wants to play, it's because the White teacher did it, or the Black teacher did it, or that Hispanic teacher did it. There are some things that happened long before Kaura began school. . . .

But now that Kaura is in school we need to work together. Now what are we going to do to make a difference in Kaura's life? But all too often, what happens is that when that child hits school and they hit one of these teachers who are not really teachers, they want you to take Kaura home and send them a better Kaura! Send them a Kaurine! These are people who do not accept that the parents are sending us their best kid every-day. They do not have another one at home that they can send us. But we have people that have not accepted that fact—that this is the product and we have to work with this product.

—African American principal

THE FOREGOING STATEMENT by an African American principal at an inner-city school illustrates the complementary influences of the two contexts that exert the greatest influence on children in their formative years: home and school. This insight can be framed in the terminology of risk: Either family risk or school risk, or both, may influence children's educational outcomes (Keogh, 2000). A third factor in the mix is individual risk, the possibility that the source of children's difficulties may lie beyond either home or school, in children's own biological makeup—that some children simply "have" intrinsic deficits, regardless of their circumstances. We contend that inappropriate attribution of learning difficulties to individual or family risk is itself an element of school risk, and that it arises from a failure to carefully consider the individual/family/school interface.

So far, this book has focused on some of the risks in schooling. The majority of the school personnel in our study did not acknowledge this element of risk. Rather, they focused on family and community roles in the "nature/nurture" argument. While many expressed a strong belief that school-identified disabilities represented genuine intrinsic deficits, the majority added the nuance that there is a "fine line" between intrinsic and environmentally induced deficits. While many school personnel spoke of poverty as the key factor, many seemed to assume that poverty was synonymous with poor parenting and lack of interest in children's education. Overall, the most powerful message from practitioners was "It [disability] comes from the home."

In this chapter we focus on school personnel's views of family contexts in children's education and on the impact of those views on children's educational careers. We present examples of these views, juxtaposed with portraits of those families that we were able to interview, visit, or both. In some cases the information we were able to glean did corroborate school personnel's beliefs about the families. In most cases our information provided a very different picture. Overall, four concerns are most striking in these stories: First, stereotypical images of families were usually based on a single piece of information that was enough to damn the family in the eyes of school personnel. Second, school personnel made no effort to counter negative beliefs with information on family strengths. Third, the families lacked the social and cultural capital to effectively challenge these stereotypes. Fourth, the accumulation of negativity around a family actually affected the outcomes for some children.

SCHOOL VOICES: "IT COMES FROM THE HOME"

School personnel's descriptions of the role of family contexts in children's school failure centered on four aspects: The "fine line" between nature and nurture, the impact of poor parenting, children's limited cultural and social experience, and caregivers' lack of support and monitoring of their children's schooling. Although we will not detail it here, there was a common sentiment among Hispanic and Anglo American school personnel that African American family and community environments tended to be more detrimental to children than those of immigrant families.

Nature/Nurture? "A Fine Line"

The delicate balance between detrimental circumstances, school failure, and special education placement was illustrated by the words of an Anglo American teacher at a predominantly Haitian school in a low-income neighborhood:

> They [the parents] really don't understand [what the school is expecting]. They can't help their children. They're not home. These children are very much latchkey kids. They fall behind. So, yes, they end up in a special education program because there's nobody there and the longer that goes on the further behind you get, and I think our hope is . . . when you get into special ed and you're working in a smaller group at your level and you get brought up to where you should be, then you get out. . . . If you continue to stay in a class with 35–40 kids, you're never gonna get what you need.

Despite this description of the interconnectedness between minimal home support, academic failure, and subsequent special education placement, the same teacher went on to say:

> I don't think you can just manufacture these deficits. You know, they're either there or they're not there. . . . These problems are really . . . they're real. . . . Whether it's from outside or within. And if it's something extrinsic that can be fixed then they get out of the program. . . . This is not a placement for life.

The belief in intrinsic deficits came through clearly in many interviews, as typified by the following statements:

> Basically . . . there are minority children who do have these problems. They're not social, and they're not administrative, and they're not due to any devious behavior. Don't misunderstand, there are children who belong in these classes because they do have problems that're intrinsic to the child.

In the simplest words:

> Some children, you know, are just born with it. . . . You know, like some children have blue eyes.

Some teachers also expressed the opinion that minority children were actually underreferred, many needing special education services and not getting them. We particularly heard this at one of our predominantly Haitian schools. For example:

> People say that there is disproportionate representation, but I don't
> see it, not here anyway. They are underrepresented. I think the
> process is too slow, takes too long, and by the time they are finally
> placed, it's too late. There are many reasons for this, associated with
> poverty, malnutrition, low-birth-weight babies.

"The Parents Are the Problem!"

While many emphasized the interplay between nature and nurture, most school personnel were inclined to blame nurture, with a focus on both family dynamics and broader societal contexts, including historical influences, economic circumstances, personal crises, cultural/social experience, and immigration status. Some school personnel spoke of families' problems in a tone of negative judgment, but others spoke with a sympathetic understanding of the impact of many negative influences on family adjustment.

The comments below, all made by personnel at schools serving low-income predominantly Black or mixed Black and Hispanic populations, placed the blame squarely on family life factors:

> The parents are the problem! They [the children] have absolutely no
> social skills, such as not knowing how to walk, sit in a chair. . . . It's
> cultural. Because most of these children have been to preschool and
> they're still so delayed. Their physical needs are not attended to.
> They're often dirty, head lice among the Hispanic children, poor
> hygiene and clothing . . . hungry, cold . . . . The big problem is
> poverty. I spend 50% of my time taking care of them other than
> teaching, and this includes downtime because of behaviors such as
> fistfights, tantrums, aggression.

> This woman asked her class: "How many kids have been exposed to
> guns?" And everyone except four kids in her classroom had either
> seen a gun, held a gun, or something.

> This child has severe behavior problems. His mother was a crack
> addict and gave him up at birth. The foster mother adopted him
> several years ago . . . and her husband, who was like the child's
> father, was shot and killed.

While there were, no doubt, factual bases for many of these statements, it was disturbing to note that, for many school personnel, labeling parents with derogatory terms seemed to be an acceptable part of school culture. One teacher, on the way from two CST conferences, rolled her eyes and exclaimed to the researcher: "The first mother is retarded; the second one is crazy!"

"A Lot of Them Think the World Stops Right There at 14th Street"

Another aspect of detrimental family circumstances reported by school personnel was what we came to refer to as "cultural-knowledge-set." This view tended to place the blame on culture and experience rather than on parents' own actions. The following statement by an African American professional at a predominantly African American school in one of the poorest neighborhoods typified this perspective:

> Most of the kids think the world stops at 10th Street. . . . I would give children a ride home in my car and they really didn't know how to get in the car, sit down, and close the door. It was hard for the child to open the door. I remember once we went on a field trip to the zoo and these kids were on the bus on the highway and they, I mean it was like the best experience they ever had to be on the bus, riding on 836 way up there and they saw all the houses and the trees and the buildings. And were like, "Wow! What's this?" A lot of them think the world stops right there at 14th Street so they don't dream.

Other versions of this theme focused on immigrant children:

> Many students come from Central or South America and they come and develop little countries or little cities within this country and most of . . . their parents are illiterate, you know, they can't read or write so they don't get the help at home. So, I feel that comes into play, not that I would place a child like that in special ed, but that comes into play where teachers lack the efficiency and want to place them because of that sometimes.

"With Parental Participation, They Will Not Be in Special Education"

The majority of teachers identified poor parental participation as a key factor in special education placement. These comments focused mostly on parents' failure to monitor homework and respond to school recommendations or requests for conferences. For example:

> I don't have a lot [of caregiver involvement] and I don't know if they understand what they're supposed to do. A lot of times they'll come

to me and say, "I haven't seen any homework," or they'll say, "They don't have homework." And then they say, "I have to look in their book bag." And I'm just wondering, shouldn't you be looking in the book bag as a parent, you know, why are you taking a 6-year-old's word for it that they don't have homework? Look in their book bag!

In the school at which African American students from a low-income area were bused into a predominantly affluent Anglo American student body, school personnel described a dramatic difference in students' preparation for schooling according to community background. The implications for parental input were implicit in the following speaker's meaning:

This is a unique community in that these children come into our school well prepared academically, and so there is a blatant, blatant disparity when you look at a child who is coming from the community and one who is coming from [the African American area].

Moreover, some personnel saw the effects of parent participation on student educational outcomes as very direct:

With parent participation, they will not be in [special ed] programs. Typically, the children who are being placed do not have any parent participation at all from caretakers.

As our case studies in later chapters will show, we did not find this last statement to be true. Moreover, despite this strong trend of complaint about lack of parental involvement, we noted that high levels of involvement in school-based conferences did occur in schools or even classrooms where school personnel made consistent efforts to "get parents in" and to develop respectful relationships with parents. We found that school personnel's efforts were far more predictive of parental response than were the parents' SES or ethnicity. For example, the success of intensive efforts to include parents was powerfully demonstrated in one school with a mixed Haitian and African American population. The counselor reported that parental turnout was "remarkably good, though not yet 100%." When asked what accounted for this, she replied, "We make a pest of ourselves!" Our observations corroborated this: Efforts to encourage parents' attendance included letters, phone calls, visits by the community involvement specialist (CIS, paid for by Title I funds), who was Haitian, and even the giving of rewards to children for taking home letters to parents about conferences. In our observations of 12 CST or placement conferences there were only 2 for which the parent did not come in.

The job of the CIS was to act as a liaison with families. These personnel were usually of the same ethnicity as the predominant group of students, and some were very effective in assuring high parent turnout at CST and staffing conferences. In these Title I schools it was the CIS and the counselors who worked most closely with the parents, and they tended to speak of families in much more understanding tones than did the teachers. For example, in one predominantly African American school, a Hispanic teacher said, "There's virtually no parent participation. Only a few cooperate," while the African American counselor estimated that 70% of the parents cooperated with school requests, despite the presence of what several personnel described as a general sense of despair in the neighborhood. This counselor explained that, for many parents who did not cooperate, "a lot of the problem is that they don't know." The CIS spoke in the same vein regarding parental participation through assistance and attendance at conferences:

> The parents are not more involved because they are not educated. . . .
> They didn't like the school when they were here. They didn't finish
> school. And it's kind of hard to be excited about something you
> didn't like, to pass it on to your children. . . . I have one parent who
> tells me she only got as far as second or third grade herself. . . . They
> are embarrassed to even let their children know. . . . It is easier to
> push a child away or talk down to them to keep them from being
> aware of the real situation. . . . A lot don't volunteer at the school
> because they'd have to watch a child read. And they don't want to do
> that because they can't read the book [themselves]. . . . I've heard
> [teachers say], "These people just want money. They don't care." The
> parents do care about their children, they just don't know how to
> deal with it or respond to it like you would.

Overall, negative indictments of families constituted the most pervasive view in the entire set of perspectives offered by school personnel in our study. Fortunately, we were able to use observations of school-based parent-professional interactions, as well as home visits and interviews, to gain some balance to these views. We were particularly interested in more close-up information on African American families, in view of the extreme negativity regarding this group. We learned that school personnel often did not attempt to gain the information needed to arrive at a true picture of family situations. Rather, they seemed to rely on stereotypical images for their constructions of family identity. We focus here on what we learned about family environments, and we refer readers to a further discussion of attempts at parent advocacy in Harry, Klingner, and Hart (2005).

HOME VOICES: "DOING THE BEST I CAN"

Our views of parents' perspectives came from two sources: school-based conferences and home visits. In this chapter we will refer to the former source only as a background to the more in-depth, personalized information we garnered from the latter. Thus, after a brief overview, we will focus on two case studies whose details illustrate the disservice that can be done to families by deficit assumptions and stereotypical thinking.

Fleeting Views

We observed many school-based conferences with parents who were obviously in dire need of help. We saw one young woman whose demeanor, dress, and apparently nonchalant attitude during the conference would readily lead school personnel to assume that motherhood was low on her priority list. We saw another who seemed desperate in her denial of her child's need for help. In the low-income, predominantly African American schools, we observed several conferences for children whose families seemed to fit the profiles described as detrimental. For example, in one school all four children whose conferences we observed had close relatives who abused drugs and who were in trouble with the law. In one conference, a grandmother, distraught by her daughter's drug abuse and incarceration, and the murder of her grandson's father, burst into tears under the school personnel's questioning.

One parent whom we came to learn a lot about, but whose home we did not visit, was Ms. Brown, an alcoholic whose efforts to participate in her children's schooling made her the butt of much amusement and criticism. In this inner-city school, an open-door policy encouraged parents to drop into classrooms and Ms. Brown frequently appeared in the classroom obviously inebriated, much to her son Jimmy's chagrin. After two CST conferences, both attended by Ms. Brown, the decision was made not to refer Jimmy for evaluation, because the multidisciplinary team felt that he was progressing as well as he could under the circumstances. A year later, Jimmy and his sister were removed from the home by the state's child welfare department because of extremely detrimental physical surroundings, and a teacher who visited Jimmy in his foster home reported that he seemed much happier. What was surprising in this case was that although school personnel had visible evidence of the mother's alcoholism, it was at least 2 years before the case was reported to the relevant state agency.

Taddeus was another child whose home was reputed to be detrimental, in this case because of a history of involvement in drugs and violence. Taddeus, a handsome, nattily dressed second grader with a wide, shy smile, was described by his teacher as "knowing nothing" and being "on the moon." Having been tested in his first-grade year and found not to qualify for special education services, he had been retained in the second grade. The teacher said that she heard that there are gangs at his home and that his cousin was killed recently, and she could not figure out why Taddeus had not qualified for special education. In our only visit to this home, the mother confirmed that a sibling and a relative had been seriously injured as a result of being "caught in crossfire." The mother's description of Taddeus was very different from the teacher's, emphasizing that, although he was not doing well at school, "he's great with his hands and can fix anything." Pointing to a child's bike in the corner, she explained that people in the neighborhood pay Taddeus "to fix bikes and things."

Miles was another child whose family we visited only once. An African American kindergartner in a low-income neighborhood, Miles was found eligible for LD services and was retained in kindergarten. On our visit to Miles's home, his mother apologized that she had no living room to invite the researcher into. Her half of the house consisted of a series of three rooms off a hallway, so the interview was conducted in her bedroom. When the researcher commented on her son's excellent vocabulary (his suggestions for zoo animals included *sea lion* and *otter*), the mother said that Miles had never been to the zoo, but learned a lot of vocabulary from the Disney Channel, which the family watched together once a week. Showing great interest in the meaning of the "learning disability" label that was being applied to her son, Miles's mother exclaimed, "Well, you see, I'm doing the best I can!"

Another parent we came to know beyond the school walls was Janey, mother of Anita, a first grader placed in special education. Janey described herself as a "hillbilly," and her daughter's father as a "wetback" (a Mexican migrant). This mother was a regular volunteer in her daughter's classroom, but was described by school personnel as "retarded." Our interviews with her revealed that she had been in a special education program herself, but her keen understanding of the special education system belied the belief that she was retarded. While acknowledging that she did keep her daughter home too often, Janey argued that the school was not doing its job. Indeed, when her daughter was placed in the LD program, Janey accurately described to us the poor instruction the child was receiving and the lack of adherence to her IEP, which we also observed.

These brief vignettes point to the range of challenges faced by families of whose lives we were able to gain only a fleeting glimpse. In search of in-depth understanding of family situations, we relied on information from the 12 case study children as well as 3 others whose families agreed to participate in interviews, home visits, or both. These 15 cases were as diverse as the entire cohort of participants in the study, but most of them did have problematic family circumstances that typified the kinds of complaints school personnel expressed about families.

Close-up Views

Although school personnel often used terms such as *single parent* or *intact* to describe families, these classifications were meaningless in light of the array of family configurations to which we were introduced. Contrary to the mainstream notion of a "single parent" family, we found that all the families we met had more than one adult in the home—whether a stepparent or members of the extended family. All had other children—whether siblings or cousins—living in the home.

The configurations of the 12 families of case study children were as follows: One Haitian family appeared to be headed by two biological parents. Two other families, one African American and one Haitian, were headed by fathers as the primary caregivers; one mother was hospitalized with a psychiatric illness and the other lived in Haiti. Another African American child lived with her paternal grandmother and an aunt, since her mother was in jail; her father was a frequent visitor to the home and participated in school-based conferences. Five children (two African American and three Hispanic) lived with their mothers; in one case the mother had a psychiatric illness and was the child's legal guardian, while the father also was involved in child care; in another case, the father was in Puerto Rico and the child lived with her mother, siblings, and an infant nephew. Two other children—one Haitian and one African American—lived with their mother and a stepfather. The 12th child lived with an adult relative and had experienced the deaths of adult family members, including his father; the caregiver he lived with was himself quite ill and passed away toward the end of our study.

Many of these configurations represent what school personnel tended to describe as "dysfunctional." However, when we stepped inside children's homes we saw another side of the picture—a side that spoke of families' caring for and pride in their children. Their ways of caring and the sources of their pride were not always consonant with what school personnel would count as important, but it was evident to us that the parents were making an effort to fulfill what they perceived to be the important responsibilities of parenthood—providing nurturance and love.

We will focus here on the family environments of two case study children whom we were able to follow extensively. Details of how the children came to be designated as having disabilities will be given in Chapter 10, where we address the social construction of the ED category. We visited these homes six times each, and we emphasize that, although we do not know the families well, our visits were enough to dispel the cloud of suspicion that had been cast over them. Certainly, their difficulties were readily evident, but so were their strengths.

Jacintha: "Bring Momma's pen, baby." Robert was an African American second grader in one of the most denigrated neighborhoods of the city. His was the school previously reported to have suspended 102 children out of a total of 603 in one year, based on a "zero tolerance" policy by which kindergartners through fifth graders were placed on 3-day, out-of-school suspension for fighting. The stereotype that influenced school personnel's response to Robert's mother was that of a drug-abusing mother who had more children than she could handle.

We visited Robert's home six times throughout the period of our research. At first, finding the house was a challenge. Located in the heart of the city, this two-story block of eight apartments was about 100 yards away from a bridge under which homeless persons frequently built their temporary shelters. The apartment was on the ground floor, with a narrow, lopsided porch that served this and the apartment next door. The entrance to the apartment was a swinging door with broken slats that, over the course of the 3 years in which we visited, eventually disappeared entirely, leaving open spaces through which one could peer into a living room that was about 10 feet square. The living room contained a sofa for two, a chest of drawers and mirror, and a playpen in which the 2-year-old slept. This room merged into a passageway that led, on one side, to a tiny kitchen and, on the other, to a bathroom and two bedrooms. Four siblings slept on two bunk beds against one wall of their room. Against the other wall was a long shelving unit covered with colorful cloth that matched the curtains. Behind the shelf covering was a collection of probably 100 children's books.

Robert's mother, Jacintha, was a petite woman whose speech and deferential manners reflected her southern origins. Warm and enthusiastic in her manner, she welcomed our research team and spoke openly of her family life and the challenges she faced. The most dramatic impression of this family was of the loving and demonstrative relationship between this mother and her children. The family interactions supported Jacintha's explanation that she had nine children because she "just loves having children." The four eldest lived in another state with their grandparents. The five who lived with Jacintha were very physically affectionate with her, as illustrated by 8-year-old Robert's lying across her lap and looking up at her as she talked with the researcher.

Three small but very telling interactions further demonstrated the competence and caring of this mother who lived in such limited circumstances. First, Jacintha's ability to organize her household was evident in a quick moment: When asked for a pen to sign the research consent forms, the mother said to her 4-year-old, "Bring Momma's pen, baby." The child went directly to a drawer in the small desk and pulled out his mother's pen. Later, as Jacintha was describing to the researcher how she loves to read to her children, one of the children ran to a cupboard against the wall and opened it, and dozens of children's books came tumbling out. On the same occasion, as the mother talked about the family, one of the children brought out a collection of small photo albums to show the researcher. Each album was filled with photos of an individual child, and in the front of each album was inscribed, "To: [child's name] from Mom and Dad with love, Christmas 19____."

This mother was often described in very derogatory terms by some school personnel. While some acknowledged that she was polite and well spoken, others focused on their knowledge that she had a history of drug addiction, or on the fact that she had nine children in all, by more than one union. The last two facts led school personnel to preconceived beliefs about Jacintha that are evident in the following two episodes. On one occasion an administrator commented that the mother had "five children here and four farmed out somewhere else." The fact that the four older children lived in another state with their paternal grandparents was verified by the researcher, who met these children one summer when they came to stay with their mother. The children's traditional southern manners ("yes, ma'am; no, ma'am,") put their city siblings to shame and contradicted the connotation of irresponsible child-rearing inherent in the notion that they had been "farmed out somewhere."

In conversations with the researcher, Jacintha spoke openly of her history of drug abuse. By her account, she had been "clean" for several years. Nevertheless, when she lost about 15 pounds over a summer, a faculty member commented that "you can always tell when she's back on drugs because she loses weight!" Our interpretation was rather different: Just a week earlier, the researcher visiting Jacintha expressed surprise at her weight loss over the summer. Turning to show off her trim figure, Jacintha exclaimed: "Slim-Fast, girl! It's fabulous! You wait right here and I'm'a get you a tin. You'll see how good it works!"

School personnel's persistence in negative and poorly based beliefs about Jacintha was puzzling and troubling because this mother consistently showed herself to be a caring and responsible parent. She attended every CST or placement conference for her child and participated in a polite, deferential, yet firm manner. For example, when her son was eventually placed in an ED program and the multidisciplinary team had to ask her to sign for permission regarding the possibility of physical restraint, she showed great concern and asked for examples of exactly what that would mean. She could always report exactly what medication her son was on and how he was responding to it. Nevertheless, some school personnel were consistently rude to her, as the following excerpt from a field observation indicates. The committee chair asked whether Robert was receiving his medication at school:

> A team member replies: "He does not get it here." Everyone looks puzzled again and the speaker, who is sitting behind the mother, mouths the word "*she*" and, pointing to the mother, makes a gesture of cutting across the throat. She is saying that the mother stopped the medication being given at school. Her facial expression as she does this appears angry and annoyed, as she scowls and points at the mother with an accusing gesture. The mother is not intended to see this, and does not. A second later, the speaker seems to realize that her lack of voice came across as a silence in the room and that everyone, except the mother, is looking at her. She mumbles something like, "It [the medication] was stopped." At this point, I do not look at the expressions of others but can feel the discomfort in the room. Everyone has seen the team member's gesture except the mother, whose back is directly to her.

The faculty member's negativity on this occasion was but another example of her vindictive attitude to Jacintha and the advantage that was taken of this mother's deferential attitude to school personnel. In the previous year, Robert had been placed on half-day suspension, and the same faculty member told the researcher that this action was taken to show the mother that she had to be responsible for Robert's troublesome behavior. Jacintha, meanwhile, had easily understood this message, explaining to the researcher that Robert was put on half-day suspension to "punish me." This "punishment" involved Jacintha being required to come for Robert at 11:00 A.M. every day, which she did for 5 months, walking approximately 10 blocks with her two younger children in tow. The half-day placement meant that Robert had to miss school sometimes when his mother had a medical or other appointment for herself or the other children, because she could not be back at school by 11:00 A.M. When it was suggested that she should go to the school district to complain about this action, Jacintha replied that she would "just leave it to God."

The principal of the school was the same African American woman whose insightful comments about a hypothetical "Kaurine" were cited as the introduction to this chapter. Yet it was the principal herself who ordered Robert's half-day attendance in school, arguing that because of his behavior he was, at that time, "not capable of benefiting from a full day of school." This arrangement remained in place from January until the end of May, despite the fact that, in January, Jacintha had signed permission for a psychological evaluation. In May, when Jacintha refused to come for Robert any longer, he was reinstated in the full-day program and evaluated for special education placement.

Grandma S: " There's nothing wrong with her. She just wants her momma!"

Kanita was an African American second grader who was placed in an ED program in an inner-city school. The stereotype that dominated school personnel's view of Kanita was that her mother was incarcerated and there were "a bunch of people living in the home." On the basis of this information, school personnel expressed the belief that the family was "dysfunctional."

Six visits to Kanita's home provided us with a very different picture. The attractively painted single-family dwelling had belonged to Kanita's paternal grandparents for more than 30 years. In this house Mrs. Smith and her husband had raised her family of six children on the prized American principle of hard work. The family's small business had, for more than 20 years, been the location of weekend and vacation work for all the children, and Mrs. Smith told us that many a Christmas Eve would find the entire family over at the business working until midnight. Mrs. Smith's father had been the founding pastor of a nearby Baptist church, which she and some of the grandchildren still attended. Mrs. Smith's children had all moved on to establish their own families, and her living-room shelves attested to the many grandchildren and three "great-grands" who now enriched her life.

At the time of the study, we learned that Kanita and one of Mrs. Smith's daughters and her child lived in this home. This family had considerable cultural capital in their community. In contrast to school personnel's view of this home as a place where a "bunch of people" lived, the strength of the extended family unit was evident in the home's function as a center for the grandchildren to come to after school until their parents could pick them up. Cousins, aunts, or uncles were frequent visitors during all of our six visits to the home.

Kanita had lived with her grandmother since she was a baby, when her mother was incarcerated. Her father, who lived elsewhere, was in close touch with his daughter and either he or one of his sisters would attend school conferences along with Mrs. Smith. At the placement conference, Kanita's grandmother and aunt both acknowledged that the child's behavior was troublesome, but when told that Kanita had qualified for an ED program, the grandmother stated flatly: "There's nothing wrong with her. She just wants her momma."

It was evident that Kanita was treasured by this family. Her school awards, sports trophies, and photos were prominent among the family mementos in the living room. Mrs. Smith loved to bring out her album in which she kept Kanita's school records and awards all the way from Head Start to the time of our study. Report cards, classroom certificates, a certificate of

Kanita's participation in a regional mathematics competition, notes from classroom peers and teachers, and Mother's Day cards from Kanita to her mother and grandmother were all carefully pressed into this album. Pride in Kanita's accomplishments was evident in the family: On one visit, an aunt, standing in the kitchen as the researchers talked with Mrs. Smith, called out to remind her mother to tell us about Kanita's excellent performance on the statewide testing. On the same day, her cousin, coming in after school and realizing our university affiliation, asked quickly: "Is Kanita going to college?"

Kanita's psychological evaluation offered a sobering picture of the power of negative stereotyping. Prior to the actual evaluation, the psychologist reported to us that this child was from a "dysfunctional family," the mother being in jail. The first 2 hours of evaluation were based on the Weschler Intelligence Scale for Children (WISC)-III, on which Kanita cooperated fully and earned a composite score of 107 with a score of 118 on the "freedom from distractibility" subscale. When the psychologist began the projective testing by asking Kanita to draw a picture of her family, the child did so eagerly, with a big smile. As the questioning on these tests focused increasingly on personal family information, however, Kanita became more withdrawn. For example, when the psychologist asked Kanita to name one of the figures, the child did so in a soft voice. The psychologist repeated, "Who is it?" Kanita replied, "My cousin." The psychologist asked, "How old is he?" Kanita's replies were too soft for the researchers to hear, but we saw her shrug several times. The psychologist asked if this cousin lived in the house and if he slept in Kanita's bedroom. As the subsequent series of questions focused on details of Kanita's bedroom, the child answered softly, gradually becoming more restless, fiddling with the tabletop and moving around in her chair.

The psychologist then turned to a series of questions about Kanita's mother, including why she was incarcerated and whether she had been on drugs. The family questions finally ended with the psychologist asking Kanita to tell her "everybody that lives in the house," to which Kanita listed about nine names. The psychologist asked Kanita if it was a big house and Kanita said yes. From these tests the psychologist went on to the sentence-completion test and the Roberts Apperception Test. By the end of the session, Kanita had slid almost halfway under her desk and was giving virtually no answers.

After the evaluation, the psychologist offered the researchers the interpretation that Kanita's growing recalcitrance was a sign of "denial of her feelings" in the context of a "dysfunctional" family. The psychologist rejected the suggestion that Kanita's withdrawal may have been indicative of embarrassment or distress, arguing that children in this neighborhood were so accustomed to having family members who were on drugs or incarcerated that they were generally quite "blasé" and would speak openly of these matters. Thus, the psychologist concluded that Kanita's resistance to the topic was not normal for a child in this social environment. Nor did the psychologist entertain the possibility that the child, like many children in inner-city neighborhoods, had likely been taught not to reveal family information to strangers, especially White strangers. Finally, it was evident that the psychologist's line of questioning regarding the sleeping arrangements for Kanita's cousin represented poorly veiled hints at the possibility of improper relationships within the family. We feel certain that Kanita's sensitivity to this insinuation contributed to her increasing reluctance to participate in the projective testing.

The outcome of the evaluation was that Kanita qualified for a placement in a self-contained ED class at a different school. Kanita's placement in this program turned out to be a "double-edged sword," since, in the hands of an effective teacher, she did very well both academically and behaviorally and was soon partially mainstreamed. However, she was so stigmatized by the ED label that her behavior in the general-education settings, though no different from that of many of her peers, was frequently interpreted as problematic. By the fourth grade, Kanita was placed, part-time, in a gifted program, where the teacher asked us if her status as a child with ED was "a mistake."

STEREOTYPES, CULTURAL CAPITAL, AND "RISK"

The two preceding cases point to the power of racial and socioeconomic stereotypes to exacerbate the difficulties of children whose families lack the cultural capital valued by schools. In both cases, school personnel constructed their images of children's families on the basis of uninformed and untested negative assumptions. In the face of the families' lack of cultural capital, school personnel used their unchallenged power to make decisions that were not in the children's best interest. These stories illustrate a statement by Skiba and Peterson (2000) that "information about inadequate family resources or family instability is used to affix blame, creating an adversarial climate between home and school" (p. 341).

"Risk" in Family Configurations

The NAS report on minority overrepresentation in special education (Donovan & Cross, 2002) emphasized the impact of detrimental social and biological influences on children living in poverty. The authors devoted a chapter to a detailed summary of findings regarding the detrimental effects of such factors as lead-based toxins, alcohol, iron deficiency, and maternal depression on the cognitive and behavioral development of minority children living in poverty. The history of American racial politics prompted some scholars to express concern that the NAS's highlighting of these issues was another version of "blaming the victim," suggesting that poor, in particular, African American, families were at fault for raising their children in detrimental circumstances. We believe that what was missing from the NAS's analysis was insight into the responsibility of public policy for many of these circumstances. Indeed, around the same time, the NAS (2002) also published a report, which detailed the extensive discrimination against minority groups in the health care system.

Another line of research on family "risk" factors is found in Nichols and Chen's (1981) family profiles, which focused on poverty; unsafe neighborhoods; large family size; residential instability; and parental characteristics, including absence, poor mental health, criminality, and substance abuse. Sameroff and colleagues (1993) developed similar profiles but stressed that it is the combination of several such features, rather than any single feature, that indicates risk. Blair and Scott (2000) applied the question of demographics directly to special education placement and found high correlations between key demographic indicators and special education placement, which, they argued, proves the lasting influence of early environments and experiences.

While we do not doubt the importance of the formative childhood years, we contend that demographics do not tell the whole story. As researchers have demonstrated (e.g., R. Clark, 1983), dynamics within families can provide protective factors that result in considerable resilience. Moreover, research on culturally responsive pedagogy shows that schools *can* make a difference (Hilliard, 1997). If children who have started life with detrimental influences are further exposed to detrimental schooling, we cannot place all, or even most, of the blame on the preschool years.

Kanita's family did not fit the profile developed by Sameroff et al. (1993). To the contrary, it was based on a strong extended family unit, supported by the flexible extended systems known to be typical of traditional Black family structures (e.g., Hill, 1971). These include grandparent involvement, adult sharing of financial and practical responsibility, and sibling responsibility. Information on Robert's family suggested that this family was indeed particularly vulnerable by virtue of several "risk factors." Nevertheless, two aspects of the story are particularly disturbing: First, school personnel made no attempt to ascertain the family strengths that did exist, and, second, decisions made about Robert suggested an attempt to undermine rather than to assist this vulnerable family.

Social and Cultural Capital

The concepts of cultural and social capital are very helpful in interpreting the interactions between school personnel and the parents in these stories. Lareau's (1989) comparison of the home-school interactions of working class versus professional parents showed how social connections and the cultural styles of parents accounted for differential reception by school personnel. Proposing an analysis of what constitutes parental cultural capital in school contexts, Lareau and Horvat (1999) offered a list of characteristics that included "parents' large vocabularies, sense of entitlement to interact with teachers as equals, time, transportation, and child care arrangements to attend school events during the school day" (p. 5). These researchers argued also that school personnel approved only those "socioemotional styles" that reflected trust in school personnel and acceptance of their recommendations.

Meeting these expectations can be difficult to achieve. As Bowers (1984) argued, because social interaction is premised on unspoken, "taken-for-granted" beliefs, parents' mastery of the "communicative competence" needed for home-school interactions requires an "explicit and rational knowledge of the culture that is being renegotiated" (p. 29). Studies by Harry and colleagues (Harry, 1992; Harry, Allen, & McLaughlin, 1995; Harry, Kalyanpur, & Day, 1999) illustrated how difficult this challenge was for Puerto Rican, African American, and other culturally or linguistically diverse families from low-SES backgrounds.

What does cultural capital look like when low income, minimal formal schooling, and linguistic difference intertwine with race in a racialized society such as the United States? Lareau and Horvat's (1999) study of contrasting interaction styles of White and Black parents indicated that cultural capital and race are often inextricable in the context of the U.S. history of racism. While traditional conceptions of cultural capital, as outlined by Bourdieu (1986), tended to focus on material and symbolic indicators of cultural capital, Lareau and Horvat (1999) attended to something far more intangible—the psychological impact of historical racism on parents' access to cultural capital and the means needed to activate that capital. Thus, they found that Black parents' knowledge of the school district's history of racial discrimination resulted in their inability to approach school personnel from a posture of trust. In contrast, White parents, not wounded by this history, generally did trust the school and interpreted any inappropriate actions of school personnel on an individual basis. Lareau and Horvat argued that in this context, being White became "a type of cultural capital" (p. 42), "a largely hidden cultural resource that facilitates White parents' compliance with the standard of deferential and positive parental involvement in school" (p. 69). These researchers did not present this as a fixed characteristic, however. Rather, their study showed that middle-class Black parents, while also suspicious of the school, mastered the interaction style that was valued by school personnel and succeeded in "customizing" their children's education without ever revealing to school personnel that they harbored misgivings based on race.

Lareau and Horvat's (1999) findings were relatively clear cut in the context of a school in which Black students were in the minority as compared with their White peers and, more important, in which the majority of school personnel were White. In our study, however, the schools that had large proportions of Black students usually also had significant proportions of Black faculty and often Black administrators. What is the role of race in such contexts?

Cultural Capital in a Racialized Society

The neighborhoods where Kanita and Robert lived reflected three commonly held criteria for stereotyping: Black, poor, and dangerous. While the school that Robert attended had a growing population of Hispanics (19%), the neighborhood had a long history of being predominantly African American. Moreover, Robert's school itself was the alma mater of many African Americans who were of considerable status in the city and who were reported to be quite involved in supporting the school's needs. However, over the years, city restructuring and funding patterns contributed to the neighborhood becoming one of the most denigrated in the city. Kanita's neighborhood was seen as more "working poor" than Robert's, but would also be considered "inner city," in the common use of that term to indicate low-income Black residents.

To what extent did race contribute to the stereotyping of these families? At face value, race does not appear to be an essential ingredient. In Kanita's case, the three key school personnel involved were all White (Anglo American ethnicity)—a referring teacher with very poor classroom-management skills, the administrator who handled the referral-team process, and the psychologist. However, in Robert's case, with the exception of the psychologist, the key personnel involved were African American—the team member who gestured rudely behind Jacintha's back; the administrator who made the decision to place Robert on half-day attendance; and the referring teacher, whose negativity and poor classroom management made it impossible to know what Robert's potential was.

If we understand racism as an insidious ideology rather than as a simple matter of prejudice between individuals of different races, it is easy to see how members of a racialized society are predisposed to make intuitive negative associations based on race, even within their own group (Bonilla-Silva, 1996; Delgado & Stefancic, 2000). This type of ingrained racism seems a likely part of the negativity we noted, operating more like a lens that colors, even distorts, one's view. Through this lens, the image of these neighborhoods as beset by guns, violence, drugs, and family dysfunction condemned all who lived in them.

We do not dispute that many detrimental influences did affect the quality of life of many children in these schools. We do contend, however, that in the family stories told above, generalized knowledge of the neighborhoods combined with minimal and superficial knowledge of these families to produce a mindset that was detrimental to the children. Looking at each family as an individual unit, we argue that these stereotypes did a great injustice to these families and children.

CONCLUSIONS

The contrast between our findings and school personnel's views of families illustrates the terrible power of stereotypes. Certainly, our observations showed the tremendous challenges of poverty, personal loss, and limited education faced by these families. We acknowledge also that there is a strong likelihood of volunteer bias, in that those families who agreed to participate were those who knew they had nothing to hide; who knew that they were, as one mother put it, "doing the best they could." So our discussion here is not intended to put forth the case that there were no families whose lifestyles and challenges contributed to their children's difficulties in school. Indeed, it seems reasonable to assume that even the strong families we met were struggling against odds so powerful as to place children at increased risk for school failure or even special education placement.

Nevertheless, we believe that our portraits of family strengths are also irrefutable and that tapping into these strengths could have made an important difference. No one knew that Miles's surprising vocabulary reflected his mother's use of the Disney Channel as a source of educational activity and family solidarity; that Robert's mother's tiny apartment, in a building for which no landlord was held accountable, housed a large collection of children's books from which she taught the toddlers "their ABCs"; that Taddeus's mother, against a background of family tragedy, took great pride in her son's mechanical abilities; or that Kanita's grandmother, cherishing and nurturing the talents of a gifted child whose mother had "chosen the wrong way," had carefully preserved all of her granddaughter's school reports and awards from Head Start until the fifth grade. Although all these caregivers came to CST conferences and participated to the best of their ability, the image of the ineffective, minimally involved parent persisted, because most of these efforts and activities did not meet the criteria school personnel had in mind when they spoke of "parental involvement."

The saddest part of these stories is that the family strengths we were able to discover in just a few visits and conversations went unnoticed by school personnel, whose views and decisions were central to these children's educational careers. This lack of recognition, a recognition supplanted by disdain and disinterest, contributed directly to decisions that were not in the children's interest and that were not challenged by any of the parents, although the parents disagreed with some of them. These parents had neither the social capital, in the form of social connections, nor the cultural capital, in the form of knowledge of rights, logistical supports, or faith in their own voice, to challenge such decisions.

In the preceding few chapters we have addressed systemic as well as personal biases that affected outcomes for children. Overall, we believe that a powerful combination of biases interwove race with poverty and marginalized family structures or lifestyles. Explicit negative biases were most evident when these factors were thought to coexist with African American ethnicity. The implications of this legacy of historical racism are enormous and should be directly addressed in teacher-preparation programs. Our findings echo Delpit's (1995):

> Teacher education usually focuses on research that links failure and socioeconomic status, failure and cultural difference, and failure and single-parent households. . . . When teachers receive that kind of education, there is a tendency to assume deficits in students rather than to locate and teach to strengths. To counter this tendency, educators must have knowledge of their children's lives outside of school so as to recognize their strengths. (p. 172)

CHAPTER 6

At the Conference Table: The Discourse of Identity Construction

I test; I write my report; I write my recommendations and I give it to the placement specialist. . . . We discuss it and we come to a decision. And we discuss it prior to the meeting just to make sure we are providing the best for the child. And once we have a unified front for the parents, we can bring them in just so they know what is going on.

—School psychologist

THE STATEMENT ABOVE typifies the argument of Mehan et al. (1986), that the special education placement conference is essentially a "ratification of actions taken earlier" (p. 164). Mehan and his colleagues emphasized that this process should not be interpreted as a "conspiracy," but as a "culmination, a formalization, of a lengthy process that originates in the classroom . . . when the teacher makes the first referral" (p. 165). They continued:

We should not disparage this process of everyday decision-making by comparing it with rational models, formal reasoning, or scientific thinking. . . . Instead, it seems more appropriate to call into question the efficacy of scientific reasoning as a model of everyday reasoning. There are good organizational reasons why decision-making occurs as it does. The decision-making circumstances assumed to exist by the rational model are not available to problem solvers in formal organizations like schools. . . . Furthermore, the rational model assumes that all the factors being considered in the decision-making calculus have equal weight. . . . But, as we have seen, a single factor, such as the space available in the program, may outweigh all others in its consequences for decision makers. (p. 166)

Certainly, the reasoning we observed in the decision-making process was far from scientific or rational, if we understand these terms to mean a process that moves logically from a particular premise or set of premises, with the intention of accomplishing a specific goal or set of goals. However, if we bear in mind that, as Mehan et al. suggest, decisions must take into account multiple individual perspectives as well as numerous organizational factors, some of which may never have been included in the original premises, then the rationale for decisions becomes easier to understand. We found that the school district we studied had, indeed, a very rational plan for decision making, but that the actual process was often driven by agendas and perspectives that could not be found anywhere in the official plan.

While our purpose is not to disparage, we believe that it is important to understand and make explicit the many forces that push decision making in one direction or another. This is critical because it shows that the overrepresentation of minority groups in special education should not be understood to mean that these children "have" more disabilities than others. Rather, we believe that institutional and personal biases and beliefs combine with political pressures to produce a pattern of minority overrepresentation.

The main premise on which high-incidence disability placement is based is that the failure of some children to succeed in school is the result of disabilities. This premise gives rise to a mindset that seeks the problem within the child. It is the responsibility of school personnel to identify those children and provide them with appropriate, individualized services in the least restrictive environment. The main goal is to remediate the children's difficulties as far as possible so as to allow them to be successful. Based on these premises and goals, the school district developed the model of "collaborative consultation," described in what follows, which would lead, when necessary, to appropriate special education placement.

THE RATIONAL MODEL

The school district required at least two conferences, and preferably three, for each child being considered for special education placement. At the first conference, the CST would respond to a referral; at the second meeting of the CST the decision would be made to refer a student for a psychological evaluation; at the placement conference, the findings of the psychologist's evaluation would be reported and a decision made about placement. Certain key school personnel were required to attend all conferences, and parents or guardians had to be invited. All personnel involved in the referral process could describe it readily, as in the following statement by a special education teacher:

> The classroom teacher will usually come to the assistant principal and say, so and so is really having problems with their schoolwork. Then

we usually will meet, but the person has to have documentation that they have spoken to the parents and that they have tried a few different strategies. This makes the parent aware of it and we see what the parents have to say. And then if there really is no change, then we meet in a group, we invite the parents and we talk about what the child is doing in class and we come up with some strategies to see if we could help the child before we do anything further. Then after 2 or 3 months we meet again to see if there has been any change, either positive or negative. And then if there really is no substantial change, if the parent is agreeable, we decide to see if there is a processing deficit of any kind that would qualify [the child] for a learning disability. We also give them a hearing test and a vision test. We want to try and rule out all kinds of things before we go that way. Then we put all of the pieces together, of course there is some intelligence testing, too, and then we see if there is a need for placement.

We rarely saw the process carried out in quite this idealized way. A few inner-city schools that had full-service programs seemed particularly effective at trying alternative strategies before referring a child. For example, in one school that served a mixture of low-income African American and Hispanic students, there were several supportive structures and approaches that fed into the CST process. At the first signs of trouble, a screening committee used a flow chart to guide the steps required to obtain assistance from outside agencies. If the problem persisted, then the case would go to the CST. This school also had informal supports that allowed counselors to respond to teacher referrals in formats such as a daily lunchtime group-therapy session.

Regardless of variations, most conferences we observed resembled the official process in terms of the chronology of steps taken, the paperwork submitted, and the personnel participating. In all cases, however, the details of interpersonal dynamics, personal and professional beliefs, and official and unofficial agendas affected both the process and the outcomes of these conferences.

PLACEMENT PATTERNS ACROSS SCHOOLS

We have noted before that the overall placement rates in the 12 schools offered no clear-cut pattern of relationships between overrepresentation and SES or ethnicity. Although we can see that poverty and ethnicity combined to work against children's success in a number of ways, we argue in this chapter that school cultures and the actions of key individuals were more important than were any objective features of children or school contexts.

We refer the reader once more to Table 1.2, at the end of Chapter 1. This table shows that similarities in SES did not predict similar special education placement rates across schools. The four-highest-income neighborhoods are placed at the top portion of the table. These schools served a range of ethnicities. In the eight schools in the lower portion of the table, Black and Hispanic students represented a range from 82% to 99% of the population, and 88% to 99% of children were on free and reduced-price lunch (FRL). In these settings, with the sole exception of one excellent school, Green Acres, several administrative issues tended to combine with poor instruction to exacerbate children's problems. Yet placement rates across these schools varied widely—from 3.5% to 9.8%.

In three schools that served higher-income populations, Bay Vista, Clearwater, and Blue Heron, the range of children on FRL was from 65.6% to 70.1%, which can be considered mid-SES, relative to the generally low income levels in this school district. In this group of schools we rated instruction as generally very good, and achievement levels were better than at the schools with higher poverty levels. However, this did not mean that children were less likely to be referred to special education. Table 1.2 shows that Blue Heron, serving a predominantly Hispanic population, was the highest-referring school, with a placement rate of 12.5% in LD, although its rate of 65.6% FRL was the lowest in the entire group of 12 schools. Bay Vista's demographics were very similar, with an FRL rate of 68.7% and a predominance of Hispanic students, yet its placement rate of 6.6% in LD was approximately half that of Blue Heron. Clearwater, whose population was predominantly Black (mixed African American and English-speaking Caribbean ethnicities), had the lowest rate of LD placement (4.1%).

Ethnicity was as complicated a factor to interpret as was SES. For example, comparing Creekside and Palm Grove, which had a predominance of Haitian students of the same SES level (more than 97% of the students on FRL), we see that Palm Grove placed almost twice as many students in LD as did Creekside (6.8% versus 3.5%). We rated classroom instruction in both schools as very variable. The four schools with mixed ethnic populations served a much smaller range in LD—from 4.1% to 5.8%.

Only one school, Sunnybrook, presented a clear picture of a combination of ethnicity and low SES at work. As the only school in the sample serving a high-SES neighborhood, 55% of the student population was White (Anglo American), 23% Hispanic, and 17% African American, the last being bused in from a low-income neighborhood. The percentage of students on FRL was only 18.5%, which was accounted for by the African American population. In this school, we did see a clear pattern of combined low SES and ethnicity as an obvious correlate of high special education placement:

Although the overall LD placement rate was low (4.1%), the rate of placement of African Americans resembled the nationwide disproportionality pattern. That is, Black students were represented in special education at twice the rate of their presence in the school population (35% in LD; 17% in the school population). Further, since we could not obtain access to the necessary records, we were unable to ascertain what percentage of students were identified as MMR or EH and transferred to schools that offered these more restrictive programs.

To summarize, neither SES, ethnicity, nor general school quality could be relied on to explain placement rates in any given school. While it is clear that these factors played a role, it was also evident that each school seemed to have its own culture of referral, one that reflected the beliefs of individual teachers, administrators, and psychologists as well as pressures from the school district.

THE CULTURE OF REFERRAL

By *culture of referral* we mean the attitude toward and beliefs about children who were not doing well in the general-education program, as well as beliefs about special education. Important beliefs included how quickly teachers and administrators assumed that low performance or behavioral difficulties were indicators of "something else" at work, whether these children were seen as "belonging" in general education, whether special education was seen as the solution either to the children's difficulties or the classroom teacher's frustrations, and whether special education placement was considered an appropriate response to external pressures resulting from high-stakes testing.

Although in all schools there were individual teachers whose referral patterns were either much higher or much lower than the average among their colleagues, each school faculty tended to show its own pattern of referral rates. Our observations and interviews revealed that administrators' beliefs and policies were greater determinants of these patterns than were the characteristics of the children themselves. This was underscored by very different rates at schools serving very similar student populations.

GUIDELINES FOR REFERRALS

The decision to refer must be demonstrably within the "disability" belief system, in that the referring teacher must feel reasonably confident that the child will "meet criteria" for one of the disabilities. For LD, this means the presence of a discrepancy between measured IQ and academic achievement. For EMR, this means an overall "flat profile," falling well below age norms. For ED, this means that academic achievement must be affected by evident emotional disturbance.

Beyond these general requirements, some schools and some administrative regions had specific guidelines. A common theme was to make the CST process "more selective." In one region this took the form of an explicit expectation that the "success rate" should be high, that is, that a high percentage of those referred should be found eligible for special education. At another school, which had a relatively high rate of placement in LD (6.6%), the process appeared to be very careful. Administrators told us that great attention was paid to details of the "referral packet," such as considering the child's social and academic history, attendance patterns, and language, before bringing the packet to a CST conference. The assumption here was that there would almost always be two CST conferences before a child would be referred for evaluation. All members but the psychologist would attend both conferences. The psychologist would attend only the second. Personnel described this process as having "a lot of checks." Nevertheless, school personnel estimated that 70% to 75% of the children did go on to a second CST.

In line with the definitions of the high-incidence disabilities, there was a common guideline that referrals must reflect an academic rather than behavioral focus. We noted that most referrals were for primarily academic concerns, and some principals stated that they discouraged referrals that were basically a matter of "your classroom management," in order to encourage teachers to distinguish between their problems and those of the children. However, an outcome of this in one such school seemed to be that the teachers who were the weakest classroom managers seldom referred and simply kept jogging along with their disorderly classrooms. We also noted cases where students were originally referred for academic concerns, but the focus of the referral system soon shifted to behavioral issues (such as with Matthew).

There were other requirements that varied from school to school. At one school a kindergarten teacher informed us, "We are not allowed to refer in kindergarten." A first-grade teacher reported that "it is the ones who have made no progress in reading." At another school, teachers were asked to refer everyone who scored below a certain cutoff on Success for All reading tests. In the vast majority of schools, guidelines resulting from the pressure of high-stakes testing were particularly powerful and will be discussed later. Despite these guidelines, as early as the first week of the school year, many teachers could point out children who might be likely referrals. The children who "did not fit" were readily apparent.

THE TEACHER AS INITIATOR; HIGH AND LOW REFERRERS

Some of these children do not deserve to be in EH, but they have already gone through the process and the psychologist makes the recommendation. I don't know if something is wrong with the assessment procedures, but I think it is much more than the evaluation itself. I think it begins with the referrals. It needs to be questioned, what has been tried to help the child? What has the teacher done? Was the parent informed?

—Behavior management specialist

Regardless of the culture of a school, the classroom teacher is normally the initiator of the referral process. The literature on the topic of teacher referral indicates that approximately 90% of students referred by classroom teachers will be formally tested and of those tested, 73% to 90% will be found eligible for services in special education (Algozzine, Christenson, & Ysseldyke, 1982; Gerber & Semmel, 1984; Gottlieb, Alter, Gottlieb, & Wishner, 1994; Pugach, 1985; Ysseldyke, 2001). Simply put, if teachers do not refer, children will not be placed, and if teachers refer, the vast majority of the children referred will be placed in special education. Thus, to the extent possible, in selecting classrooms for intensive observations, we tried to select a high- and a low-referring teacher in the same school.

Patterns of teacher referral were as variable as was everything else in this study, with the exception of one common thread: The highest referrers were White, Hispanic or both, while Black teachers tended to refer less often. It was not clear what was behind these differential rates. In Chapter 3, in our discussion of school contexts, we referred to a school in which there was a clear pattern of higher referrals by White teachers. Here, the White AP suggested that the African American teachers "don't believe in special education and don't trust the process for Black kids." The African American Placement Specialist offered an alternative explanation:

Well, I think [it's because] the Black teachers can handle the Black kids better. They don't need to refer as much. . . . Because, you know, the Black kid is . . . hollering louder than anyone . . . so when they [the children] cut an attitude, you [Black teacher] know how to really go with it. But . . . an Anglo teacher would be offended or afraid of it, wouldn't even try to resolve it because she feels threatened by it. . . . The children only respect you if they see that you're there and you're consistent. If not, and they see your fear . . .

In contrast, one White administrator expressed the opinion that some Black teachers' style of discipline was too harsh. An African American administrator at another school believed that some Anglo American teachers just did not understand the children's situations and rushed to the notion of disability, displaying "referral fever." The most common theory was that it was mainly the strong teachers who referred a lot, the teachers who "cared." One school counselor typified this view, saying that referring teachers "have taken time out of their schedules to do a seven-page referral, and care desperately enough for children that need help."

As noted earlier, we did not detect systematic evidence of a simplistic ethnic bias in referrals. In the schools with predominantly Black or Hispanic students, there was little mixture in the classrooms, so there was no "other" group with whose referral rates we could compare. In these schools, there were some teachers who consistently referred high numbers of children, while others, teaching similar students, referred very few. Moreover, where there were Black and Hispanic groups together in a classroom, we usually noted no pattern of ethnic bias in referrals. In the only school in which African Americans represented an ethnic and low-SES minority group pitted against high-achieving, wealthy White students, there was a clear pattern in which referrals of African Americans were double those of White students. In this school it was evident that high standards were affecting referral rates. These variable patterns led us to develop an impressionistic typology of teachers that seemed to reflect teachers' philosophies, personalities, and/or implicit racial preferences.

Strong, High-Referring Teachers

Some of the strongest teachers we observed were high referrers. Others were not. In one inner-city school serving a predominantly Haitian population, we selected a very strong third-grade teacher who was Anglo American and a veteran teacher of more than 20 years. In that year, she referred 15 children from her classroom or her SFA reading group, in all, more than a third of her students. These were all referrals for low academics, since this teacher's excellent instruction and classroom management seldom allowed for behavior problems to occur, even with the inclusion of one child who made himself a pest to the rest of the school. These referrals had very mixed results. At the end of the year, six had qualified, two parents had not signed permission for evaluation, one child was placed in an alternative-education class, two moved to other teachers, one left the school, and three were to be tested in the subsequent year. In the following year, the school cut class sizes in half for the early grades and this teacher then had approximately 19 children. Despite the smaller class size, by October she had already referred seven or eight children, more than one third of this class. That year, she seemed to have a better "success rate"—five were tested and did qualify for special education. Several faculty members believed that this teacher referred far too many children.

At another school, the teacher we formerly referred to as Ms. Q was exceedingly similar to the one described above, except that she was Hispanic and much younger. This teacher told us that one year she had made so many referrals that "they" called her "downtown" to explain why. Her explanation was simple. The children needed help "desperately." She reported that she referred approximately 10 children from her class every year and said she had a "high success rate" among those who were evaluated; most qualified for LD, but a few for EMH. She felt that she had a good sense for who had real problems. She spoke scornfully of the many teachers who "can't be bothered" to refer because "it's too much paperwork." She believed that special education was an effective intervention and that many children do return to the mainstream.

As we reported in Chapter 3, despite Ms. Q's evident preference for Hispanic over Black students, her referrals were proportionate to the ethnic makeup of her class. Further, while we did not always agree that every child she referred was really problematic, many were, and we were impressed that she used the CST in line with the school district's ideal of "consultative collaboration" with parents, in which alternative strategies were suggested and implemented. We observed conferences for six of her students, and in five cases she subsequently felt that the parent conference and the strategies had helped and these children were doing better.

Strong, Low-Referring Teachers

The tendency for African American teachers to be relatively low referrers was evident across the schools serving low-income populations. Some, but not all, of these were very strong teachers. In one such school, the African American counselor (who had been a classroom teacher for 11 years and had just become a counselor) exclaimed:

> I have never written a referral on a kid. *Never.* I always feel like I can work with them. Some probably should have been referred, but I found a way to get them to respond. So, I haven't, I have not referred any children.

Two excellent Black teachers in another school offered different, sometimes contradictory opinions on referrals. The kindergarten teacher said she mostly thought that, unless it was an emergency, kindergarten was too early and the children needed a chance to catch up. However, in the 2nd year, when she became a member of the CST team, this teacher referred three children.

Two of these were for seriously low achievement and were later placed in EMH, and the third was a child who had been absent 28 times for the year and was retained and placed in LD pullout. When interviewed, the teacher said that she didn't think that being on the CST had changed her attitude to special education but that these three children really needed help.

The other very strong Black teacher offered several comments on the CST process, mostly negative. While she said that children with problems should be referred "earlier," not left until fourth grade to be referred, she also felt that the first grade was a bit too early. However, she was critical of the quality of special education services—she said that in her 23 years as a teacher, she had known only two children to exit special education. She felt that this contributed to a high rate of dropout among Black kids, and so she herself did not like to refer because of the stigma and ridicule the children endure when placed in special education. She concluded by saying that special education is a "big-time failure setup scapegoat!"

Weak, High-Referring Teachers

School personnel seldom spoke of this group of teachers, but we observed several. These teachers demonstrated both poor instruction and poor classroom-management skills. Ms. E, the "passive"-type teacher whom we described in Chapter 3, reported that her steadily increasing referral rate was now at about half her class. She attributed her African American students' problems to their family lives, but her classroom was typical of those in several inner-city schools—disorganized and inconsistent in discipline. This was the type of classroom from which our ED case study students, Kanita and Robert, were referred, with no acknowledgment at the CST conferences of the classroom situation that had allowed their behavior to escalate.

A White first-grade teacher, whose classroom practice we described earlier as an example of diminished opportunity to learn, also referred at a high rate. In her ESOL class in a predominantly Haitian school she referred seven of her students. Noting that it takes two teachers to fill out the forms, and frustrated by the slow pace of the referral process, she explained that many of her referred students were still not placed by second or third grade. Like other teachers with high referral rates, she saw herself as an advocate for her students, believing that special education would benefit them. She also blamed the school's practice of "pushing to get the fourth grades tested and placed [before the high-stakes testing]" while neglecting the needs of younger students. She said, "It is a vicious cycle because they never catch up. Students don't get the help they need until fourth grade and by then they are really low. . . . For so many years they have been playing catch-up and it is just a self-filling prophecy."

Weak, Low-Referring Teachers

These teachers were all too common in the inner-city schools, including those with lower referral rates. In many of these classrooms, taught by teachers of all ethnicities, there seemed to be no concern about the quality of their work and no concern about whether children made progress. Indeed, these seemed to be the teachers whom one principal described as "just coming in for the paycheck."

However, in other cases, low-referring weak teachers *were* conscientious and caring. For example, Ms. S, a Black third-grade teacher at a predominantly Haitian school, saw special education as something to protect students from, not push them toward. She explained: "I don't refer kids for behavior. I only refer them if they are really low, when they need one-on-one." Although by all accounts she had a very "low" class, she did not make any referrals that year. She had five students who had already been retained and three more who would be retained that year. Although she herself had not referred any of her students, other teachers (that is, SFA) had referred two. In fact, 16 of her students were on the school's active Retention/Request for Evaluation Status Report because they had been referred by others or in previous years. At least five of these had been referred for a CST meeting the previous year (or earlier) but because their current teacher had not also referred them, their cases were still on hold. When questioned about this, she said that she was not aware that most of these students had been referred by a previous teacher. Like high-referring teachers, she saw herself as an advocate for her students. Yet her advocacy played out in different ways and she made tremendous efforts on her students' behalf. In the case of one boy, for example, rather than going to the CST committee, she tried to solve his problems herself by gaining parental permission to tutor him after school twice a week. Another student who was obviously quite intelligent despite his acting-out behavior had been referred to the CST for emotional and behavioral problems by a previous teacher. Ms. S did not follow through on the referral, instead pushing to have the boy placed in an honors class. She noted emphatically:

> And they can't kick him out. . . . He can do the work . . . they want him to sit quietly, but he can't. I don't care, as long as he does the work. If he has any problems in the class, I tell him to come here. He lies on the floor by my desk and does his work. I tell him, "When you feel like you want to throw chairs, come to me." I talked with the

teachers about his problems. I pleaded, "Don't kick him out! When he gets on your nerves, send him here."

To summarize, the referral process relied more on teachers' and administrators' personal beliefs about special education than on children's performance. Good intentions notwithstanding, the lesson learned was that we could not assume that referral rates or patterns reflected a systematic process.

ALTERNATIVE STRATEGIES

In addition to initiating a referral, teachers were responsible for following the referral or the first CST conference with the implementation of specified "alternative strategies," designed to address the child's needs, rather than going on to evaluation for special education. The quality of the strategies seemed to vary both by teacher and by team. All too often, the requirement was undermined by teachers' beliefs that they had already done everything needed. Indeed, some had. At one school the psychologist suggested preferential seating, positive reinforcement, and redirection as strategies, yet these were exactly the techniques the teacher had already reported using. At another school, one of the high-referring, strong teachers used a set of strategies that included after-school tutoring and daily progress reports to the parents. She commented at one meeting, "Now I think I've got the whole class on daily progress monitoring." In the best schools, the everyday instructional and behavior management strategies used by teachers simply demonstrated "good teaching," such as working at the back of the room with a small group of children, sending regular notes home to parents, having parent conferences, and using a "conference"-style method that allowed individualized attention to children's work.

Far more often, however, we noted a tendency to treat the "strategies" as a routine, meaningless requirement. The worst example we saw of this was a conference in which the consultation form noted the following "strategies": "write first and last name without model; identify rhyming words; hold book, paper, scissors"—all of which were simply instructional goals, not strategies. We seldom saw meaningful strategies listed at this school, and all of the six CSTs we observed were focused either on getting permission for evaluation or on discussing whether to retain or send the child to evaluation. In conferences in several schools, the possibility of retention was treated as an alternative "strategy" to evaluation for special education. Perhaps the most telling comment we received from a teacher about strategies came when the researcher asked her about the status of a particular child. She looked across the room at the student and said, "Who? Roberto? Oh, I think he's on strategies now."

"QUALIFYING" FOR SPECIAL EDUCATION:
A ROCK OR A SOFT PLACE?

You meet criteria or you don't meet criteria. The testing stands on its own.
—First-grade teacher

We have shown that the referral process was more of a reflection of teachers' and administrators' personal beliefs and practices than of children's performance. However, when it came to the moment of psychological assessment, school personnel expressed confidence in the gate-keeping role of this event. The preceding quote typified this view, and dissenting voices were rare.

Elsewhere (Harry, Klingner, Sturges, & Moore, 2002), we referred to the widespread perception of the psychological assessment as the idealized "rock" of special education; the point at which hard science determines whether a disability is present. We recall Bronfenbrenner's (1977) statement that researchers who do not attend to ecological validity get caught "between a rock and a soft place, the rock being rigor and the soft place being relevance" (p. 15). This is exactly the error of the belief that fixed "criteria" can ensure an empirical determination of essentially intangible, hard-to-measure human processes. We believe that traditional psychology, no matter its pretensions, is a "soft" science, whose softness is an advantage in teasing out the ambiguities and contradictions of human thought and emotion. This does not mean that psychology's outcomes are not valid, but they must be understood within the confines and the possibilities of an informed uncertainty. In their statements to us, some psychologists expressed their awareness of this. Regardless of what they told us, it was evident in their practice.

When a child's referral actually got to "the table," it was clear that neither "rationality" nor "science" were in control. Rather, we noted six "soft places" that informed, influenced, and at times distorted the outcomes of conferences on eligibility and placement: school personnel's impressions of the family, a focus on intrinsic deficit rather than classroom ecology, teachers' informal diagnoses, dilemmas of the disability definitions and criteria, psychologists' philosophical positions, and pressure from high-stakes testing to place a student in special education. We will treat some of these in depth here, but will hold specific discussion of others until later, when we show how they applied to individual children.

School Personnel's Impressions of the Family

We have already devoted an entire chapter to the power of school personnel's explicit belief that "dysfunctional" families were the chief cause of children's school difficulties. Despite the presence of some sympathetic voices, this belief often made it difficult to disentangle views of the family from views of the child. As we also showed, these views sometimes directly affected referral, assessment, and placement outcomes for children.

Classroom Ecology

Perhaps the most detrimental practice we observed was that CST conferences typically took no account of the ecology of the classroom from which the child was being referred. The assumption seemed to be that the problem was necessarily in the child, not in the environment. Typically, no one asked whether a teacher's instruction or classroom management might be an important contributor to a child's difficulties. This was a serious omission, as was evident in the referrals of two of our case study children, Kanita and Robert, whose classrooms were so ineffective that children had little alternative but to be, at best, inattentive, and at worst, troublesome. We will say much more about the absence of attention to these contexts later.

Overall, it was ironic that school personnel readily sought the source of children's problems in their home environments but seldom in their school environments. As we show elsewhere in this book, all too often we saw the latter as a powerful contributor.

Teachers' Informal Diagnoses

Mehan and colleagues (1986) found that the psychologist was accorded the greatest status in placement deliberations. However, literature on the effects of teacher referrals point to teacher judgment as one of the most influential factors in assessment outcomes (Gerber & Semmel, 1984). In our study, these two patterns seemed to converge, in that, although the psychologist's judgment was definitive, there was considerable team pressure on psychologists to meet their colleagues' expectations.

As full members of the referral and placement teams, psychologists had to balance their role as an expert with their role as a team member. We observed different approaches to attaining this delicate balance. Some psychologists engaged in an interactive style with team members that included casual conversation about cases before or after conferences. Others seemed to maintain some distance. More specifically, the most interactive of the psychologists whom we observed would sometimes directly invite teachers' opinions about the source of a child's learning difficulties, for example, asking, "Do you think the difficulties are just a reaction to the home situation, or do you think there's an intrinsic problem here?" This approach indicated the "expert's" respect for the opinion of those who knew the child better, implicitly acknowledging the limitations of formal testing. The downside of this approach, of course, was the likelihood of undue influence of the teacher's opinion. Occurring at a preliminary CST conference, this conversation affected whether the child's referral would go forward to evaluation or go back to the classroom for "alternative strategies." It also affected the psychologist's expectation regarding the child's condition.

When psychologists did not agree with, or act upon, the views or recommendations of the referring teacher, team relationships could become strained. For example, on one team, faculty dissatisfaction with a psychologist's finding that a child had ADHD rather than an emotional disturbance was followed by an outcome that smacked of considerable manipulation. Robert's behavior had been perceived as so troublesome that he was placed on a program of half-day school attendance that lasted 5 months. Neither teachers nor administrators could fathom how Robert could fail to qualify for an EH placement. The psychologist's determination of ADHD resulted in Robert's eligibility for services under Other Health Impaired (OHI), which meant that he would be served in a part-time, pullout program in his home school. However, Robert's IEP failed to include any specification for a behavioral plan, and the placement soon proved unsuccessful. The psychologist felt impelled to "update the psychological" and qualify Robert for a self-contained ED placement. Without systematic behavioral support, Robert didn't have a chance to succeed in the pullout placement. We suspect that this was an example of the considerable, though covert, power of the team. He was ultimately moved to an ED program at another school. We will tell more of Robert's story later.

Psychologists' Philosophies

Psychologists evidenced three main philosophical orientations that had powerful implications for their practice: Their preferences for some testing instruments over others, their beliefs about the importance of cultural and linguistic diversity in their testing, and their beliefs about the efficacy of special education.

With regard to assessment of children suspected of having an emotional disturbance, this school district required the use of projective tests such as the Roberts Apperception Test, the House-Tree-Person, and others. We have referred before to the unreliability and subjectivity involved in projective testing (Gresham, 1993; Knoff, 1993; Motta, Little, & Tobin, 1993). Our discussions with psychologists revealed that, while they generally had confidence in the tests, their approaches to administration varied. For example, those who used the Thematic Apperception Test reported using it in different ways, such as using all items in the test or using only a few selected items. Similarly, some would routinely complete a battery of four or five tests, while others would select one or two and terminate the testing if the child seemed to be scoring well—that is, not indicating signs of emotional disturbance.

With regard to IQ testing, psychologists' selection of instruments reflected their beliefs about the nature of their craft. Despite current understanding in the field that IQ tests assess children's learning, one psychologist, who used the WISC III, offered the opinion that the IQ tests do measure "inborn intelligence." In contrast, many expressed concern about the applicability of these tests to culturally and linguistically diverse students. Some of these psychologists selected instruments such as the Kauffman Assessment Battery for Children (KABC) or the Differential Ability Scales (DAS), which, by being "less verbally loaded," are thought to be more appropriate for children from diverse cultural and linguistic backgrounds.

Psychologists' preferences for certain tests were intertwined with their views of the relationship between testing contexts and children's cultural and linguistic experiences. Some psychologists spoke of the limitations of standardized American tests in assessing the capabilities of children from low-SES backgrounds or from localities such as Haiti and parts of Central America. In the case of Haiti, for example, quite apart from cultural differences, poverty and limited schooling made these tests particularly inappropriate. Further, the American practice of placing children in grades according to their chronological age meant that Haitian and other immigrant children were often placed at a level far above the level they had been at in their home countries. This presaged certain failure, which, after a short time, would come to be interpreted as an indicator of disability. Psychologists' attempts to give such children the benefit of the doubt often resulted in what teachers perceived as a juggling act, whereby "easier" IQ tests would be used to allow the child to earn a higher IQ score, so as to gain the required discrepancy between IQ and academic achievement. Gaining this score, the child could "qualify" for an LD program rather than the more stigmatizing EMR program.

The foregoing concern was related to psychologists' third philosophical orientation—their view of the efficacy of special education or their preferences for one categorical placement over another. One psychologist said that she often put children in special education to "save" them, because she trusted that the smaller class size and relative individualization would improve the child's rate of progress. To the contrary, another psychologist believed strongly in keeping children in the mainstream wherever possible, especially those with behavioral problems, because placement in an ED program would almost always be very restrictive. She was also very reluctant to designate children as EMR because of the high likelihood of mistaking the impact of poverty and diverse cultural and social experience for evidence of low intelligence. This psychologist also emphasized the effect of the relativity of standards across schools and neighborhoods.

We concluded that many of the processes we saw were truly professional, with psychologists bringing extensive information, responsiveness, and insight to a difficult task. In all cases, the outcomes we saw varied with the three sets of beliefs outlined above and with the other pressures described in this chapter. Some psychologists seemed unduly influenced by preconceived beliefs about children and families. Some were more influenced than others by their colleagues. We saw some prejudice, much concern, and many social pressures that ran in different directions. Overall, the arbitrariness of the process was frightening. We did not see science.

Skrtic (1991) defined professional work as "complex work . . . that is too ambiguous, and thus too uncertain, to be reduced to a sequence of routine subtasks" (p. 86). Agreeing with this, we do not argue that special education decision making ought to be "scientific." We do not believe, in fact, that there is a rock. Rather, we believe that an informed and caring subjectivity should guide well-trained professionals in making decisions about services for children. We note, however, that much of the arbitrariness we saw in the process is the result of the unnecessary requirement for the assigning of a categorical disability.

High-Stakes Testing as a Filter for Disability

During the years of this research, special education students' scores on state-wide testing were not included in the state's rating of schools. These rankings bring sanctions and rewards in the form of funding, vouchers for children to be moved to other public schools or private schools, and, no less important, perceived status in the community. Thus, it became important for school personnel to identify those students whose performance might "bring down our scores."

A new definition of disability. The policy in place during our research made a mockery of the construct of disability as the criterion for placement in special education programs. It demonstrated two points we made in Chapter 1: First, it is paradoxical that costly, specialized services, attained through powerful parent and professional advocacy, should come to be seen as detrimental to minority groups because of stigma and questionable efficacy. This paradox becomes more intense when the low achievement of minority students results in their being seen as "having" disabilities, instead of their receiving instruction appropriately tailored to their needs.

Second, we referred to the trajectory of special education and the education of minority groups as reflecting a "collision course." In this district, high-stakes testing and special education had become the crossroads for this collision. Many administrators openly discussed changes they had instituted because of new accountability measures. For example, when one principal was asked whether she thought the state testing and the state grading plan had actually influenced the referral process, she replied:

> Yes. Very definitely it has because when we looked at our scores this year we had no zeros, thankfully. We will take writing for an example—we had no zeros, scored on a zero-to-six scale. But we had ones across the board—*those are our special education students who have not been identified.* Those kinds of scores count in our school's [grade]. They pull our score down, just one factor in the total of the fourth grade, and it brings your score down. *And one student can make the difference between one letter grade and another*, and then that stigma is attached not only to that classroom, to the students, but to the entire school. Where it might be one or two students that if they had been identified early enough, [their scores] could have been factored out of the total results. So that is a very telling statistic and yes, it does emphasize our making sure that we identify children with special needs prior to the fourth grade. (emphasis added)

The notion that struggling students are actually "our special education students who have not been identified" represents, in essence, a new definition of disability. By this reasoning, low achievement came to be synonymous with special education eligibility—in short, with disability. The drive to identify special education students prior to the year they would first take the state's high-stakes tests was described explicitly by principals determined to improve their schools' grades. Though we have multiple examples of this, we will focus on one inner-city school principal who predicted at the beginning of the project that the state's accountability plan would affect referrals:

> I think you're going to see a greater number [of students referred]. I think that principals are going to feel their backs against the wall and whatever it's going to take to make sure that the school is achieving, that's what they're going to do. . . . I know as a principal I'm looking at all options at this point. Where can we see growth and where are we going to put our energies and what must be done in order to do this . . . looking at everyone.

A year later, soon after schools' "grades" had been announced and this school had earned a D, the same principal said:

I've told the teachers that we've got to identify those children who should be getting special education help and get them over there. We know darned well they should be there so let's get on with it. . . . This is the reality. It's a matter of survival now!

A teacher in that school reported that there was "a big push to test as many as possible so they won't qualify for the [high-stakes tests] in a couple of years." At the end of the final year of our research project, the school's ranking had moved up to a C. An interview with the principal confirmed that she had set out to ensure that children who needed services were tested to see if they would qualify for special education. She felt that the effort had been successful and that "it was about time," since too many children previously had been left in general education long after it was evident they were years behind. She believed that this strategy had contributed to the school's new ranking.

This principal's efforts were admirable in many ways. She instituted a program of testing every child at the very beginning of the school year to determine their reading and math levels, followed by weekly testing and official posting of scores. This was supported by intensive small-group instruction, described as follows:

We took the teachers who did not have classroom responsibilities . . . the reading leader, the Success for All reading tutor, the system locator, the computer facilitator. . . . Each was assigned a classroom and they went with the teacher and took 10 to 15 children or however many and took them out of that classroom and they worked with them on those skills. We double dosed them in reading or math. Everyone has reading for an hour and a half, from 9:00 to 10:30. From 10:30 to 11:30 every day, the children receive [high-stakes-test] reading skills. And those are the skills that they need to pass. Then fourth grade receives another hour in writing. Math for fifth grade was done differently because they receive their hour and a half of reading and then they receive a double dose of math, regular math, and then [high-stakes-test] math. . . . That and prayer!

A serious limitation to the program described above was that, while general-education students received more intensive, small-group tutoring, the opposite occurred in special education classes. The reassignment of general-education and special-area teachers to reading instruction for extended periods meant a reduction in the resources that usually allowed for small-group special education instruction. Special education teachers found themselves with groups of students larger than the groups in general education.

Overall, high-stakes testing actually changed the nature of the referral process in schools in which principals took such actions. Normally, the process placed the responsibility for referral in the hands of teachers. As we have explained, however, teachers showed great variability in their willingness to refer. Principals who were trying to "identify" all the special education students before they were tested felt vindicated in their efforts when they discovered that there were children in the fourth grade in their school who could not read, and whom everyone seemed to have ignored up until then. The principal cited above simply took this matter into her own hands:

> A lot of teachers don't like to [refer]. What we have done this year, we've tried to have patience with them. But we know that they are a problem and we have our AP go in and we do it for them.

This process, then, directly affected referral rates. Yet when asked if it would be correct to say that the high-stakes-testing demands had actually increased special education placements, this principal replied that since the children "had to qualify" for those services, this qualification would confirm that they really needed them. She then noted the excellent skills of their psychologist. This psychologist, however, had been observed to be under considerable pressure to place a child in an LD program although the child had not met the "discrepancy" criterion. This was one of the ironies in our findings: Principals and teachers felt justified in increasing their referrals because they thought psychologists would only identify those students who actually met criteria. Yet it was evident that some psychologists did succumb to the administration's pressure to place students. One told us that she did her best to respond to this pressure by choosing instruments that would be more likely to "find" the suspected disability. One of these, a test commonly reputed to be unreliable and biased, she referred to as "her secret weapon."

It was not only the failing schools that felt this pressure. In one of the highest-achieving and highest-income schools in the sample, a special education teacher told us that there was a significant increase in the number of fourth graders entering the special education program. When asked why, she replied, "[High-stakes] testing, of course. The teachers are under a lot of pressure."

Do the ends justify the means? The intensive search for failing children was not without some strengths, since it provided principals with a lever to force attention onto students who previously had been "passed along" without ever attaining grade-level academic skills. Some principals described this pressure as an opportunity to redress this disservice to children. If children did improve, then it is difficult to argue that the ends do not justify the means.

In contrast, our observations of special education classrooms indicated that there was little reason to believe that such placement would be more appropriate than most effective general-education classrooms. As described earlier, in one school, an excellent remedial program for general-education students took away from the promise of small groups in special education classes. Ironically, if not for the desire to remove failing students from the mainstream, the remedial program could have been used for everyone. It could have become, simply, the model of general education implemented in that school by a bright and motivated administrator. It could have been accomplished without the need for an arbitrary border between normalcy and disability. Instead, the model that emerged resembles the UK system described by Gillborn and Youdell (2000) as "a form of educational triage, a means of rationing support so that some pupils are targeted for additional teacher time and energy while others are seen as inevitable casualties of the battle to improve standards" (p. 14).

The "accountability" pressure on schools in this state is tremendous. As educators, we agree that some version of this type of accountability is needed and appropriate. However, the extent of pressure placed on schools by the state-ranking plan, tied to the results on high-stakes tests, is extreme. All too often, we saw clear examples of many teachers' statement that they no longer had the professional autonomy to adjust either the content or pace of the curriculum to the needs of their students.

CONCLUSIONS

In concluding our consideration of the discourse by which schools constructed "disabled" student identities, we find that the work of both Mehan et al. (1986) and Skrtic (1991) point to central ironies and paradoxes in special education service provision. Skrtic maintained that the goals of special education are essentially those of an "adhocracy"—"a problem-solving organization in which interdisciplinary teams of professionals collaborate to invent personalized programs" (p. 185). Such a system requires maximum flexibility, based on the principles of innovation and problem solving, in contrast to standardization. However, Skrtic argued, two other models have affected special education: the culture of a professional bureaucracy, in which highly trained individuals work alone to perfect standard goals, and a machine bureaucracy, which attempts to further standardize by developing "an organization in which worker behavior is controlled by procedural rules" (p. 184).

In our research we saw the interaction of these competing models at work. Psychologists' professional interpretations of children's complex needs were hamstrung by fixed "criteria" for categorical placements. Placement specialists' attempts to develop individualized educational programs were defeated by a climate that emphasized only compliance with legal requirements. School administrators, trying to keep their schools and reputations afloat, created "triage" sorting systems to decide which children could be saved and which sacrificed. General-education teachers, stressed by large class sizes and inequitable administrative practices, put their faith in an idealized vision of special education that was very unlikely to be realized. And family members were largely excluded from the discourse because of negative stereotypes and because seeking their genuine participation might further complicate a process that everyone wanted to simplify.

The impact of high-stakes testing on special education referrals was one more example of the machine bureaucracy at work. In this case, the extreme sorting process mandated by the NCLB act worked against the best interests of children whose achievement was toward the weak end of the learning continuum. The drive to find "our special education children who have not been placed" resulted in appropriate interventions for some and very inappropriate interventions and placement for others. Indeed, to frame the issue in terms of that quotation was to confound low achievement with disability.

In an adhocracy, it would be appropriate that decisions should reflect what Mehan et al. (1986) referred to as "everyday" rather than "scientific" reasoning. Everyday reasoning, as long as it is well reasoned, would be a natural part of problem solving. We understand that the variable, often inequitable, circumstances of schools will limit the possibility of systematic decision making that proceeds from clear premises and principles. However, that very inequity and variability is the reason for the field to move toward the most flexible service provision possible. Perhaps learning disability should not be conceived of as a condition that can be measured by the same yardstick for all children. Perhaps troublesome behavior cannot be categorized as either disturbance or deliberate noncompliance. Perhaps mental or developmental delay does not mean that children need to be in separate programs. Perhaps there is no rock.

Certainly, one size should not be expected to fit all in a multicultural, multilingual, society where wealth is so inequitably distributed and where the legacy of centuries of racism is still palpable. For the most vulnerable of children to be placed at increased risk of decisions that may negatively affect their educational careers, indeed their identities, is to impose upon them one more inequity.

CHAPTER 7

Bilingual Issues and the Referral Process

It's easier to determine if a disability exists in a bilingual program.
—Counselor in a bilingual school

IN THIS CULTURALLY and linguistically diverse school district, careful attempts have been made to address the challenge of ensuring that language-learning processes among children whose native language is not English are not mistaken for learning or other disabilities. The referral process for these students is similar except for the additional involvement of a Limited English Proficiency (LEP) Committee, a bilingual assessor, and an ESOL teacher.

As with the district's official referral policies, the written guidelines for English-language learners (ELLs), that is, bilingual students not yet fully proficient in English, were excellent. However, our findings regarding the efficacy of this system were quite mixed, suggesting that, once more, much had to do with the quality of the school, the knowledge of key players, and the culture of referral. Although school personnel seemed quite knowledgeable about the district's referral policies for native English speakers, and could explain them articulately, we noted much more confusion regarding the process for ELLs.

THE RATIONAL MODEL

One AP explained the process clearly:

> The first thing to do with an English-language learner is address his language proficiency. Is it a situation where a child is having difficulty with language? So at the LEP committee [the committee set up to monitor ELLs' progress], we look for alternative strategies, and we try to get the parent involved in any tutoring that the child might

need. . . . We consider whether or not we need to reclassify the child's ESOL level, or that he needs a little more time, some strategies, some alternatives, and then we continue monitoring him. Children aren't just dropped when they exit ESOL, but they are monitored for 2 years. And during that time they still have to be going to the LEP committee before they go to a CST, because it might still be a language issue. After a certain amount of time if we see that the child is still having difficulties then we ask for assistance from the CST.

At the first CST, if the child is at an intermediate level of English proficiency (ESOL Level 3 or 4), he is referred to the bilingual assessor for evaluation in English and his native language. The students who are in ESOL 5 and are at the 32nd percentile in reading or lower and have been exited from the program for less than 2 years are also evaluated. According to one bilingual assessor, the reason for this is that

if a child is brand new, and is an ESOL Level 1 or 2, they do not need to be evaluated by the bilingual assessor. . . . You cannot evaluate them based on their English, you have to go based on their home language. So, if the child has not been here a sufficiently long time to acquire the second language, the evaluation must be based on information or the input that you have on their home language. A bilingual psychologist tests them in their native language only.

However, this policy not to refer students at ESOL Levels 1 and 2 to a bilingual assessor was changing during the years of our investigation. We were told that schools now had the option of asking for a bilingual assessment for students who are ESOL 1 and 2.

The report from the bilingual assessor is supposed to be completed and sent to the psychologist before the second CST meeting. Bilingual assessors administer the Brigance Inventory, written and oral narratives, a social-language inventory, and perhaps additional standardized tests. A bilingual assessor explained:

You have to look at it holistically, and ask when the child arrived, where was he born, how long has he been in ESOL, what kind of support he has received, is he attending the bilingual programs? Is he in an ESOL self-contained class versus a pullout program? You need to look at all of these things.

The required process is based on Cummins's (1984) well-known distinction between cognitive academic language proficiency and basic interpersonal communicative skills. Thus, the bilingual assessor's evaluation determines whether the child is still in the process of learning formal academic language and whether the child's academic difficulties might be caused by other factors in addition to those associated with language learning. The psychologist takes this into account in assessing the child.

INADEQUATE ASSESSMENT

The preceding description reflects an idealized version of a process that we rarely saw implemented in this form. In reality, the bilingual assessors were backlogged, and we detected little direct evidence of their influence. We never saw a bilingual assessor attend a CST meeting or placement conference. When questioned about this, we were told that this was "because of the level of work to do. We have over 200 referrals per person in the office per year." This heavy workload was reflected in the very long waiting periods typical for bilingual assessments. The presence of these professionals at CST and placement conferences was sorely missed. Even when it had been determined that a child could be tested in English, this did not negate the fact that English-language-learning issues were still relevant to understanding his/her problems. We rarely heard any mention at all of the bilingual evaluations. And with the exception of one psychologist who frequently questioned teachers and others about issues related to language acquisition, we rarely saw evidence that these factors were considered when referral or placement decisions were made.

Our research site was not unique in this regard. Ochoa, Rivera, and Powell (1997) surveyed 859 school psychologists who had some experience conducting bilingual psychoeducational assessments. They indicated that they frequently omitted critical factors such as consideration of the student's native language and the number of years of English instruction. Only 1% attempted to determine if a discrepancy occurred in both English and the student's home language.

STAFF CONFUSION

Another barrier to effective implementation was confusion among those responsible for carrying out the process. Although some school personnel seemed quite knowledgeable about district requirements, many seemed uncertain. At one school the AP who was in charge of the referral process did not seem to know the difference between the bilingual assessor and the bilingual psychologist, referring to them interchangeably. When asked for the name of the bilingual assessor, she provided the name of the psychologist instead. Other personnel also seemed confused about the role of the bilingual assessor and the purpose of testing. At a CST meeting at another school, we noted the following:

> I asked the counselor to clarify the role of the bilingual assessor for me. She says he will test the child's academic skills in Creole, to see if he has learned them in his native language. She explains this for a couple of minutes, then pauses and looks a bit doubtful. Then she turns to the team members and comments that maybe that's not right, since he may not have learned those things in Creole yet. They nod. The conversation drifts off.

At a third school, the psychologist stated emphatically, "The district will not allow psychological testing of young children at ESOL Levels 1 and 2." At yet another school, the psychologist explained to a CST team, "He can't be referred anyway until he's ESOL Level 4." The teacher asked if the child could be referred for a bilingual assessment, and the psychologist responded, "No, his ESOL level is too low; they won't accept it."

This issue of when to refer a child certainly caused confusion. When we questioned the district administrator responsible for establishing ELL policy about whether there was a rule stipulating that beginning-level ELLs should not be referred, she responded, "No, not at all. No, no. At every meeting, in fact at every regional or AP meeting that we have gone to, we say it. All children have access to any categorical program." At another point in the conversation she said:

> One of the issues in terms of ESOL students is that we [in general around the country] wait until the students become proficient in English. But that doesn't happen too much in this district. We sometimes don't really have "underreferral." I think that in the average schools overrefer. That is my perception of what we have out there.

An additional challenge seemed to be the beliefs of individual practitioners. Although the professionals with whom we spoke were knowledgeable about Cummins's (1984) assertions that it takes up to 7 years for a student to acquire cognitive academic language proficiency in English, some confided that they did not really think it took that long. When questioned about this, one bilingual psychologist explained,

> It depends. If they've been taught and if you ask me about an immigrant, a Columbian who is coming without the language, by the 3rd

year they should be able to have social[-language proficiency in English]. . . . So if they have started here since kindergarten and they have heard the language every day, they should be able to learn it like any other student. So even though they switch [to using their native language] at home, it doesn't matter. You see, I was born in [a Spanish-speaking country] but I went to an American school all of my life. So I know what it is like [to learn English]. In my head I have the experience, so I expect [students to acquire English quickly].

DIFFERENTIATING BETWEEN ENGLISH-LANGUAGE ACQUISITION AND LEARNING DISABILITIES

It is notoriously difficult to differentiate between normal second-language acquisition and learning disabilities (Gonzalez, Brusca-Vega, & Yawkey, 1997; Ortiz, 1997). This distinction is particularly problematic among children who do not seem strong in either their native language or English. One bilingual assessor explained how challenging the process is:

My role as a bilingual assessor is to determine if the child's difficulties are due to [learning a second] language or due to other factors. Sometimes it might be something I don't know. Sometimes I don't have all of the facts in front of me. Sometimes the discrepancy is so thin. Maybe if they give him more time, he'll make it. Maybe we will give him 2 years and with more time we'll see a change. Maybe sometimes we know that 2 years will not help. Sometimes it is just kind of struggle to see.

In part, placement decisions are difficult because no test of language proficiency has yet been developed that can adequately let us know when a child whose primary language is not English is ready to be tested only in English (Figueroa, 1989; Ortiz, 1997). Even children who demonstrate English proficiency on language-assessment measures still typically demonstrate a low Verbal IQ and high Performance IQ profile. If a child was transitioned prematurely, for example, from a bilingual or ESOL program to a regular classroom, this is likely to have had a negative impact on achievement and also depress scores on tests of intelligence. Authors such as Trueba (1989) have challenged the practice of blaming low achievement on low IQ, stressing the importance of looking further at the context within which underachievement occurs. Yet, as described in earlier chapters about our case study students, we saw little evidence of such considerations. Although the bilingual assessors seemed quite knowledgeable about these issues, because they did not attend CST meetings or staffings, they were not in a position to share their expertise.

Personnel at our school with a full bilingual program expressed the opinion that it is easier to identify students with learning disabilities when they are in a bilingual program, "because you can tell if they are having difficulties in Spanish, their native language, as well as in English. You can determine if the child's difficulty is due to confusion learning a new language, or something broader that is apparent in both languages." In addressing this issue, one psychologist explained:

> At [ESOL] Level 3, you start forgetting the native language so the child may have poor vocabulary in both languages, so it is hard to tell if it's a learning disability. Then the tests that are in Spanish are based on norms for monolinguals and these kids are not. So you just do the best you can. . . . The kid falling between proficiency in both languages does poorly. Only in a full bilingual program is the kid likely to adequately maintain both languages.

VARIABLE REFERRAL RATES

The phenomenon of "high"- and "low"-referring schools applied as much to schools with high percentages of ELL children as to those with mainly monolingual populations. Indeed, among the four predominantly Hispanic schools, LD placement rates ranged from 4.2% to 12.5%. In the two predominantly Haitian schools the rates were 6.8% and 3.5%.

The most common explanations for varying placement rates had little relevance to differences between children. Rather, they reflected differences in school personnel's beliefs about special education, beliefs about English-language acquisition, knowledge of the process, and also how busy the person was. The district-level administrator quoted earlier noted that school-level administrators have a lot of control over how the process is actually carried out in their schools. The issue of "high referring" versus "low referring" was tension filled. At one of the high-referring schools, the counselor believed that its rate should be viewed positively:

> We are considered a high-referral school. The district was saying that there were too many referrals. . . . But if the teachers identify more kids that they suspect may have a problem, then they have to work harder because they have to do a lot of paperwork. We have to work harder because we have to do more meetings. But we are trying to help the kids so we don't mind. But then, by the same token, the

psychologist needs to test more. The staffing specialist needs to do more staffing, because it affects everybody. When you are considered high referral, it's not good. You are definitely not looked upon favorably.

By contrast, district personnel shared concerns about other schools they considered to be low referring. One bilingual assessor expressed the view that at some schools "not enough" children were being placed. Another said that for a few years they had received no referrals from one of our schools— "Zero!"

The bilingual assessors with whom we spoke speculated about why some schools are reluctant to refer:

There are many reasons. Sometimes they are cautious to refer a child . . . because they don't want to do all of the paperwork and find out that the child doesn't meet criteria for services. And there are a lot of cases like that . . . Maybe it has to do with the person in charge of the referrals. Some people do not believe that the child belongs in special education and say, "Let me give that child a chance." Some people see special education as a negative thing.

PARENTS' ROLE IN THE PROCESS

We were also told that parents' reluctance to place their children in special education and parents' misunderstandings about the process were additional challenges. Issues we noted concerned the use of translators, as well as parents' beliefs about their heritage language.

Misunderstandings Due to Inadequate or Sporadic Translation Services

Despite the great presence of Spanish-speakers and Haitian Creole–speakers in this region, the district provided translations of some, but not all, official documents. Translation of CST and placement conferences generally was provided by the classroom teachers who were present; the counselor; or, at some schools, the community involvement specialist. However, this depended on the population in each school. In one 99%-Hispanic school, all members of the CST team, with the exception of the AP, spoke Spanish. This presented a tremendous advantage for parents; all the conferences we observed were conducted in Spanish. It was rather awkward, however, for the AP and severely limited her role.

In most schools it was not difficult to find a Spanish interpreter, but interpreters for Haitian Creole were much harder to come by, and occasionally no one was available to translate. From what we could surmise, those who translated had not received any special training in how to translate the results of a psychological evaluation. We noted that there were misunderstandings when adequate translation services were not provided, even when parents seemed to speak English well, as in the example below from a CST meeting with a Haitian Creole speaker:

> The AP reviews the information on the form. She asks if this was Antoine's first time here at school. The father replies yes. . . . They seem to misunderstand him to be saying that Antoine just started here this year. So the teacher asks, "Didn't he come to kindergarten here last year?" The father asks the interpreter, "What she say?" She translates and he tells her, "Yes, Antoine was here last year." [Later, the translator needed to leave and the meeting continued without translation services.]

A community involvement specialist who was the usual translator at her school spoke about her scheduling difficulties:

> I went to about three [CST] last week. They had already scheduled the time and they never let me know beforehand. . . . It is a scheduling issue; it is hard, when you schedule a parent to come to a CST, that takes parents from work and you cannot ask them to come back. So when they are there they are trying to do as much as possible. But usually I am there to translate or Mr. M. He's the Creole-speaking visiting teacher, and some of our teachers are also there and they speak Creole.

Parents' Attitudes Toward Their Home Language

Information on the attitudes of some Haitian parents toward the importance of Haitian Creole was a poignant reminder of how societal attitudes toward devalued minority groups can be internalized by group members. In this city, where Spanish is a highly accepted language, we never heard of Spanish-speaking parents denying their home language. We heard this only in the case of Haitian Creole speakers who sometimes would indicate to school personnel that their children spoke only English when in fact the children spoke both Creole and English. The following conversation is about parents' attitudes toward speaking their home language and letting their children participate in the Home Language program. The Haitian community involvement specialist reported that some parents only wanted their children to learn English but that she was able to change their minds by pointing out the benefits of being multilingual. She explained:

> Oh, definitely, yes. We have some of them like that. The first time they really don't know what is going on, they are like, "Haiti, I am ashamed of it, so I don't speak Creole; Creole never helped me and I don't need Creole when I come here." . . . But when they come to register, they are asked, "Do you speak another language at home?" and then they put "yes." . . . If you have "yes" . . . the child needs to go to ESOL, then they need to go to Creole classes. But some of them when . . . they put the "yes," we put the child in those classes and then they come back and say, "My child doesn't speak Creole, why did you put him?" "But that is what you answered in your form." And then they say, "No, I don't want them to speak Creole." Once, I remembered that she couldn't speak English and I asked her why she didn't want her daughter to learn Creole. She said, "No, because Creole is not important for my child, she will stay in the United States. She needs to speak English." And then I told her, "To me it is an opportunity to learn another language. She knows how to speak English but as a parent it is good for you to teach the child Creole because when you go back home one day that child will not want to speak to your mom, to the grandparents, to the friends." And she was taking it in, and I said, "You see where I am now, why do you think I am here? That is because I speak Creole, I speak French, and I speak English. If I didn't know how to speak Creole they would have never put me in a position like this." And I told her, "And we have a Creole class at night, and we have a lot of professionals, doctors and lawyers, in that class because of the needs of the community and they need to speak to the community. They have to learn the language." . . . She was like, "Oh, that is true." They said that they didn't know, and then they want their child in that classroom. . . . If it is good for their child then they are OK. Once I explain it to them then they are OK with it.

CONCLUSIONS

Overall, we noted several instances of concern. Although personnel appeared to be well trained, individual children's language needs were not as central to the referral process as they should have been. We noted that even in schools in which bilingual issues seemed to be well understood by key players, children's language needs and the influence of their limited proficiency on learning and behavior were not discussed at CST meetings or placement conferences; nor were they written into evaluation reports. We detail specific examples of this in subsequent chapters. It seemed that personnel felt that once a child had been through a bilingual assessment, there was no more need to attend to this feature.

Although, nationally, ELLs are only marginally overrepresented in LD categories, emerging evidence suggests that subgroups of ELLs may be particularly vulnerable to misclassification. In their study of the placement rates in special education of ELL subgroups, Artiles, Rueda, Salazar, and Higareda (2002) found that those students classified as lacking proficiency in both their first language and in English were heavily overrepresented. As indicated in Table 1.1 in Chapter 1, this district reflects the national pattern, with Hispanic students slightly overrepresented in the LD category. Although we did not look at patterns of Hispanic subgroup representation in any systematic way in our study and cannot say whether any subgroup of the ELL population was over- or underrepresented, our data do suggest that the referral process when applied with ELLs was variable and confused.

We have focused in these two chapters on the discourse by which children's school identities were officially determined. Although we noted many informed professional opinions that were appropriate to such discourse, it seemed that decisions were all too often undermined by the tension between professionalism, administrative and workload pressures, and the demand for categorization of students. In the following three chapters, we narrow our focus to detail the processes by which individual students were determined to be eligible for special education services. We focus also on the outcomes of those decisions.

CHAPTER 8

Constructing Educable Mental Retardation: Cracks and Redundancies

The placement specialist informs Mrs. Carey [the referring teacher] that Mercedes does not qualify for any special education program. The school psychologist tells Mrs. Carey about Mercedes's achievement and IQ scores. One is too high and the other is too low. Therefore, she doesn't qualify. Mrs. Carey says that she doesn't believe that Mercedes is not EMR. The psychologist tells Mrs. Carey that she gave her the test that would render the lowest scores (trying to qualify her for special education services). Mrs. Carey is visibly upset. She says that . . . special education is "all backwards. Basically, you mean to tell me she is too low for to qualify for the LD program and too high for EMR? So, she is just going to fall through the cracks? Then what is she going to do in middle school? I won't be there to watch over her anymore." Mr. Talbot explains that they have the same [placement] procedures in middle school. The best he can do is write a note for them to look over her case in middle school. . . .

Mrs. Smithe, the special education teacher, states that Mrs. Carey's extra help with Mercedes probably led to an increase in her achievement scores. The school psychologist agrees. . . . Mrs. Carey responds incredulously, "Are you saying that it is my fault!?" She continues about the nightmare she has about these students being overlooked. The special education teacher says, "You taught them too well." Ultimately the team recommends peer tutoring for Mercedes.

IN THIS AND the next two chapters, we address the cracks and the redundancies that plague the high-incidence categories in which CLD students are overrepresented. We begin with the EMR placement process, looking at the dysfunction that arises from overly rigid diagnostic criteria and from the inability to provide special education services without "proof" of disability.

"FALLING BETWEEN THE CRACKS"

The conundrum faced by Mercedes's assessment team captures two essential shortcomings of the categorical construction of EMR, LD, and ED: First, these disabilities are conceptualized as fixed conditions whose distinctive characteristics will lead to the correct diagnosis. Second, children cannot receive specialized services without "qualifying" for one of these categories. This medical model of disability does not translate well into the complex and social contexts of education. A number of obvious contextual issues arise: Did the child have adequate opportunity to learn or to correct early learning difficulties? Is the child's social behavior a temporary expression of emotional distress? How consistent and how severe does this behavior have to be to be considered a disturbance? Are peer-group pressures contributing to the problem? Can parents be of assistance? As in the case of Mercedes, could a teacher such as Mrs. Carey make a difference?

Unfortunately, the field has not sought answers in the social contexts of schools (Keogh & Speece, 1996). Rather, in support of the categorical model, it has turned to definitions, operational criteria, and futile efforts to measure intangible characteristics. These attempts continue to fail. Efforts to crystallize the distinction between LD and EMR have focused on identifying a discrepancy between academic achievement and cognitive potential (as measured by an IQ score) and on ruling out competing etiologies such as other impairments or environmental disadvantages. But identifying the discrepancy required for an LD diagnosis means waiting until the child is old enough to demonstrate academic competency, which also means waiting till he/she is old enough to fail. Appropriate interventions may be introduced too late. These criteria also mean that children from low-income circumstances may not be considered for the category partly because of the exclusionary definition and partly because the cultural content of IQ measures may make it difficult for them to score high enough to achieve the required discrepancy (Collins & Camblin, 1983).

Mercedes's case presents a somewhat convoluted version of the LD/EMR conundrum. In her case, although the psychologist gave Mercedes an IQ test on which she expected her to gain a low score, Mercedes did better than expected and scored too high to qualify for EMR. It seems that an effective teacher had interfered with the profile by teaching Mercedes so well that her academic scores were too high for her to display the "discrepancy" required for LD eligibility. This case illustrates perfectly Gergen's (1994) argument that the "increasing entanglements" (p. 143) of the mental health professions often defeat the best of intentions.

For decades, the discrepancy criterion and the exclusion of "environmental disadvantage" resulted in Black and low-income students being more likely to be designated EMR than LD. In recent years, the EMR-LD shift has resulted in the use of LD as a catchall category and a diminution of the use of EMR across the board (MacMillan et al., 1998). Indeed, in the 4 decades since its introduction, LD identification rates have increased almost sixfold, while the rates of placement for all ethnicities in EMR have been reduced by almost half (Donovan & Cross, 2002). Despite the reduction in numbers, the EMR category continues to display severe overrepresentation of African Americans, who are more than twice as likely to be identified in this category than are students of other ethnicities (Donovan & Cross, 2002).

CROSSING THE BORDER: FROM DELAYED DEVELOPMENT TO MENTAL RETARDATION

It is well known that children found eligible for the EMR category nowadays are likely to be more impaired in overall cognitive development than were those children represented by cases such as *Larry P. v. Riles* (1979). The criterion of an IQ score of 70 as an indicator of "significantly subaverage" general intellectual functioning, accompanied by impairments in adaptive behavior, are much more stringent than was the pre-1970s cutoff point of 85 on an IQ scale. With the current standard, it is expected that children identified as EMR will show significant differences from their peers who are labeled LD.

In our study we did find that the children labeled EMR seemed to reflect that qualitative difference, but this observation was sometimes called into question, by late educational intervention, inadequacy of the assessment, or poor teacher quality in either general or special education, which resulted in limited opportunity to learn. Each of our four case studies in this category illustrated at least one of these limitations. Leroy, an African American kindergartener, represented an exemplary placement process, including early referral in kindergarten by an excellent teacher, a thorough assessment, and placement within the kindergarten year. Leroy did seem to meet the academic and functional criteria for EMR services. The downside to this case, however, was the final phase—extremely poor quality instruction and classroom management in his special education classroom. In contrast, Bartholomew, whose first language was Haitian Creole, was not referred until the third grade, when an excellent teacher expressed intense frustration at the fact that this child had been passed along the grades although, in her words, "he doesn't know his alphabet. He doesn't know the sounds. He knows numbers but he can't add and subtract single digits!" Clearly, lack of early response to this child's cognitive and linguistic needs complicated the apparent evidence of EMR. We will focus on the other two children, Clementina and James, whose cases illustrate more mixed configurations of the placement irregularities we noted.

Clementina

Clementina was a third grader of Puerto Rican parentage, at an inner-city, predominantly Black school with a growing Hispanic population. It is not clear what her ESOL level was when she was in her third-grade ESOL class, but by the time of her placement conference in the fourth grade, she was considered fully proficient in English and was evaluated only in English. According to her mother, she had spoken only Spanish at home until she started school at age 5.

We observed Clementina over a period of two years. In her general-education third-grade class she impressed us as a child who was minimally interested in her schoolwork and only occasionally participated in class activities. Each of the following examples is from a different day's field notes during that year:

> The teacher asks Clementina, "What are you writing about?"
> Clementina responds, "I don't have no journal." The teacher says, "This is not an art class. You'd better write."
>   I go over and check Clementina's work. She smiles mischievously and says to me, "I'm not doing my work." I ask her, "Why not?" She says, "I don't feel like it." . . . She is just sitting now, looking at Floyd. . . . Clementina is still sitting at her seat, doing nothing.

The third-grade teacher was concerned about Clementina, saying that she "has really changed, become very aggressive, and is not the sweet little girl she used to be." Clementina was absent for weeks at a time because of head lice and, at one point, because of ringworm. The teacher perceived the family circumstances as very detrimental, saying: "The mother is retarded, and can't even sign her name, and she has eight kids. Her older sister is 14, and now having a baby. The grandmother takes care of her."

Our observations of Clementina in her fourth-grade general-education class showed her performing much the same as in the third grade. She participated only minimally and when she did join in she appeared to be parroting what her peers were saying. The teacher expressed puzzlement and frustration over the fact that she had been promoted to the fourth grade, saying:

> Last year Clementina got all Fs in reading but then she received a C [at the end of the year]. A D is passing, so she got promoted. I don't know how, for Clementina reads on a first-grade reading level. She is

low. . . . I've been trying to help her with her writing, getting her to use the prompt when she writes the answer on the [statewide test]. In that way she can get a one and not a zero. The whole process I find very frustrating.

The outcome of Clementina's evaluation in the fourth grade was an EMR placement, with a full-scale IQ score of 51 on the WISC-III. Her academic work was assessed to be at the kindergarten level, with some letter recognition but no word recognition, and simple addition but no subtraction skills. The psychologist commented that there was "nothing remarkable, no mental delays, she smiles when you look at her but she does not speak. She forgets things very easily." We found this description of Clementina as having "no mental delays" rather curious, because "mental delays" are precisely what a score of 51 and other aspects of her profile would indicate.

Despite the fact that Clementina's family members agreed that she had "mental problems," other aspects of her case compounded the picture of an inappropriate placement process. First, it turned out that Clementina had been referred by her kindergarten teacher and it had taken 3 years for the first CST to be held and 4 years for her to be placed. Another problematic aspect was the excluding behavior of school personnel toward Clementina's family members at the CST conference and the unsatisfactory nature of the information shared at the placement conference. The CST conference lasted about 5 minutes. When questioned about this, the classroom teacher said, "They rushed through it because they figured the parent wouldn't understand anyway," explaining that they thought the mother herself was "retarded." The following notes are from the placement conference:

> The classroom teacher said, "Let me see the record." Clementina's cumulative file was passed to her. As she looked through the papers, she exclaimed in surprise, "The kindergarten teacher referred her! Clementina was referred at kindergarten!" . . . The placement specialist asked, "Is this the first time she's been staffed [placed]?" She then looked at the AP. The teacher responded, "Yes." The placement specialist said (incredulously), "Clementina was referred a long time ago. But the placement conference just took place today?" Once again she looked to the AP for a response. The AP said, "It's because of the bilingual assessment. You know how long those can take. We were waiting for that to be done." The placement specialist responded, "So the bilingual assessment is what held up the process."

Despite the casting of blame on the bilingual assessment, neither the results of that testing nor information on her ESOL level were mentioned at the conference. Nor could we locate these reports in Clementina's files. By the time she was formally evaluated, she was considered fully proficient in English and the bilingual assessment was not required. Also missing from the conversation and from the files was a record of her scores on the Scales of Independent Behavior, a test of adaptive skills required for EMR eligibility.

The missing information and the shocking delay of 4 years in following through on this child's referral casts doubt on the entire process and on the ultimate label of EMR. Recalling Mercedes, the student whose story opens this chapter, the question arises of whether Clementina would also have improved in the hands of a Mrs. Carey. Of course, if she had, she might simply have become one more casualty of the EMR/LD "crack." Our point is that if there were no categories, there would be no cracks in the system, and such children as Clementina and Mercedes could have been provided appropriate interventions as soon as the need was identified.

James

James, whose primary language was Haitian Creole, was referred early. The first-grade teacher who referred him, however, was the same one whom we previously described teaching an ineffective lesson on the five senses. This was a self-contained ESOL class in which no ESOL strategies were observed. The teacher told us that James had never been in school before and that "he wasn't learning anything." By the spring she was quite concerned that he had not yet been evaluated. She told us that his pediatrician had asked if he was in a special education class yet and had said, "You know, he needs to be." The teacher also thought he needed to be in a full-time EMR class and was frustrated with slowness of the CST process. The school recommended retention, but the teacher thought James would only see this as a punishment and "might totally turn off, whereas now he at least tries."

James's first CST meeting was held in April of his first-grade year. He was not retained, after all, but by the end of his second-grade year he still had not been evaluated and his second-grade teacher was quite frustrated. Showing us a sample of his work, she pointed out that "he could barely write" and said that she "didn't know why the first-grade teacher sent him like that."

Our testing of James on the Woodcock Johnson-R in the spring of his second-grade year revealed skills in the kindergarten range and in a chronological-age range from 4½ to 6. The tester noted James's distractibility and apparent incomprehension of many of the questions. However, noting that James had a bad head cold and also his status as an English-language learner, the tester commented that factors such as the possibility of ear and upper-respiratory infections and second-language acquisition issues could be complicating the picture. He concluded, "There is not enough information to make a clear judgment as to the cause."

During our observations of James throughout his first- and second-grade years, we seldom saw him engaged in academic work, but his classrooms were so chaotic that many other students were not engaged either. In his first-grade class, he was typically one of the students who were yelled at and sent to stand in the corner for being inattentive and off task. Regarding his behavior, one researcher wrote, "He appears very eager to please. He likes receiving extrinsic reinforcement: praise and tokens. Every time he appears to have gotten into trouble, it can be attributed to someone else doing something to him." We did observe him engaging in tasks such as playing a matching game on the computer, copying words and their definitions out of a children's dictionary, and copying math word problems from the board. Neither of the last two seemed meaningful to James and he was not expected to solve the math problems.

James's history revealed indicators of developmental delay. According to his mother, he was "born at 6 months; he walked late and talked around age 3." She said that she took him to a psychologist, who asked if he was in a special class and was surprised that he was not. The mother was receiving SSI for James, which would indicate that he had already been diagnosed with a disability.

James was finally tested and placed in EMR during the fall of his third-grade year. We believe that James was functioning at a lower-than-average cognitive level and that services at the EMR level were appropriate. However, we have concerns about the referral and placement process. The instruction and classroom management in the various classes in which we observed James (including his Success for All [SFA] reading classes) were not conducive to learning—thus we doubt that he received adequate opportunity to learn. He certainly started school behind his peers, but it appeared that little was done to help him progress. Also, as with other case study students whose home language was other than English, it seemed that language and cultural issues were not sufficiently considered or addressed. This was James's first year in school, and he was still at a beginning level of English proficiency. The following excerpt from his CST meeting illustrates the inadequate attention given to these considerations:

> The teacher continues with information about some of James's academic difficulties and the AP joins in quickly and says that "a lot of the children in ESOL" have these difficulties. The teacher interjects, "But I think it's more than that. It's more a matter of higher-level thinking. . . . My real concern is that when I give a direction he gives me a blank look, like he doesn't understand . . . he's lost." She

adds, "His behavior isn't one of the worst, but he has a problem sitting still. . . . I don't push him too much." The AP nods, saying, "He's probably working to his potential."

We are not convinced that the circumstances of James's instruction were adequate to support knowledge of what his "potential" really was. The teacher's lack of understanding of the needs of second-language learners leads us to ask, for example, whether James's "blank look" was, simply, incomprehension of English.

CONCLUSIONS

What is needed in education is a seamless system that is prepared to respond to children at their level when they enter school. Certain assumptions of the American school system present particular challenges for immigrant children performing at the weak end of the cognitive-abilities spectrum. In the case of children coming from Haiti, many are disadvantaged by the lockstep, chronological-age system by which children are placed with their age group regardless of their educational levels. Many such children may not have been to school prior to their arrival in the United States, and Haitian personnel explained that even for those who were in school, it cannot be assumed that they were learning at the grade level expected for their age, since in the Haitian school system students are not promoted until they have mastered the required level of each grade.

James was a Haitian American boy who had not had the benefit of preschool or kindergarten; nor had he spoken English upon entering school. Yet he was placed in the first grade in a regular class of up to 30 children, with ESOL support of questionable quality, and was expected to rise to the occasion. We contend that whether or not James "had" mental retardation should not be the issue. Indeed, his progress was further delayed by the fact that he had to show evidence of this disability in order to receive placement in a smaller class with a specially trained teacher. While James was referred in a timely fashion, the weak instruction he received from his referring teacher in the first grade gave him minimal opportunity to begin to catch up. A similar year in the second grade only compounded his problems. In Clementina's case, the bureaucratic process was even more detrimental, making it impossible to know what her potential really was.

There are many possible reasons why the determination of these children's eligibility for special education instruction was so delayed. It may have been because of some school personnel's desire to protect children from the stigma that comes with the EMR label, or their reluctance to engage in the arduous paperwork required for the referral. It could also be because of an overloaded system that makes process delays inevitable. In commenting on these cases we may be accused of being too critical.

It may seem that we are seeking perfection, always offering caveats to any positive conclusions. The truth is that we seldom saw exemplary practice in relation to special education placement. Either early instruction was poor, limiting children's opportunity to learn, or the placement process was faulty, through delays or inadequate assessment procedures, or the special education class into which the children were placed proved to be of minimal benefit.

Beyond those cases that did "cross the border" were the many students like Mercedes, who fell between the cracks, becoming what one administrator referred to as the "PDK" (pretty dumb kids) group, whom she perceived as needing a program of practical "survival skills." Another teacher, referring to this group as the "borderline retarded child, who doesn't qualify for any program," asserted, "It is the responsibility of the regular education teachers to fill those gaps." We believe that this is one more group of children to whom the current categorical system does a grave disservice.

CHAPTER 9

Constructing Learning Disabilities: Redundancies and Discrepancies

I can qualify Germaine for LD. . . . His reading was OK but his math was very low. His Verbal IQ was low. He doesn't really have a learning disability, but with this [special education] teacher, he'll get the nurturing and individual attention he needs.

—Psychologist

THE QUOTE ABOVE represents a school psychologist's attempt to "protect" a vulnerable child from falling through the cracks of the educational system. Germaine was referred with suspicion of an emotional disturbance, based on the classroom teacher's skeletal anecdotal report of "strange" behaviors, which were listed as "playing with pencil," "looking at pencil," "smiles to self," "talking to self," "writing on desk," "fingers in mouth," "sitting on feet in chair." The teacher's awareness that the child had a parent with a psychiatric illness seemed to have played more of a part in her suspicions than did the child's actual behaviors.

The psychologist quickly discerned that the child's answers to projective tests were clearly within the realm of typical, middle-class norms for child rearing: Germaine reported appropriate discipline from his parents and showed a clear sense of responsibility for his actions. But the child was slightly behind academically and his occasional misbehaviors in class indicated that he was very sensitive to teasing by his peers. Our observations of Germaine in the LD class into which he was placed indicated that the psychologist's expectation was correct: He did flourish in the hands of an excellent, nurturing special education teacher. However, this placement was truly an anomaly for the teacher, since Germaine was on grade level in reading and less than a year behind in math. In fact, his reading was so ahead of the rest of the group that he had to be sent to the intermediate special education class with fourth and fifth graders. Nevertheless, at the end of the year the special education teacher felt that he should remain in special education for the supportive small class, in which he would be under less social pressure from his peers.

In effect, the protective strategy of LD placement succeeded in providing this sensitive child with small-group instruction tailored to his learning and behavioral needs. Germaine's father, who was the primary caregiver, was very pleased with the outcome and felt that the school had indeed done the very best for his son.

DILEMMAS OF DEFINITION AND ASSESSMENT

Germaine's story reflects what has come to be referred to in the field as the "comorbidity" of learning disability and emotional disturbance: the fact that children often present behaviors and learning patterns indicative of both disabilities. Throughout this text we have used the term *ED*, since it is the federal category and would be recognizable to readers across the country. However, in the state in which we did our research, concerns about definitional ambiguity in the category of Emotional Disturbance are reflected in the state's establishment of two categories—Serious Emotional Disturbance (SED) and Emotional Handicap (EH)—in an attempt to determine the intensity of service needed. The SED label, seen as a subcategory of the EH umbrella, is reserved for students thought to require comprehensive mental health and psychiatric supports within a psychoeducational program. The distinction was introduced primarily to allow for additional funding for the more intensive category (Hart, 2003). Thus, it is the milder category of EH that represents the "high incidence" category in this state.

A key issue with eligibility for the Emotional Disturbance category is that the disturbance must be creating an "inability to learn." Meanwhile, for the child to qualify for services under the Learning Disability category there must be evidence that his/her inability to learn is not caused by other conditions, such as emotional disturbance or mental retardation. Because of this categorical construction of learning difficulties, one of these conditions must be identified as the primary cause.

School personnel turned to a number of strategies to solve this classic "chicken or egg" dilemma. The psychologist referred to above, using judgments that seemed to be based on commonsense middle-class norms for social behavior and attitudes, was impressed by Germaine's openness to personal questions about his family and by his clear-cut answers to questions about right and wrong and about appropriate punishments. By contrast, in the case of Kanita, the African American second grader whose strong extended family had supported her through her mother's incarceration, the same psychologist was suspicious of the child's reluctance to discuss her family, of her indications that corporal punishment was appropriate, and of references to "hitting" in some of her projected interpretations. Based on these responses, the psychologist found Kanita eligible for services in the EH category. However, as we will detail further in Chapter 10, Kanita's immediate change in behavior in her EH class, along with her rapid academic progress and subsequent placement in a gifted program, indicated that all she needed was a solid, structured teacher who challenged her strong intellect.

Our research was conducted during a period of increasing uncertainty among scholars and policy makers about just what the criteria should be for qualifying students as having learning disabilities. The report published by participants in the Learning Disabilities Summit (Bradley, Danielson, & Hallahan, 2002), the report of the President's Commission on Excellence in Special Education (2002), and Donovan and Cross (2002) all recommended looking closely at current eligibility criteria. Procedures for identifying LD are changing. In the newly reauthorized IDEA, states may choose to discontinue the use of the IQ-Achievement discrepancy formula and eliminate the requirement for IQ tests as part of the special education identification process. One option is that states may use response to intervention (RTI) criteria as part of the identification process instead. The NAS report (Donovan & Cross, 2002) argued that appropriate and intensive interventions should be initiated in response to poor achievement, rather than there be a waiting period to "prove" the child eligible for a disability label. The current categorical system ensures that children who do not meet criteria often "fall between the cracks" and are left to languish in unresponsive general-education classes.

In this school district, there was an attempt to avoid the implication of intrinsic deficit through framing the question in terms of whether the child would "qualify" or "be eligible" for special services. This language allows that there could be any number of reasons why the child has come to this pass and that the school's purpose is simply to provide appropriate services. As one psychologist in our study explained, his job is not to diagnose a disability but to determine what services, if any, the child needs. The school district uses the language of "services" and "placements," not of "disabilities."

In day-to-day professional and family discourse, however, qualifying for special education services is seldom conceptualized in this way. For most people, the meaning of the event is the discovery of a disability within a child, proving that his/her failure reflects some deficit that makes the child qualitatively different from others. This was the common understanding among the school personnel in this school district, who did not express any awareness of the controversy over the discrepancy criterion for LD.

CROSSING THE BORDER: FROM LOW ACADEMIC
ACHIEVEMENT TO LEARNING DISABILITY

Our information on children across all the schools presents a portrait of tremendous variability in the types of learning difficulties and in the reasons for, and the processes by which, children were placed in LD programs. Three issues predominated: the comorbidity of behavioral and learning disabilities, along with school personnel's preference for the LD category as a protective device; the influence of local (within-school) norms for academic achievement; and, related to the local norms, the absence of any clear criteria for referral. We will illustrate each of these with exemplars of children we followed closely, noting, once more, that these represent only a fraction of the cases examined.

Learning Disability as a Protective Strategy

As in the case of Germaine, cited above, the comorbidity of behavioral and academic difficulties was a common theme across the schools. Most often, the outcome seemed to be mainly a matter of psychologists' preference. In this section we describe the situation of Paul, a kindergartner who, like Germaine, displayed reading achievement close to grade level and indicated no sign of either processing deficits or an IQ/achievement discrepancy. Both children's referrals occurred because their behavior was seen as troubling, though not severely noncompliant. In both cases, the psychologists' determination of LD reflected a desire to protect these children from the pressures of a general-education classroom and from the stigma and isolation of an ED classroom.

Paul was a 6-year-old Hispanic first grader, at a school serving a predominantly middle-income, Hispanic population. At ESOL Level 4, Paul was referred at the end of kindergarten primarily for concerns about his emotional and behavioral functioning. Two CST meetings were held for Paul during his kindergarten year, at which his kindergarten teacher described him as impulsive, distractible, and needing constant supervision. At his second CST meeting the psychologist strongly recommended that he be seen by a medical doctor regarding medication for hyperactivity. When Paul was evaluated at the end of the year, however, a different psychologist, though also noting hyperactivity and possible depression, explained that she did not write the latter in her report because of a reluctance to see the case "go EH, " which would mean a "more restrictive" placement. At the placement conference, she stated that Paul had been referred for "poor academic performance," when in fact this was not the case, and that he qualified for LD because of "learning process deficits," despite the fact that Paul displayed an IQ/achievement discrepancy that went in the opposite direction from the one required by eligibility criteria. That is, his academic achievement as tested by the WIAT was higher than his composite IQ score, as follows:

> WISC-III: Performance 90, Verbal 83, Composite score 85
> WIAT: Reading composite score 98, Basic reading 94, Reading comprehension 97, Spelling 101, Math composite 85, Math reasoning 84, Numerical operations 97.

Further, the fact that Paul's primary language was Spanish and that, at the time of testing, his ESOL level was 4, was not mentioned in the evaluation report.

Our administration of the Woodcock-Johnson scales confirmed that Paul was at or above grade level in all but Applied Math Problems, where he scored at midkindergarten level. Observations of Paul over a 2-year period revealed that he did have trouble concentrating and was easily distracted and frequently out of seat. We saw widely varying behavior and task accomplishment by him and it seemed that his completion of tasks depended on how well he could concentrate on any given day. Eventually his parents withdrew him from this school and placed him in a private school where he did not receive special education services. We were not able to follow him to this placement.

Like Germaine, Paul's case revealed explicit manipulation of assessment findings to fit the psychologists' judgment of the most appropriate placement. Neither child met the criteria for LD. In Germaine's case, we know that the psychologist's good intentions had the desired results. Both cases illustrate professionals' attempts to find the best solutions for children but, in doing so, proving the incompetence of the categorical system to meet children's needs. As we have argued before, children, particularly those who belong to an already stigmatized group, should not need a false disability label to receive appropriate instruction.

Learning Disability as Relative to the Peer Group

Although we have argued that diminished opportunity to learn placed children in the inner-city schools at risk of school failure and unnecessary special education placement, this was not the only source of risk. On the contrary, in schools that had higher academic standing and expectations, we saw referrals of children who would most probably not be referred in schools with lower academic standing. Ironically, the raising of the bar in the "better" schools, along with school personnel's belief in sorting children by presumed ability, meant that being in a "better" school did not protect children from unnecessary special education placement. The cases of two children in such a school reiterate the issue of comorbidity, but also illustrate our second issue regarding LD: the influence of local norms on referral and placement practices.

Matthew and Austin, two African American second graders in a high-achieving, high-SES, predominantly White school, were referred by an African American teacher with strong instructional skills and a warm but firm management style. Besides being the only African American boys in the class, Matthew and Austin stood out by virtue of always being seated separately from the rest of the class—Austin next to the teacher's desk and Matthew at the back, sometimes with an aide working with him for part of the time.

The two boys were very different in all aspects. During the period of our research, Austin lived with a relative who had a terminal illness and who died some years later. Toward the end of our research Austin's father also died. In class, Austin was very attention seeking, seeming to use an exuberant personality to cover insecurities about his work. Whenever he paid attention and understood what was happening, he worked well, but he could be quite disruptive both verbally and physically. Matthew was much quieter, but was generally inattentive, easily distracted, and often out of seat. We learned that he had witnessed the death of a sibling and had received some counseling services to help him deal with this trauma. The teacher was very patient with both boys and tended to ignore consistent out-of-seat behavior from Matthew, but not from other members of the class. She described him as a "sad child" who could not concentrate and needed a smaller class.

Matthew and Austin differed from their peers in terms of their academic levels. Austin's scores stood out because they ranged widely, suggesting that he would do well when he tried and very badly when he didn't. Matthew's scores were more consistent but were the lowest in the class and he was always behind the rest of the class in completing his work. Of four math test scores posted on the wall, Austin's were 90, 9, 62, 4. Matthew's were more consistent—70, 74, 72, and 0 (we do not know if he was absent for this last test). Most of the other students regularly scored between 75 and 100 and each tended to have consistent scores, whether higher or lower.

Official referral records noted that both boys were referred mainly for behavioral difficulties, but the placement outcomes represented the opposite of the teacher's expressed concerns: Austin, whose referral statement cited "disordered school behavior," was given a battery of tests usually used for children suspected of having an emotional disturbance. He did not qualify for EH, however, and was placed in a pullout LD program in the same school. It was noticeable that the language in his record changed distinctly after the evaluation results were in, stating that he had been tested in order to assess his poor general academic performance and his difficulty in specific learning areas. Matthew's evaluation report stated that his academic achievement was found to be average but that he showed "serious learning difficulties." This statement was puzzling, since his academic scores were higher than his IQ scores and he was not found eligible for LD services. Given the same battery of projective tests as Austin, Matthew *was* found eligible for EH services in a self-contained class. He was moved to another school.

Matthew settled quickly into his EH program. Writing samples of his work demonstrated appropriate conceptual, writing, and spelling skills for a child just beginning the third grade. We have already introduced the reader to Matthew's "I have a dream" composition. His composition about his summer plans was equally appropriate both conceptually and technically:

> My summer
> Week 1: June 18th–24th
> I will be with my nephew having so much fun playing game and riding on bikes but he's not riding one because he's just two year old.

Austin's work was not as impressive. Most of our samples were of routine work rather than creative writing, perhaps because he often left his work unfinished. His handwriting was more uneven than Matthew's, sometimes mixing upper- and lowercase letters. It showed spelling errors but no signs of letter reversals or difficulty forming letters, although his sentences were poorly structured. The following excerpt is from his notes on two science experiments. Writing within the confines of a dittoed sheet with rectangular frames, Austin seemed to be working carelessly, "squishing" his answers into the frames:

> I noticed that the potting soil
> see a litte white thing in it . . .
> Tap the Baking tray softly, the harder
> Baking tray was tapped softly it was Doing No happened
> call through the tube softly, then louder
> I noiced when the baking tray Was tapped louder happed
> I was juimp

In contrast to this, a copy of Austin's freehand drawing of the globe with the lines of latitude and longitudes was excellent, showing no signs of difficulties with visual perception. He earned an A for that assignment.

In comparing these two students, we believe that Austin showed learning difficulties that could indicate a mild disability or simply inattention and insufficient practice. Behaviorally, he was certainly the more troublesome student, and it seemed that his need for attention was what deterred him from making better progress. We would not have been surprised to see him placed in the EH program. Matthew, by contrast, was not very disruptive at all, although it was reported that he occasionally had tantrums and seemed to "shut down" whenever he was confronted. We believe that he would, as the report said, have benefited from a smaller class in which he could get more individual support. Although it seemed clear that he did have some emotional difficulties, he seemed to fall into a more gray area, and his rapid progress in the behavioral program suggested that he had adequate control over his behavior once individual support was provided.

Matthew's and Austin's peers in the second grade were generally performing well above average for the grade. By this standard, these two students' achievement just below grade level appeared low. Although we were not able to ascertain whether there was any explicit attempt to use special education as an alternative to having low-scoring students "bring down" this school's state ratings, this seems quite probable in light of the fact that it was common practice in many schools. Alternatively, it is also possible that the high-achieving norms of the school simply infiltrated teachers' consciousness, with the effect of an implicit raising of the bar regarding general-education expectations. That low-income African American students might become ready targets in the sorting process would not be surprising in view of their differential preparation for schooling. Matthew and Austin's teacher would likely be as affected by these standards as would any of her colleagues, even though she was herself African American.

What was quite certain was that Matthew's and Austin's scores and classwork were well above those of second graders referred for learning difficulties in our lower-income schools. We turn now to some illustrations of this point.

Learning Disability as Anything

The influence of local norms on referrals is one specific example of a widespread issue concerning the lack of clear criteria for referrals. Our examination of children's work indicated that there was no stable pattern of learning difficulty among children designated as LD. Rather, the children referred seemed to reflect four "types" or profiles. We have already illustrated the type characterized by comorbidity of LD and EH characteristics. The other three types did not typically display social or behavioral difficulties, but showed a variety of academic profiles, as seen in the following: first, those children who fit the classic definition of LD, showing severe discrepancies between their academic progress and their overall cognitive functioning; second, children whose work was characterized by low overall achievement and slow, steady progress; and third, those whose academic achievement seemed to be more of a lag, possibly related to absenteeism or other contextual circumstance.

"True LD." The term "true LD" was used by several school personnel to refer to children whose learning difficulties resulted in "unexpected underachievement." Some personnel felt that the "true LD" kids represented only a small portion of those who were placed. We concurred with this opinion.

Jonas, a student in a school serving a predominance of Hispanic students of mid-SES level, was an example of a child with "true LD." Entering the second grade unable to read, Jonas was described by his teacher as having trouble "learning little simple things," and his writing showed minimal understanding of the phonetic code. In response to a written prompt for a letter, he wrote:

> Dear Madeline, Ae hop bat uo foe god and uen uo sen pop bat us fone and uoo ro ros seen on tehr and a uen e un to the fr and the bods lapr et us fn un ur uf mi and a col a hap uo feo god.

He was found eligible for LD services in a pullout program when he started third grade.

Manuel, a Hispanic third grader at a school with a predominantly Black, low-income population, had good listening-comprehension and verbal skills, but was quite low in reading and writing. Manuel was a quick study, as long as no reading or writing was required. His auditory comprehension was among the quickest in the class, and his keen attention and verbal articulation contrasted greatly with his weak reading. His barely legible writing showed some mastery of common words and of an attempt to spell phonetically:

> I will like to be a DocTor because you can wen A los of mune and dey can heg you win you siTsk and you can breeing The kids to The DocTor win dei or siTsk And You cAn hAs fun.

Manuel participated actively in class discussions. This excerpt is from an SFA lesson that the teacher said was supposed to be on Level 2.2 (the second half of the second grade). Manuel, she said, was "way below that." The lesson was about a boy whose grandfather was coming home from hospital after having a stroke, which had affected his memory and his initial recognition of his grandson. Toward the end of a very lively lesson, our field notes read:

After they've read for a bit, the teacher starts some more questions. "How would you feel if you were his grandchild?" There is silence for a few seconds. Manuel offers, "I'd be upset 'cause he might be sick and I'd get sick and I can't go to school." The teacher says she understands this because Manuel may be thinking that his sickness is catching, but really it's not. Other kids say, "I'd be sad 'cause he wouldn't know me"; "Scared, that he might say something awful and sound like a monster." Then she asks, "As a child, what would you do?" Manuel says, "Give him his medicine." Others say, "Take care of him"; "Give him soup." The teacher comments supportively on just about every opinion. . . . The story goes on: "A tear is coming down Bob's [grandfather's] face when he watches the boy playing with blocks." The teacher asks them why. Manuel says, "'Cause . . . my opinion is, he's remembering him as he sees him play with blocks."

Low average but making steady progress. In contrast to Manuel's display of a discrepancy between oral and academic performance, we observed children, such as Delia and Marc, who typified more of a "low average" profile. We will focus on Delia, a quiet, diligent second grader in a predominantly Hispanic school, who was similar to Manuel in that her compositions showed weak attempts at phonetic spelling, with some apparent reversals, but her handwriting was neat and legible. She wrote:

I will met wtet ther in the manu oufes gras. (I will meet her there in the main office.)

Did the hrse fyl aseep uend are the tree waey eating har? (Did the horse fall asleep under the tree while eating hay?)

Unlike Manuel, Delia's comprehension was evidently lower than that of her peers, as exemplified by the following field observation:

In this class, Delia was still quiet and studious, but not very participatory in question-answer sessions. When she did respond, her answers tended to be a bit off target. It was not clear whether this was a matter of poor comprehension or poor verbal expression. For example, when asked to give a sentence with the word *Braille*, she hesitated a long time and when the teacher prompted her by asking what kind of person uses Braille, Delia finally said, "They can't see but they listen." This answer contrasts greatly with the succinct reply offered by another child: "Blind people use Braille to read." In reading out loud, Delia read quite well but with a couple of mistakes such as saying *she* for *his* and *through* for *though*.

A native Spanish speaker, Delia attained an ESOL level that was documented at Level 4, but that was found by the bilingual psychologist to be at Level 5. Using the Differential Ability Scales (DAS), the examiner found Delia's general cognitive ability to be in the low-average range, but noted that these scores might be an underestimate of Delia's global intellectual skills. Delia's scores on the Woodcock Johnson placed her word recognition and math calculation in the low-average range and her written skills also in the low average, with quality and fluency noted as "extremely below average" and lower than expected given her overall cognitive scores. These results, along with findings of a cognitive-processing deficit, qualified her for LD services in the pullout program. By granting that Delia's low cognitive score could have been an "underestimate," the psychologist allowed leeway in interpreting whether the child met the discrepancy criterion for LD. While we cannot say for sure, it seems likely that she was more like those who used to be called "slow learners" in a previous era of special education.

Slow starters. Of our LD case studies, both Miles and Anita exemplified children whom we refer to as *slow starters*. This term indicates that the children seemed to have missed important early opportunities to learn school material, through either excessive absences or ineffective teachers, and were behind academically.

Anita, who was of mixed Hispanic and Anglo American ethnicity, attended a school serving low-income Hispanic and African American children. Her chronic absenteeism in the first grade seemed to contribute to her low achievement and she was placed in an LD program in the second grade after repeating first grade. Samples of her work show immature but clear handwriting with poorly developed language skills. Using a rectangular writing frame, she wrote:

> Brid live and nest
> Thye have Feather
> To FlY and warm the eggs
> Brid hav mon in Dad
> TheY KeeP They eggs
> Warm i Save
> Wintiwind TheY KeeP
> The eggs warm
>
> When I Write I Should
> AlWays make it neat. MY

Teacher will be happy and
My WorK Willook Nice.

Anita's mother, Janey, after several observations in her child's special education class, was dissatisfied with the frequent absenteeism of the teacher and with the general-education teacher's view of Anita as "not her student." Janey moved Anita to another school at the end of her second-grade year and we were not able to follow her further.

Miles, an African American kindergartener in an inner-city school in which teacher quality was extremely variable was fortunate to be taught by Ms. L, the African American teacher whose effective strategies for teaching school culture we cited earlier. She referred him because of his lack of basic alphabetic and math concepts. On working with Miles, we agreed that these concepts were missing, but we noted that he had an excellent vocabulary, which his mother explained was augmented by the family's regular viewing of the Disney Channel. It seemed that Miles would learn quite quickly with some individualized instruction. He showed himself to be very determined to try and to complete whatever task he started. We noted that Miles had missed 28 days of his kindergarten year. The decision was to retain him in kindergarten and have him evaluated for special education. The outcome of the evaluation was that he qualified for 12 hours of LD services a week, and he was described by the psychologist as a "very bright, charming" child who had a learning disability.

In the fall, the special education teacher started Miles with coloring tasks that were far below his level. In one of our early observations of him in this class, he pointed to his first-grade classmates and remarked to the researcher, "I can add and subtract like them but they put me back in kindergarten." Within a month of Miles's placement, his special education teacher seemed to agree with him on this. By October he was working on the first-grade math book, and the teacher anticipated that he would soon have mastered his IEP goal of knowing numbers 1–20, which was a kindergarten goal. Our end-of-the-year interview with the special education teacher confirmed that Miles had, as expected, done very well. His math and reading were then on first-grade level. He had mastered his IEP goals and was by then doing additions up to 20. The teacher thought she would most likely mainstream him for reading in the fall but keep him in special education for math to give him additional support.

Overall, we believe that Miles's difficulties in kindergarten/first grade were related to absence from school. In Miles's case, while we do not believe that he "had" a learning disability, we do think that the intensive instruction by an excellent special education teacher, and possibly his kindergarten retention, made the world of difference to his being able to catch up. On the one hand, this case exemplifies what can happen when appropriate interventions are introduced early, not waiting for the child to fail. On the other hand, there was little reason to believe that Miles needed a special education program. We believe that the kind of "tiered" intervention currently proposed by researchers such as Vaugh and Fuchs (2003), and possibly a repeat of his kindergarten year, would have worked, without need for a disability label.

CONCLUSIONS

We believe that some children have learning disabilities that require specialized interventions. We believe also that most children will benefit from good instruction and supportive classroom contexts within general education. Of all the children described in this chapter, those who reflected features of "true LD" were clearly in need of intensive instruction, preferably through small-group or individual tutoring, or both. The others displayed a range of needs that we believe could have been addressed in the general-education classrooms of strong, nurturing teachers.

Several issues worked against even the best teachers. One was class size—30 being a typical number across the schools. Another was administrative pressure to remove weak students whose scores would depress schools' ratings on statewide tests. Another was the pressure of what we have referred to previously as a "culture of referral" within a school. This feature can be driven by explicit or implicit concerns about standardized testing, or it can be an ingrained belief that children who do not quite fit really "belong" in special education. Delia was such a child. Miles was out of sync with the school's lockstep system.

On the other side of the picture is the likelihood that the protective motive evident in the case of both Germaine and Paul also drove many other referrals and maybe even worked to children's benefit. Paul's parents moved him to a private school soon after his LD placement so we do not know the outcome. Both Germaine and Miles benefited from a program of excellent instruction. The teacher who referred Austin and Matthew was very accommodating to them within her general-education classroom and told us that she hoped, as did many teachers, that the smaller class sizes in special education would help.

Despite all these caveats, we cannot support the uses we saw of the LD category as a catchall for students who seemed not to fit. The application of the category was arbitrary and often simply inappropriate. The apparently clear-cut criteria of discrepant cognition and achievement along with deficient information processing were circumvented or ignored, as desired, by assessors; and the referring teachers' recommendations were as likely to be either overwhelmingly influential or not at all influential. In Germaine's case, it proved beneficial that the teacher's view had no impact; in Kanita's case, as we will see in the following chapter, it was unduly influential. The process was so variable that it was impossible to tell if children were getting what they needed.

We do not know the long-term outcomes for all these children. We know that Austin continued to have problems that were exacerbated by the subsequent death of the caregiver with whom he lived. Given the extreme experiences of family loss experienced by this young boy, we believe that he must have needed intensive emotional support. Not "qualifying" for the EH program, an LD program was not what he needed, and his special education teacher reported that he was becoming increasingly angry. By contrast, the EH program into which his classmate Matthew was placed emphasized behavior control, not emotional support, so we have no reason to think that it would have been helpful to Austin.

In Matthew's case, the fact that his "emotional disturbance" all but disappeared overnight leads us to the third disability conundrum. In the chapter that follows we focus on the subjectivity evident in four children's placement in the ED category and on the double-edged sword of their "troubling" behaviors being rapidly removed and then replaced by a stigmatizing cloak that would prove very difficult to discard.

CHAPTER 10

Constructing Behavior Disorders: From Troubling to Troubled Behavior

There is pressure from the administration and teachers to remove kids, who are not EH, who are a pain in the neck. They get into a lot of fights. They are disruptive, but that is not EH. They are conduct disordered. . . . Some kids are so far gone that they are just criminals, instead of kids.
—School counselor

T HE QUOTATION ABOVE calls attention to a crucial concern in identifying students as having emotional disturbance: The challenge of distinguishing between behavior that is troubling to those in authority and behavior that indicates that a child is truly "troubled" (Leone, Walter, & Wolford, 1990). This distinction, as is usual within special education's categorical mindset, results in a need to determine whether behavior reflects a deliberate refusal to conform to behavioral expectations, or whether it is beyond the child's control and beyond normal responses to adverse circumstances.

The means of making this determination vary widely and depend on the preference of psychologists or on state or school-district regulations (Hosp & Reschly, 2002). In this school district, projective testing was the required approach. The subjectivity inherent in the process of interpreting the meanings behind a child's stories or drawings was exacerbated by the relativity of local norms. According to one teacher in a school serving a low-income predominantly African American population:

Social-emotional problems are difficult. A lot of it depends on the school. You put a child in another school, [gives an example of a higher-SES school]. They would be considered EH. They wouldn't be considered normal if they got into a fight because that's a very upper-middle-class school. They rarely have fights and a deficit problem might be if a child talks out in class and doesn't finish work . . . [In

this school] the only kids I would place would exhibit psychopathology. . . . Then, you have some people who would say that it is
unusual for a child to talk about killing people and drawing guns.
Here, that is reality. It is the way they live. It is not EH. If they were
to draw pictures of daisies and picket fences, they would be crazy!

This, indeed, was the thinking of the psychologist who inferred that
Kanita's reluctance to reveal her family problems indicated a "denial of her
feelings," since most children "in this neighborhood," were quite "blasé"
about events such as a parent's incarceration. Both the psychologist and the
teacher quoted above illustrate the danger of assuming that children's social
circumstances will dictate how they think.

Most of the children we saw referred for behavioral problems were of
the "pain in the neck" variety. The referral often reflected the teacher's poor
classroom planning and management, as in the case of the kindergarten children whose behavior was transformed when they entered the music class.
Despite the obvious variability in classroom contexts, the environment of
the regular class was seldom taken into account when children were referred
for their behavior.

We have already introduced three of the four children who were placed
in EH programs: three African American children—Matthew, whom we
described in the opening and foregoing chapters, and Kanita and Robert,
whose families we described in our discussion of the discrepancy between
school personnel's views of families and our own. In this chapter we introduce a Haitian American girl named Edith.

The outcomes for the four children placed in EH programs were dramatic:
All appeared to have their behavior transformed after placement in these self-
contained settings. There are two possible interpretations of this—either the
children never had any internal disturbance leading to the noncompliant or
troublesome behavior, or the programs into which they were placed were excellent and were exactly what the children needed. In the following summa-
ries of these case studies, we will offer our conclusions regarding these two
potential explanations. We note also that although all four met the expectations of their behavioral programs, after 3 years of this placement, only one
child returned to the mainstream. We will highlight briefly the key aspects of
Matthew's story and will then focus on the other three children.

MATTHEW

As was the case for children in all the EH programs we observed, Matthew's
entire classroom experience was framed by a behavioral token-economy

system. Despite the fact that the teacher and teacher assistant in his EH classes were less nurturing, and instruction was less effective than in the classroom of the general-education teacher who had referred him, Matthew settled quickly into the EH program and proved quiet and compliant even when he had finished or was bored with an activity. The only reports of behavioral difficulties occurred in the cafeteria. Nevertheless, our follow-up study indicated that after 3 years of consistently satisfactory behavior, there was still no sign of mainstreaming for Matthew.

It is difficult to know what was really going on with this sensitive child who had experienced serious family loss. It could be that the size and structure of the EH class accounted for his improved behavior. However, there could also have been other social factors at play. For example, in his general-education class Matthew may have been affected not only by the high achievement levels of his peers but also by their high income and valued racial status. In his "I have a dream" composition, Matthew's keen perception of "helmets" as symbols of wealth among bike-riding children in the school showed his sensitivity to his social situation. In his general-education class he had been one of only two African American boys in the class and was performing at the bottom of the class, though close to grade level. By contrast, in his EH class, which typified the overrepresentation of his group in this program, 8 of the 10 children were Black, and Matthew's behavior and academic level earned him the reputation of a "star" in the eyes of the teacher.

We acknowledge that it is speculation to wonder if Matthew's progress may have been related more to the familiar social environment of the EH class than to his status as a child with "emotional disturbance." Nevertheless, this question indicates that such contextual information could be more important in understanding a child's difficulties than are decontextualized "tests" through which a psychologist who does not know the child or his family purports to interpret the internal states "projected" by the child onto the external world.

Matthew's record in the EH class was the same as those of the three students we will describe next. Within a very short time, all were functioning consistently at the top level of their behavioral programs. We do not believe that this sudden turn in behavior is consistent with emotional disturbance.

KANITA

Kanita's transformation in her EH program was even more dramatic than Matthew's. In her first-grade class we had observed her to be stubborn, resistant or even hostile to the teacher, and provocative to her peers. In our first visit after 2 weeks of her placement, Kanita's behavior was so compliant that the teacher asked if we knew why she had been referred.

Unlike Matthew, Kanita had the good fortune to be in the hands of a very good teacher who moved her quickly to part-time mainstreaming, where her behavior was seldom an issue. Nevertheless, it was evident that the bar had been raised for this "EH child," to the extent that typical third-grade behaviors such as passing notes or making fun of other kids were enough to warrant a report to the EH teacher and, at one point, a return to the EH class. Because of this, the team decided to keep Kanita for a 2nd year so that she could get the support of the EH teacher. In the 3rd year, Kanita was fully mainstreamed and placed in a part-time gifted program, but her EH teacher managed to keep her on an IEP, "just in case." In our discussing this with the teacher, she commented that Kanita knew when to behave and tended to take advantage of weaker teachers. The teacher acknowledged that Kanita's behavior was actually no worse than that of many of her general-education peers, but the teacher did not want to release her from the program only to "see her back in my classroom the next year."

In contrast to the EH teacher's misgivings about Kanita's readiness to be without an IEP, the teacher of the gifted program reported that Kanita displayed no behavior problems and was doing very well in her work. The teacher of that program asked us, "Do you think she was misplaced [in the EH program]?"

How did Kanita get to the EH program? She had had a history of emotional outbursts in her kindergarten year, during her placement in the class of Ms. L, the excellent kindergarten teacher cited earlier. This teacher told us that she saw Kanita's difficulties as being a response to her mother's incarceration, and that the strategies the teacher devised for helping Kanita overcome these outbursts had worked quite effectively and consistently. However, the teacher stated that in Kanita's first-grade year she "put the school in an uproar." This teacher said that she had not expected Kanita's difficulties to prove so severe and was surprised when she qualified for EH services.

The environment of Kanita's first-grade year was, however, very inadequate for a child with emotional difficulties. The first-grade teacher was Ms. E, whom we referred to in Chapter 3 as practicing "passive" classroom management. The first time we observed in her class it was obvious that she made next to no effort to intervene in early signs of misbehavior and typically did not respond to it until it was nearly out of control. Our observation of Kanita in this classroom, around the same time as her referral, revealed a very disjointed lesson to which only a few children seated near the front were paying attention. Most children were restless and distracted, and Kanita and one or two others stood out as verbally oppositional to the teacher, while another student simply stood at her desk with her back to the teacher and appeared to stare at the wall throughout the period without any attempt by the teacher to redirect her attention. The following is an excerpt from the observation field notes:

> The teacher begins a lesson on synonyms. Her voice is loud as she tries to talk over the noise in the class. . . . Soon after she asks a question, students at the computer request help and other distractions occur so that she is not focusing on any one thing. She then walks out of the classroom for something and when she returns she asks another question about synonyms. During this lesson there is little student involvement. Some are looking at what their classmates are doing at the computer. At least one student is cutting paper, while others look aimlessly around the room. . . . The boy sitting next to me keeps talking to Kanita, who is at the computer. Someone tells the teacher that Kanita is doing Math Corner on the computer and the teacher tells her not to. Kanita replies that she is going to do it anyway.
>
> A child near me tells his neighbor to behave and says, pointing to me [the researcher], "She writin down what you do." The neighbor looks around and replies, "She ain't writin bout me, she writin bout her!" [pointing to the teacher]. A child at his table starts singing Aretha Franklin's "Respect."

Although we observed this classroom only once while Kanita was in it, we observed the teacher again in the following year with a different group and noted exactly the same (lack of) management style.

Kanita, the only "success story" of our four EH students, exited the EH program when she entered middle school. Nevertheless, we are concerned that a child should have to experience such a stigmatizing label in order to receive an appropriate educational program—indeed, in order to get back on track. Based on our observations of Kanita in her first-grade classroom, we concur that she was a "pain in the neck." So was her teacher. In contrast, Kanita's quick perception that good behavior was required in the EH class resulted in an immediate change in her behavior.

We conclude, first, that with an effective general-education teacher, Kanita's behavior would not have deteriorated to the point of her requiring a referral. Second, this was a bright child whose scores on the WISC-III defied the sociocultural bias of that test (she achieved a combined score of 107 with 118 on the freedom-from-distractibility subset). Had she been placed in a class with a strong teacher whose expectations were high, she might well have been perceived as "gifted" rather than "disturbed." Finally, the power of the psychologist's preconceived and erroneous belief that Kanita's family was dysfunctional resulted in an evaluation that was truly a travesty. In summary, Kanita's success resulted from her good fortune in being placed in the only high-quality EH program we observed.

ROBERT

As in Kanita's case, the first thing we noted about Robert was that he was referred to special education from a very ineffective classroom. In the first grade, Robert had been marked as having behavioral problems that seemed to become worse the following year and resulted in his referral.

Our first recorded observation of Robert was in the fall of his second-grade year. The atmosphere in this classroom was extremely negative and exemplified our concern with the validity of a referral coming from such a classroom. Although the class was team-taught, there was minimal individual attention given to any child and almost total reliance on repetitive seat work, which was seldom monitored. When instruction did occur, it was offered by the younger teacher, Ms. J, who, despite a nurturing approach to some children, was largely ineffective. The older teacher, Ms. P, reserved her participation almost totally for discipline, which usually amounted to harsh reprimands, insults, and threats, such as: "Do you want me to snatch you!?" or, yelling at Robert, "I don't appreciate your acting like somebody crazy today! Did you take your medicine? I can't take this every day. I will get on the cell phone and call your momma." Robert first appeared in our observational notes that fall in the following context:

> Marvin, one of the students we have been following from [his first-grade class] last year, is seated at a lone desk facing the wall near the front of the room. He is doing nothing. If he has a reading book it is not in evidence on his desk. He stands and looks around. I go over to him and ask if he should be reading. He shrugs and says no. I walk away and soon he is wandering around the room talking to various children. Ms. P is seated at her desk talking to a parent and Ms. J is standing facing the class. Neither teacher pays any attention to him. The noise level is increasing.
>
> After about 10 minutes, Ms. J starts calling on some children to read their books out loud to the class. Several volunteer but many do not appear to have heard the request and continue to chatter to their neighbors. After about five children have read their books aloud, the teacher tells a boy to collect the books. The chatter increases even

more. Marvin is still wandering around and Jose is also out of his seat. Ms. J reprimands Jose. . . .

Every now and then, Ms. P looks up and reprimands the class sharply . . . they quiet down immediately but as she returns to her conversation with the mother they soon start talking again. At one point she tells Jose, "I'll take you to the cafeteria to your momma. That'll stop that smiling!" Another child, Robert, whom we had also noticed in the first-grade class last year, is also wandering around.

Our observations through the fall confirmed that the negative ambience and ineffective instruction were typical of this classroom. In January of that school year, both Robert and Marvin were placed on half-day school attendance because of their behavior, with a referral to the CST. Marvin's mother became angry and pulled him out of the school, while Robert's mother accepted the decision and he remained on this arrangement for 5 months. In our earlier discussion of families, we explained that the arrangement for Robert to attend school only from 8:30 to 11 A.M. continued for 5 months, until his mother, Jacintha, refused to come for him at 11:00 A.M. any more. At that point he was referred for evaluation. Most shocking was that his records revealed that his mother had signed permission for evaluation in January.

When Robert returned to school in May that year, it was clear that no one, including himself, expected appropriate behavior from him. At this time, Ms. P's approach to Robert's misbehavior was to send him to stand at the front of the room where he did basically whatever he pleased until she noticed him again and offered some reprimand that would quiet him for a few minutes. This teacher was often out of the room, and although the co-teacher said she did not agree with putting Robert to stand at the front, it was not her decision. The following excerpt illustrates the scenario:

Ms. J is standing behind the screen at the back of the room. I hear her talking to someone and I think perhaps Ms. P is there with her, since I don't see her anywhere else in the room. Soon I realize that Ms. J is talking on her cell phone behind the screen. She remains there for about 10 minutes. I realize that Ms. P has left the room.

There is steady, though not too loud chatter in the room. Robert is at the front, standing and playing around the teacher's desk. Ms. J comes from the behind the screen, still talking on her cell phone as she walks toward the front of the classroom. She puts the phone away and then yells at Robert, "No! Not at my desk!" She tells him to get away from her desk. He moves away from the desk and remains in constant movement, kneeling, standing, then walking over to a girl seated near the front. He stands next to her watching her. He is always on the move but is not really noisy. Soon, he stands at the front, swinging his arms. . . . Then he walks around the front of the room chatting to kids. She tells him to go back to the front. He does, stays for about 5 minutes, then walks around again. Ms. P has not returned.

Our final observation of Robert in this classroom toward the end of the school year noted the following:

Robert is standing toward the front of the room. He is hopping up and down with his shoes off [all the children have their shoes off to be weighed and measured for some reason]. Then he puts them on and is quiet for a few minutes. Then he starts rocking from side to side, hops, jumps, walks over to stand in line. He looks over at me and grins. . . . Soon after this, Robert is doing flips on the floor and crawls under a desk. The line of standing children blocks the teachers' view of him.

Robert was evaluated twice, which reflected a continuing controversy over what his label and services should be. The psychologist's first evaluation of him determined that he had no emotional disturbance but was exhibiting behaviors typical of attention deficit/hyperactivity disorder (ADHD), such as impulsivity and lack of reflective approach. Because of these findings, the psychologist referred Robert to a doctor and he was designated as having ADHD. This allowed him to be served under the category Other Health Impaired (OHI), and placed, within the same school, in a pullout class that served children eligible for various high-incidence categories. His IEP, however, did not include a behavioral plan, and although his behavior proved better in the hands of a skillful special education teacher, it was still challenging, and he was still being troublesome in his general-education placements. Some months later, after an occasion when he threatened to harm another child, Robert was reevaluated by the same psychologist. He was found to qualify for an EH placement and placed in a self-contained program in another school. Thus, he proceeded to the most restrictive environment without appropriate behavioral interventions having been tried.

This child's story raises several important concerns. First is the issue of medication. All school personnel who worked with Robert described his behavior as being variable according to whether he was taking his medication, and they expressed the belief that he often was not. His mother supported the medication plan but tended to withdraw the medication when Robert complained that it made him feel ill. The ensurance of compliance is not always within the power of the school, and parental ambivalence when children express discomfort with medication is common.

The second issue, classroom quality, certainly *was* in the hands of school personnel. The negative effects on Robert of this unproductive classroom were exacerbated by the third issue, the administration's decision to place Robert on 5 months of half-day attendance at school. From the point of view of the school's responsibility to provide appropriate educational opportunity, this decision was unconscionable. School personnel's awareness of the dangers of the neighborhood was evident in that they did not consider it safe for Robert to walk home alone outside the regular hours, so they requested the mother to come for him personally every day. When Robert returned to full-day school in May, he was more of a "pain in the neck" than ever.

Fourth, despite Robert's obvious need for behavioral support, no behavior plan was written into Robert's IEP when he was placed in the special education pullout classroom. In a class of only about 12 children and a competent teacher, such a plan would have been feasible. Further, the school had Robert's mother's full agreement to the placement, which she hoped would help to curb his behavior.

Finally, the most disturbing aspect of Robert's story is the outcome at the end of his primary-school years. After the end of our funded research project we did not see Robert during his fourth-grade year. In his fifth-grade year, Hart (2003) obtained permission to resume research on him for her doctoral dissertation. Observations and interviews with Robert, his mother, and his teachers indicated that Robert put out more effort in all areas than did his peers and was consistently compliant with the behavioral program, maintaining full points for extended periods of time. In this program children would lose points for minor infractions such as turning around in their seats, whispering to a neighbor, or asking a classmate for a pencil without permission. Robert's only periods of challenging behavior occurred when he had not taken his medication. Despite Robert's success in this very restrictive placement, he was not mainstreamed for any elective or content-area classes, and at the end of the fifth grade, he was sent to an even more restrictive setting—a totally separate school for students with emotional disturbance.

EDITH

Like Kanita, Edith was a child whose story supports the hypothesis that she had no emotional condition that warranted an EH placement. Of greatest concern was the fact that Edith showed no behavioral problems at home, as explained by her mother and verified by our home visits.

Edith was born in the United States, of Haitian parents. She was a third grader when we first saw her, and she stood out among her peers because of her height and unusual attire—somber, conservative skirts and blouses required by her religion. These features made her appear quite atypical in her class of African American and Hispanic children. She was described by her teacher as "different" and was referred for evaluation because of poor academic achievement. However, near the time of her evaluation, there was an incident in which she reacted to her peers' teasing by threatening to kill herself. This event caused the psychologist to focus on emotional rather than academic issues in her assessment and Edith was found to qualify for an EH placement.

Since Edith did not stand out in the classroom in terms of her behavior or academic level, her placement in an EH class came as a shock both to us and to the school counselor who told us about it. It was a shock also to her mother, who expressed adamant disagreement with the evaluation:

> Edith is not handicap! [emphasis on *handicap* in a raised voice]. I tell them at school, Edith do lots for me at home. I send her to the store, she get everything I need, no problem. She listen at home and do what I tell her. She behave. She have no problem in the brain. She fine. I pray to God and she fine. I have six children. Two in college, two in high school, doing fine. I have a 4-year-old and he doing fine too. All of them fine, Edith too.
>
> There was these kids, bothering Edith every day, that's why. Edith come home, she cry every day. I go to the school, the principal don't do nothing about it. They tell me Edith have problem. So I take her to doctor. He say she fine. No handicap. I take her to another one. Same thing. I take her to three doctor. They all say she fine! They [school personnel] say Edith say she want to die, so she have problem. I tell them, kids been bothering Edith every day and she cry, she upset. That why she say that. Doctor say she fine. She fine with me at home. She go to church every week. She walk with her cousins. She sing in the chorus at church. She going to be in a play at church in December 25. Edith, she OK. She fine. She need help with her reading and writing, but she not handicap.
>
> I went to the school [placement conference]. I am not agree with them about Edith. They tell me Edith cannot read and write, and she have problem. . . . They say she stay in program one year. She still there. If she need help to read, they should help her.

We began observing Edith again in her self-contained fifth-grade EH placement and followed her into her placement in middle school. Both these placements were extremely restrictive, her only potential contact with children in general education occurring at lunch. Hart's (2003) follow-up study reported that, across 16 classroom observations (including regular-education homeroom, special classes, and EH classrooms), and observations at lunch and during transition periods, there was never any sign of Edith's behavior being problematic. The only report we had from school personnel in the elementary education EH setting was that she once had to be "taken down" (physically restrained) for telling lies. State regulations on the use of physical restraint indicate that this was not an acceptable sanction for lying.

The first issue in this case was that the entire placement process reflected family stereotyping. Unfounded assumptions related to Edith's family and culture resulted in disregard of family information. Our visits to Edith's home confirmed her mother's claim that Edith functioned well and normally within her family. On one occasion, a researcher accompanied Edith to Sunday school, which she attended with her cousins and in which she participated fully and appropriately. It is clear that school personnel's perception of Edith was based totally on her social difficulties in school, which defies the requirement that the disturbance should exist across settings or that information given by the family be taken into account.

The second issue was the lack of attention to context in the referral process. It was reported by her referring teacher that Edith was initially referred for learning difficulties, but the psychological assessment, conducted by a Hispanic psychologist, focused on a report that Edith had threatened to kill herself. Without any attempt to investigate or correct the peer-group dynamics that led to Edith's frustration, the assessment "revealed" underlying emotional issues, which resulted in an extremely restrictive placement for this child who, in her home and community, functioned no differently from her peers. The parent attended the conference and expressed her disagreement, but her views concerning Edith's emotional state and needs were disregarded, and Edith was placed in the EH class with promises from school staff that the placement would last "about a year" and would assist Edith "with her reading."

A third issue brings Edith's situation in line with that of Robert—the question of the efficacy of the EH program and its ultimate outcome. Hart (2003) reported extensive evidence of inappropriately restrictive settings and ineffective, rote instruction that did not address Edith's language needs. Although she demonstrated little, if any, propensity toward angry outbursts, she was instructed solely in the EH class because of her "inability to deal with the frustrations of the mainstream." Like Robert, Edith often maintained the top level of the behavioral system and her cumulative file showed no instances of behavior referrals.

CONCLUSIONS

Two overwhelming conclusions emerge from our study of the four children placed in EH classes. First, classroom contexts were most often not taken into account either in the decision to refer or in the assessment itself. The referral processes for Kanita and Robert did not raise questions of whether or to what extent negative classroom environments were contributing to these children's behavior. No one thought to address the extreme teasing that led to Edith's threat to kill herself. And no one raised the question of the potential effects of the busing policy on Matthew, a sensitive African American boy whose on-grade academic achievement seemed inferior in a class of high-achieving, wealthy, White peers.

Second, with the exception of Kanita's program, the EH programs we observed defied the law's requirement for the least restrictive environment. Even in Kanita's case, the stigma of the EH label worked against initial efforts at mainstreaming her and it was only her teacher's persistent protection and advocacy that enabled her eventual return to general education. This very protection, of course, echoes the words of the psychologist who had referred both Kanita and Germaine, who put children in special education "to save their lives." It can certainly be argued that these two children were "saved" by these actions. Nevertheless, we think that if this is to be the job of special education, it should not be done under the guise of disability.

Overall, we do not believe that the changed behavior of Robert, Kanita, Edith, and Matthew proved that they needed a self-contained EH class. They needed to be in smaller classes with good teachers who were sensitive to their social and emotional needs and structured in their approach. In Edith's case, the placement was particularly inappropriate from the point of view of the evaluation results. If Edith's threat to kill herself had been serious, she would have needed a much more supportive environment than the "file the line" classroom into which she was placed. Conversely, Austin, whose case we reported in Chapter 9, was truly in need of emotional support, but was placed in an LD program.

Kanita was the only student whose EH placement was helpful to her, and she was the only one who exited the EH program. Kanita's "success" story points to the power and the pain of special education. A good teacher, small class size, a structured but challenging curriculum, individualized supports, and an openness to recognizing the child's strengths are all within the purview of the IDEA. We believe that Kanita benefited from, but did not need, this classroom. Two years after the initial placement, she functioned without a hitch in a classroom of about 22 children designated "gifted," in the same school from which she had been referred. We believe that she could have done that in the second grade.

These students' stories underscore the negative results of a construction of disability that focuses on identifying within-child deficits. As we argued in our earlier discussion of assessment, there is great danger in this approach, especially when it is reliant on controversial, subjective projective testing. Our research dramatically endorses the arguments of several scholars who have called for an emphasis on school response and context rather than child-centered labeling (Keogh & Speece, 1996; Montague & Rinaldi, 2001). Further, the importance of effective classroom management in the first grade has been shown to have a lasting effect on children's behavior (Kellam, Ling, Merisca, Brown, & Ialongo, 1998). Recently, there has been a great deal of concern with the punitive and "zero tolerance" approaches to such issues. Skiba and Peterson (2000) and others have argued for zero tolerance to be replaced with "early response" strategies too numerous to detail here. Central to all these proposals is a preventive principle that combines individualized response with supportive rather than punitive schoolwide policies and a commitment to functional assessment of behavior. Skiba and Peterson state:

> The technology of functional assessment, for example, enables school personnel to better understand the "communicative intent" of challenging behavior (Brady & Halle, 1997). In a zero tolerance environment, however, teachers and administrators may be less interested in understanding communicative intent than in ridding schools and classrooms of troublesome students. (p. 340)

Robert's school exemplified the zero tolerance approach. This was the school cited earlier as suspending more than 100 students in one year, with a required suspension for fighting. This applied even to kindergarten and first graders.

Finally, we conclude that despite good intentions, the concept of "emotional handicap" as practiced in this state is not tenable. The existence of the EH category encourages school personnel to assume child deficits without examining context and to place children who are troubling to teachers or peers in separate settings that defy the law's call for the least restrictive environment. The reification of these negative labels in the eyes of school personnel results in school careers marked by exclusion.

CHAPTER 11

Into Special Education: Exile or Solution?

Disproportionate representation is a problem if the quality and academic relevance of instruction in special classes block students' educational progress, including decreasing the likelihood of their return to the regular classroom.
—Kirby A. Heller, Wayne H. Holtzman, and Samuel Messick,
Placing Children in Special Education

OUR RESEARCH was premised on the argument of Heller et al. (1982), that overrepresentation of culturally and linguistically diverse students in special education must be considered a problem if either the precursors to, or the outcomes of, placement are inappropriate or inadequate. In other words, how did the students get there? Was it worth it? The preceding chapters have presented our answers to the first question, concluding that the process was so variable and subjective as to be inequitable. We have reserved this chapter for close attention to the second question.

SPECIAL EDUCATION BENEFITS: IDEAL VERSUS REALITY

The two statements below represent the ideal versus the reality of special education in this district:

> If you get them placed correctly, and get them whatever they need, early on, they have a chance. You know, get them counseled, or get them reading or doing math and writing, you know, whatever it is that they need. (High-referring, first-grade general-education teacher)

> With special ed, there are large numbers in the classroom. And we write these wonderful individual education plans. When I was going

into special ed, my professor talked about five kids in a classroom . . . and you'd get to do so much and it all made sense—IEPs, and five kids, and being able to work with them and build them, then let them fly. . . . But special ed teachers have a lot of responsibilities . . . paperwork, authorization, and on and on. And they have no assistance in the classroom, as far as a paraprofessional, you know, it's just them and 20 kids and IEPs. . . . You walk into a special ed classroom and everybody is doing the same thing. So . . . where's the individualization? The material is probably at a lower level, but everybody is doing the same thing. . . . I guarantee you, in more than 90% of the classrooms. . . . How can you expect me to individualize when I have 20, 25 kids? (Placement specialist, former special education teacher)

The first quote above captures the essence of most general-education teachers' expressed beliefs about the value of special education placement. In a few cases, we saw these expectations realized. More often, we saw the picture described by the special education teacher who had become a placement specialist. Overall, the "big picture" of special education programs was not encouraging: large class sizes, teacher shortages, undifferentiated instruction, poor teacher quality, poor curriculum quality, undue restrictiveness, continuing stigma in EH programs, and, at the end, a low rate of exit.

In the previous section we outlined the basic outcomes for the students we were able to follow closely. To summarize: Of the students designated LD, Miles and Germaine, placed in the same special education class, did well. Miles, described as a "bright" child with LD, exemplified what the psychologist called "early intervention." A slow starter, he caught up in a year, repeating kindergarten with an excellent general-education teacher and spending 12 hours a week with an excellent special education teacher. We do not believe Miles had LD; we believe that excessive absenteeism in his kindergarten year set him back and excellent instruction caught him up. We believe that his need for early intervention could have been met without psychological assessment and without the assignment of a disability label. We believe the same for Germaine, who, referred in the second grade and almost on grade level in reading, was out of place academically in his primary special education class. But, a sensitive child who had experienced serious family loss, he benefited from the gentle manner of the special education teacher. Austin, by contrast, did not do well in his special education pullout program. In fact, he did much better in his general-education homeroom of 30 than in the resource room. It seemed that with his extreme experience of family loss, what Austin needed most was a strong connection to his teacher; once more, the teacher made the difference. Marc was in a pullout program with 16 other students; he was quiet and compliant, and made steady but slow progress in an uninspired, nonindividualized program. We do not know the outcomes for Anita and Paul, since they were both moved by their parents to other schools.

Of the students placed in EH programs, Kanita blossomed in the strict but supportive environment provided by a strong EH teacher who recognized her potential for a gifted program. We believe that Kanita would have done just as well in the class of any structured, challenging general-education teacher. Like Kanita, Matthew's and Edith's "emotional disturbances" disappeared upon placement in their EH classes, where they became immediately compliant with strict behavioral management systems. Matthew, whose work was just below grade level when he entered the program, became a "star" in contrast to his lower-achieving peers. Edith, who had no behavioral difficulties in her home and community, continued into middle school in an extremely restrictive setting and never received the appropriate literacy instruction she desperately needed. Robert improved as long as the program was able to enforce his medication regimen. Despite his progress, he was placed for middle school, in an even more restrictive setting—an entire school that served only children with emotional disturbance.

The three children placed in full-time EMR programs were destined to remain there. It seemed that Bartholomew developed health problems that would probably diminish his progress. Clementina seemed much happier in her well-run special education class. She was an enthusiastic participant in class activities, and the teacher stated that "Clementina is one of the smartest in her group. She is a good fit. She will catch up." She stayed in this class for 2 years, but we do not know what happened to her when she moved on to middle school. Leroy, in a primary special education class where he would remain for 3 years, was not likely to improve much in the chaotic environment we observed. We were not able to follow James into his special education setting.

This picture of mixed outcomes indicates that there were circumstances in which special education placement proved a blessing. In others, it was no worse, and no better, than general education placement. In the worst cases, it was disastrous. Overall, we concluded that the most important factor in these outcomes was the teacher. However, there were several factors that mitigated against this benefit, and others that made it difficult even for good teachers to perform well in these programs.

Class Size

The belief that special education programs provided small class sizes with individualized instruction was not generally substantiated by our observations.

This was most obvious in classes referred to as Varying Exceptionalities (VE), which served those children perceived to have a range of high-incidence learning difficulties. These classes contained a mixture of children designated as having any of the three high-incidence disabilities, although they were predominantly LD, with a few children labeled EMR, and occasionally a child labeled EH. These classes could be self-contained, where children spent most of the day, or resource classrooms to which students came for up to 12 hours a week. Most typically, these classes ranged between 16 and 24 children.

In one inner-city school serving a predominantly Black population, the Intermediate Special Education teacher exclaimed: "At 9:00 A.M., there are 21 to 23 kids at my door." This situation reflected a plan in which all the fourth and fifth graders who received LD services came to the LD resource room for 2½ hours for instruction in the same Success for All (SFA) reading program used by their peers in general education. Thus, the special education instruction they received was a poor imitation of what they received in the regular classroom. Moreover, students in this class represented five SFA levels, so the teacher had to "juggle instruction and seat work" for her 21–23 students. The theoretical advantage of individualized instruction envisioned both by the SFA program and special education were offset by this large number of students.

In another school, in which the principal was determined, at all costs, to improve the school's grade in the state's evaluation system, an intensive attempt to assist general-education students had some very detrimental effects on the special education program. The numbers in the LD program were already very large (9.8% of the school population). Worse, however, was the administration's decision, in the semester prior to the high-stakes testing, to schedule all the special education children to stay with their special education teachers from 9:00 A.M. till noon every day, while all general-education teachers would focus on test preparation with small groups of students. This brought the LD students' special education programming to 15 hours a week instead of the 12 required by their IEPs, and some students, who should have gone to LD for reading and language arts only, were required to stay with the LD teacher for math also. The last arrangement reflected the fact that, since those students already had an LD label, their scores would not "count" in the school's assessment. These arrangements shortchanged the special education students of appropriate math instruction, of the least-restrictive-environment requirement, and of the IEP requirement for small-group instruction while in their special education class.

As in our findings about variability in general school quality, class sizes suggested a pattern of SES inequity in special education. At the school serving the highest-income, mostly Anglo and Hispanic population, we saw the smallest class size in the entire sample—two resource rooms that ranged from

6 to 12 children each. Paraprofessionals were more likely to be present in the higher-income schools, apparently paid for by money raised locally. By contrast, at one inner-city school serving a predominantly Black population, the average size of an LD class was 13–16. At another in a nearby neighborhood, there were, in the first year of our study, 2 VE classrooms, a primary and an intermediate. But when one teacher resigned, both classes were combined under one teacher and this remained so for the entirety of the following year. At another school in a similar neighborhood, resource room size was 17–24 students. In some of these inner-city schools, the special education teachers started out with comparable class sizes, but when a vacancy occurred, it was harder to fill, thus resulting in larger classes for varying periods of time.

These classrooms typically had no paraprofessionals. In one inner-city school, the self-contained VE class had 19 students, 4 designated MR and 15 LD, across all grade levels from second to fifth. The principal reported that the VE class must be up to about 24–25 to get a paraprofessional and that this self-contained class had never had more than 22–23. The principal did not consider this a problem, since the teacher was excellent and there were no "uncontrollable" children in that class. Our perception was that the teacher was indeed excellent and did manage quite well, but that the class size seriously negated these children's IEPs and the law's mandate for individualized instruction.

Classrooms for students designated as having EH or EMR generally had smaller numbers and often a paraprofessional. These classes typically had no more than 12 students, usually with a paraprofessional for at least part of the day. An exception to this was one school serving a low-income, African American population at which the EMR self-contained intermediate class included 19 students, with a paraprofessional.

Individualized Versus Undifferentiated Instruction

Very often instruction in VE and resource classrooms was indistinguishable from that in general-education classrooms. The claim of individualized instruction was completely negated in schools in which special reading programs such as SFA were used, since reading instruction in the resource room used the same SFA texts as general-education classes. Math instruction also was mostly "whole class," though we did see a few exceptions. The following example of routine, whole-class instruction is from a school with a predominantly Hispanic population, where we generally noted a high quality of instruction and management in the general education classrooms. Students did not appear to be following the lesson at all, since the instruction was so unclear.

10:10 A.M. There are 13 students total—aged 6, 7, and 8, in first and second grades. The teacher is teaching a whole-class lesson. Students are working at their desks, completing a workbook page—there is some talking. The teacher says, "If you can hear me, clap once. . . ." Walking around looking at students' work, she says, "I told you three times to write your name, you haven't done it yet, now do it." She instructs students to "find the number for your age and circle it" in their workbooks. . . . She then returns to the board and asks, "Who is 7?" and writes the names of students who raise their hands. One student says that he is 9 and another student says, "No, you are 7." The teacher says, "Ask your mom." Next the teacher writes the names of the 8-year-olds. She makes a bar graph. I hear a student say under his breath, "We don't care about that." . . . The teacher says, "The problem is that you are not listening—it is very important to listen to me so you know what to do."

[Observer's comments: I don't think the students followed this lesson at all—it wasn't clear what the teacher was trying to show, and she didn't really explain it. All students seem to be doing the same thing (no differentiated instruction). Students are quite wiggly.]

Several teachers emphasized that large class size was a serious deterrent to individualized instruction, and our observations showed that the amount of individuation did seem to correlate with the number of students present in the class—the more students there were, generally the less instruction was differentiated. In one of the EMR classes we observed we did notice small groups working at different centers and at different levels in a well-structured environment. In the following example of a resource room in an inner-city school with otherwise variable instruction, there were only two students in the room and the teacher provided one-on-one instruction. This was a math lesson; class size was much larger during reading (up to 18 students):

1:00 P.M.: Three students are leaving as I enter the room. One, a kindergartner named Gerald, remains. He's sitting at the kidney-shaped table. The teacher counts with him, pointing to and "reading" large numerals on cards posted over the whiteboard. The 8 is missing. When they get to 8 the teacher acts surprised that it is missing and asks in exaggerated fashion, "Where is the 8?" Another student comes in at this point, and the teacher stops to give him a paper and direct him to sit down and start working. She goes back to working with Gerald. She writes on the whiteboard: "1, 2, 3, 4, 5, 6, 7, 8 [circled]." He is supposed to circle eight animals in his workbook. The other boy asks, "Do I do the back?" The teacher responds, "Um hum," and goes over and checks his work. The kindergartner is coloring the animals on his workbook page. Now the teacher comes back and asks, "Finished?" Gerald nods. The teacher checks his work and says, "Very good." She writes a happy face and Gerald says, "Happy." The teacher says, "OK, now count with me." They count, and this time she circles the 7 and asks Gerald to come up to the board and write a 7. The teacher says, "Very good, that is another star." She draws the star under his name on the board—he now has two. Next Gerald is supposed to color seven balloons out of nine on the page. I ask the teacher if this is how many students she usually has now, and she tells me that one is absent. Gerald has colored all nine of the balloons in his workbook, and the teacher explains to him that he needs to cross out two because he has colored too many. She helps him cross them out, with her hand over his, and then asks him if he understands. He nods. She tells him that now he can play on the computer. She then works with the other student.

This situation represented the placement specialist's ideal vision of special education –"IEPs and five kids." Clearly, differentiated and individualized instruction was possible where there were good teachers and small, even reasonable numbers in a classroom. However, this scenario was rare.

Teacher Quality

In comparison with general education, where we saw a clear pattern of weaker teachers in the lower-income, Black neighborhoods, the pattern was similar but not as clear-cut in special education. While it was true that the schools serving higher-income populations did have consistently more effective teachers, several of the inner-city schools also had some excellent special education teachers. However, they also had some very weak ones.

In one inner-city school, for example, we observed a teacher in a resource room with 10–12 students offer routine, whole-class instruction that resulted in considerable boredom and inattentiveness on the part of the students. The teacher made no effort to improve students' responses by changing seating, adjusting the task, or engaging the children at the back of the room. We summarize the lesson as follows:

Throughout the lesson, only three girls seated at the front were participating. Other behaviors included a boy in the back interacting angrily with a peer, a boy in the front fiddling and failing to respond to specific requests from the teacher. When the lesson moved on to choral reading, the researcher observed that the girls in the front read very well, and actually carried the group reading. Round robin reading also revealed one very poor reader. The lesson was based on an SFA text, with sentences such as "Don gets Pit Pat. He gets the sock." The researcher's note ended: "There is so much idling taking place that I can see the overwhelmed look on the teacher's face. . . . She turns to me and sighs heavily, and says 'I have a lot of antsy kids.'"

We were often struck by the rote, low-level quality of some of the instruction we saw. For example, we observed several times in the resource room at another school with a predominantly African American population of higher SES than that of the inner-city schools. The 16 fourth- and fifth-grade students with LD in the class were generally on task and well behaved, yet frequently were occupied completing workbook pages and doing low-level work such as coloring. In one observation, the teacher was giving a spelling test of words such as *ran* and *sat*, which seemed to be at an early first-grade level, even though the students we were following were working at an upper-second-grade level or higher.

At another school, this one mostly Hispanic, we observed Paul, one of our case study children, in his resource room. We were struck by the low level of the work.

During this single observation, Paul completed two "color and cut" activities (one an alligator to go along with the story "The Lady with the Alligator Purse" and one a Christmas bell). He also took a "spelling test" with the words listed on the board for students to copy, and did a sentence-completion activity, with the answers written next to the sentences that were to be copied. Paul completed all these activities without any difficulty.

Nevertheless, we did see some very effective teaching in some classrooms. One of the most effective lessons took place in a school that was, otherwise, characterized by some of the worst instruction we observed. This was in a self-contained special education class in the predominantly Haitian school featured as providing limited opportunity to learn. The teacher herself was of the same ethnicity as the students. This lesson was characterized by student engagement and higher-level thinking, even though the students themselves seemed to be functioning at a fairly low level:

As I enter the classroom, one boy holds out his hand and introduces himself. He then shows me a bulletin board about Mexico and says,

"The teacher is good and teaches us a lot, like about Mexico and Black people and what they've done, and the rainforest." 8:50: The teacher has written on the board: "May 20, 1999. The destruction of the rainforest cause [sic] Jane to . . ." She asks students to write in their journals. They do so quietly, without a sound, apparently accustomed to this routine. The children are bright eyed, well groomed, friendly. . . . The chalkboard has a poster with rainforest animals on it. Books about the rainforest are lined up along the bottom. . . . 9:06: The teacher asks Joselyn to share and "show her beautiful picture." Joselyn shows the class her picture, then gives me a big smile and goes back to her seat. Charles comes up to read what he has written: "The destruction of the rain forest cause Jane to cry." The teacher tells him that his picture is nice, to show it, but he doesn't want to, saying that his other drawing is better. The teacher says again, "It's nice, go around and show it." She asks, "Anyone else? Don't be shy." . . . Another boy shares and says that the destruction of the rainforest "cause Jane to die." Another student (a girl) adds, "Maybe from stress."

Teacher Shortage

In some of the highest-need schools, teacher shortage severely affected teacher quality. It was in these schools that principals had the hardest time finding permanent replacements, or substitute teachers, when teachers left. As mentioned, some principals solved this by combining two classes under one teacher. Another strategy was to staff the class with a series of long-term substitute teachers. We observed one substitute special education teacher twice during SFA reading instruction. When the researcher entered the classroom, the substitute teacher told her, "I don't know what I'm doing." The room was quite noisy and chaotic, with very few students actually reading.

VARIABLE QUALITY IN EH PROGRAMS

We have already described the main outcomes for the four students placed in EH programs. At one end of the spectrum was Kanita's classroom, in which the emphasis was on work and learning within a structured behavioral program. At the other end of the spectrum was Edith's classroom, where the curriculum was essentially behavior modification—or, to put it bluntly, what we heard referred to as "boot camp." We will detail here some features of Edith's program, to indicate how detrimental such placement can be.

Although Edith was placed in EH because of perceived depression and possible suicidal tendencies, her EH program was of the "boot camp" nature and seemed designed much more for her classmates with acting-out behavioral problems. Our observations of this classroom were rife with negative, even insulting phrases from the teacher's repertoire of reprimands, such as: "Heads down!" "Bury your face!" "File the line!" "You're off level, you just got three extra days!" "PE is canceled!" "Stand in the corner!" "Give him zeroes! "You and me will be on the floor." Additionally, school personnel were observed imposing physical-intimidation tactics, such as walking menacingly toward students, grabbing student's faces, banging a chair or desk en route to deal with an off-task student, and the use of physical restraint with students "for becoming verbally disrespectful." It was evident that this climate was dictated mainly by the lead teacher and aide, but when a new teacher was transitioned and tried a more thoughtful approach, it was difficult for her to be taken seriously either by the students or staff.

Overall, daily instructional and organizational routines removed the locus of control from the students. Such routines included supervised breakfast in the cafeteria at a later time than that of the general-education population; supervised bathroom breaks, with teachers accompanying all students to the bathroom at regimented times; the requirement that students "file the line," or keep a specified distance of 3 feet between themselves and the student directly in front of and behind them; and the requirement that students line up for out-of-class activities by behavioral level. It was clear that these fifth graders were being exposed to a class environment that would in no way prepare them for the normal routines of the mainstream. Edith did not receive specialized instruction in reading, or counseling for depression.

Robert's and Matthew's EH programs fell between the extremes of Kanita's and Edith's, and were far from exemplary. While not totally reliant on "boot camp" tactics, the curricula in these programs were generally unchallenging and repetitive. Given their main focus on children's ability to earn points in the behavioral program, there seemed to be little emphasis on teaching and learning, and it was all the more surprising to see that the majority of the children in these classes, despite their designation of EH, were able to sit quietly through periods of minimal instruction and boring, repetitive routines. Once more, we were left with serious doubts as to the presence of emotional disturbance in most of these children.

RESTRICTIVE ENVIRONMENTS

School personnel's approaches to mainstreaming children varied from school to school. In general, however, little mainstreaming took place, whether from resource or full-time programs. Self-contained EH and MR programs evidenced significant concerns with meeting the requirements of the least restrictive environment. With just a few notable exceptions, self-contained programs were set up to allow the minimum movement outside the classroom and little if any modification to meet the needs of individual students. The impression given at the placement conferences was that if a child was considered eligible for such a program then it meant that this was the level of restrictiveness needed for that child. Yet our data indicated quite the opposite for some children.

EH Programs

We have already indicated that Edith's placement in the EH program was totally inappropriate for her. Indeed, bearing in mind especially that the designation EH in this state indicates the milder end of the SED spectrum, the restrictiveness of this program was inappropriate for any child designated EH. Students in this program, after eating breakfast separately from their nondisabled peers, returned to their classroom no earlier than 9:05 A.M. and as late as 9:15 A.M. Thus they had 35–45 fewer instructional minutes than did their nondisabled peers, who were able to eat breakfast in the cafeteria prior to school. Moreover, students in this program attended only PE with the general-education students, a privilege that was frequently withheld in order to punish misbehavior. When the students did make it out to PE, the special education teacher accompanied the class to "show his face," thus keeping the students in line. Instruction in music and art was delivered to these students in the self-contained setting. Despite the teacher's protestation that he was "a big advocate for inclusion," none of the 14 students in Edith's class was mainstreamed in any subject area. When asked about Edith's possible return to the mainstream, the teacher said, "Maybe she'll be *partially* mainstreamed by high school."

Fortunately, such restrictiveness was not uniform across all the schools. Kanita's program was quite different. With an excellent teacher in the self-contained classroom, these students "went out" to mainstream settings according to their needs. From the start of her placement there, Kanita was mainstreamed for PE and other special classes. When, after only a couple of months, it was evident to the teacher that Kanita's behavior was fully compliant in the self-contained classroom, the general mainstreaming process began.

Finally, one of the most disconcerting aspects of these programs was that they were often a dumping ground for any child perceived to have behavioral difficulties. Thus, students who were perceived to be depressed and suicidal were "thrown in" with students with conduct disorders and other acting-out behaviors, and then treated similarly, as in Edith's case. We consider this one of the most disconcerting aspects of the EH category.

EMR Programs

The EMR programs we observed were also quite restrictive in that students were rarely mainstreamed. For example, we have already noted inappropriate restrictiveness in Bartholomew's EMR program. In direct contradiction of the recommendation in the child's placement conference, the teacher's insistence that her students "do not go out" deprived Bartholomew of his right to participate in the Creole language program that would have been his only opportunity to use his home language during the school day. This was particularly troubling for several reasons: First, this child was at ESOL Level 2 and it was evident that the teacher (a Hispanic woman) had great difficulty understanding his speech. Moreover, he was the only Creole speaker in his class, all the other children being either African American or Hispanic. During one observation, in response to a prompt of "I love to . . ." Bartholomew dictated to his writing partner, "I love to go to BCC" (acronym for the home language program). The teacher at first did not understand either what he had said or what his partner had written, and when the researcher interpreted it to her she commented, "Bartholomew can't handle going out to other classes. He has to stay here with me."

The restrictiveness of the EMR and EH programs reflected and reinforced the reification of these disability labels. One evident outcome was a raising of the bar regarding these children's performance and a pervasive view that the children "belonged" in these restrictive programs. Kanita ultimately succeeded in defying the pervasively low expectations of her as an "EH child" in the mainstream. The other three children designated as EH were not given this opportunity. Hart's (2003) follow-up study of Kanita, Robert, and Edith offers a detailed portrait of the sticking power of this label for the last two children.

LD Programs

Despite the widespread use of part-time programming for students designated as LD, there were also several self-contained classrooms. In these programs, the issue of the "velcro" label was often evident. With the exception of the school with an inclusion model where we saw a great deal of mainstreaming, we noted few attempts to return children to the general-education environment. In one inner-city school serving a predominantly Haitian population, a special education resource teacher explained that although they did both partial and full mainstreaming, with a requirement on the IEP to monitor students' progress, there was often not enough time to do this properly. The teacher of the self-contained VE class in the same school reported that she had four students whom she wanted to mainstream, but the principal told her to put them in the resource room program for reading, which she did. The teacher commented, "I don't think that's really mainstreaming. . . . but I have to take what I can get—whatever." In the school in which the principal had instituted a rigorous testing-and-placement process in order to improve the school's rank on the statewide grading, a teacher reported that it was becoming increasingly difficult to mainstream successful LD students.

LOW RATE OF EXIT FROM SPECIAL EDUCATION PROGRAMS

The foregoing review of the restrictiveness special education brings us to the very low rate of exit from special education programs. Those with whom we spoke about this issue told us that students rarely exited from special education during elementary school. One LD teacher shared that she was not in favor of dismissing students until they were at least in middle school:

> Now our policy is to recommend that the parents keep the child [in special education in elementary]. They should spend time in special education classes until they make some kind of adjustment in middle school and if they do really well in middle school then you pull [them out of special education]. Because it is a big adjustment to go from here to there in an environment where they have five or six classes and they go from class to class. I can think of two students in the past that did need special education in elementary, they needed that extra, and when they got into middle school they were dismissed. A couple of them did get promoted into honors classes. So it depends, but that is rare. It really depends on the child and how they push themselves.

In this chapter we have addressed the issue that was at the heart of the famous decision in *Larry P. v. Riles* (1979/1984)—the judge's concern that special education placement not be tantamount to relegation to "dead end" programs. In this school district, good special education programs did exist and it was evident that children placed in such programs did benefit. "Dead end" programs, however, were far too often in evidence.

CONCLUSIONS

Overall, our main concern was that "special" education was too often not at all special. Rather, the programs were marked by routine and generic, rather than individualized, instruction; teacher shortages; widely variable teacher quality; unduly restrictive environments in some programs, especially EH and EMR; and unduly large class sizes in classes for students with LD.

In terms of VE classrooms, the best programs we saw were generally in the higher-SES neighborhoods, not necessarily because they had the best teachers but because the teachers in those schools tended to have smaller class sizes and paraprofessional support. Excellent teachers in lower-income areas were often negatively affected by large class sizes and no support from paraprofessionals. While class sizes were generally more manageable in EH and MR programs, a combination of teacher quality and restrictive philosophies frequently limited the programs' effectiveness. The obvious least-restrictive-environment violations were striking.

Finally, we reiterate that a great deal of what happens in any given school depends on the principal. In our discussion of administrative issues we reported in detail on what we referred to as the anomalous school (Green Acres) in our table showing the relationship between SES and teachers with master's degrees. In terms of special education quality, we found this school to be, once more, anomalous, with an excellent special education program despite the low-SES population being served. Another anomaly was evident in the predominantly Haitian school that seemed to have the highest percentage of weak general-education teachers but effective special education teachers.

It was evident that the general approach to special education was that the child was expected to fit the program rather than the other way around. This was exactly the opposite of the individualization envisioned by the IDEA. The idealized beliefs expressed by many general-education personnel regarding the value of special education were not borne out by our study. To conclude, the likelihood that special education placement would "block" rather than facilitate students' educational progress undermines school personnel's faith that this program would provide a remedy for the learning and behavioral difficulties of Black and Hispanic children in this school district. This was especially true for those who also suffered economic disadvantage. Moreover, for the EMR and ED categories, special education placement was tantamount to exile from the mainstream of the educational system. These are the categories in which Black children are overrepresented nationwide and in this school district. Such outcomes strongly support our view that patterns of overrepresentation in these categories are, in the final analysis, inequitable.

Conclusion

That would be nice if we didn't "leave no child" behind. But we have so many problems to deal with: low students, home problems, discipline and behavior.

—Second-grade teacher in a high-poverty urban school

T HREE YEARS OF intensive qualitative study of the placement process in 12 elementary schools in a large, multicultural, urban school district point to problems at both systemic and individual levels, to the need for refinement of procedures, and to problematic human factors in decision making. The issue of overrepresentation is very challenging because of its complexity. In all cases, we noted several potential explanations for special education placement that went well beyond the notion of intrinsic deficits or disabilities in children.

FINDINGS AND RECOMMENDATIONS

Our study demonstrated the processes by which 12 schools in this multicultural, multilingual school district contributed to the district's pattern of overrepresentation of Black students in all three high-incidence categories and, to some extent, of Hispanics in the LD category. In the light of the model we adapted from Heller and colleagues (1982), we conclude that disproportionality in this school district is indeed a problem because of the numerous inequitable factors influencing all phases of the placement process. These inequities related to the three main phases of the process: children's opportunity to learn prior to referral, the decision-making processes that led to special education placement, and the quality of the special education experience itself. Specifically, our main concerns were poor teacher quality; large class size; detrimental administrative policies regarding curriculum, instruction, and discipline; subjectivity in psychological-assessment practices; pressure for special education placement because of high-stakes testing and the state's grading plan; arbitrary application of eligibility criteria; tardiness in placement processes; and restrictive or ineffective special education programs.

We refer to these negative impacts as inequities not only because they contributed to inappropriate or unnecessary special education placements, but also because there was a clear pattern of their being more in evidence in schools serving low-income, predominantly Black students. This pattern of inequity constitutes a form of institutional bias, wherein schooling reinforces rather than mitigates the effects of poverty and racism. The possibility of personal bias based on racial or social class prejudice seemed to us inherent in certain schooling situations, but was difficult to substantiate. Overall, we believe that what is needed is a firm commitment by the school district to policies and practices that will strengthen schools in poor neighborhoods, standardize the criteria on which referrals and eligibility decisions are made, and ensure an equitable assessment process. We do not deny that some students need more assistance than others—but we believe that for the majority of students this support can and should be provided within general education. Certainly, students need, and deserve, a consistently higher level of instruction than we saw in the schools serving low-income populations, whether in general or special education.

While some of our case study students who were placed in special education did display learning or behavioral deficits, the explanations for their difficulties were not simple. There were a few whose deficiencies seemed likely to be inherent in the child's cognitive or socioemotional makeup. For most, however, the school circumstances surrounding their learning and development provided a strong competing explanation. For some, the most detrimental circumstance was inadequate opportunity to learn, resulting from poor instruction and ineffective classroom management and schoolwide disciplinary policies. For others, decisions were influenced by the school setting in which the student was placed and by his/her performance relative to the norms of the local situation. For all, there were systemic influences that filtered down to the individual child through various avenues from the larger society. Indeed, the barriers to the effective implementation of the school district's seemingly sound referral and placement policies were to be found at local, state, and federal levels of the ecology of education. Below we describe these and offer several recommendations for improving outcomes for culturally and linguistically diverse students at each of these levels.

Federal Level

Findings. At the broadest level is the conceptualization of IDEA itself, which requires a determination of disability for a child to receive special education services. This premise of intrinsic deficit too often leads to an inappropriate, even manipulative, search for features that can "qualify" a student for services. This conceptualization of the child's needs is too often unfortunate because it results in the child being characterized mainly by a disability label. The stigma and decrease in self-esteem that can result from this is exacerbated by the fact that the special education program may further limit the child's opportunity to progress in a society that places a premium on formal schooling. The very separateness of special education encourages an artificial border, which, once crossed, results in social and educational exclusion.

Recommendations. We recommend that, at least for children with high-incidence learning and behavior difficulties, special education should be reconceptualized as a set of services that are available to children who need them, without the need for a disability label. The current conceptualization of special education as requiring a search for intrinsic disability has not succeeded in adequately serving the needs of students who are performing at the low end of the general-education spectrum. We recommend a reexamination of the eligibility criteria and procedures used for finding students eligible for special education services in high-incidence disability categories. As we describe in some detail in this book and elsewhere (Harry et al., 2002), we found the application of eligibility criteria to be exceedingly uneven. Identifying students (to get them help, or for whatever other reason) often seemed like trying to fit a square peg into a round hole.

We suggest eliminating the IQ-discrepancy formula as the primary criterion for LD and setting clear reading- and mathematics-performance criteria for referral for a special education evaluation. With the reauthorization of IDEA, it appears that the identification criteria for LD will change substantially to a focus on how students respond to research-based interventions as part of a multitiered model (Vaughn & Fuchs, 2003). While we support these efforts, we urge caution and careful consideration of issues related to cultural and linguistic diversity when making eligibility determinations as part of a response-to-treatment model.

State Level

Findings. At the state level, our study raises serious concerns about the unduly negative results of high-stakes testing on children who are performing at the weaker end of the educational spectrum, but who do not necessarily have a disability. Because special education was seen as a way for schools to keep their scores from being depressed by low achievers, many children were inappropriately determined to have disabilities instead of receiving the intensive regular-education support they needed. We also observed inequities in the ways schools were funded. In addition, we noted concerns about the inadequate preparation of teachers for inner-city schools.

Recommendations. We recommend reexamining accountability measures, including how high-stakes test results are used to evaluate schools. Like others, we are concerned that high-stakes testing is affecting culturally and linguistically diverse schools in disproportionately negative ways (Hilliard, 2000; Kohn, 2000; Townsend, 2002; Valencia & Villarreal, 2003). High-stakes testing of English-language learners should take account of the primary language in all phases of testing, including opportunity to learn the material, test administration, and interpretation of the scores (Heubert & Hauser, 1999). We recommend placing more weight on year-to-year improvement rather than absolute comparisons across dissimilar schools and strongly support efforts to include the scores of students receiving special education services when holding schools accountable.* We also advocate for standards-based reforms that are culturally responsive and not premised on high stakes (Townsend, 2002). Rather than punishing low-scoring schools, we suggest placing greater focus on teachers who excel, in spite of barriers, and providing additional support for teachers and schools in need of assistance (Hilliard, 2000).

We urge careful scrutiny of governmental policies and mandates related to school financing. We know that across the nation educational resources are not equitably distributed across schools and districts and that culturally and linguistically diverse children living in high-poverty areas are more likely than their peers to attend schools that are inadequately funded and staffed (Donovan & Cross, 2002; Parrish, Hikido, & Fowler, 1998). As one counselor in our study noted:

> They should give the inner-city schools more, not less—the kids come with nothing, and the teachers need to buy them things. We need more money just to get them the things that they need (that others take for granted). At other schools, if they don't bring their supplies, they get suspended, but you can't do that here.

More money would allow districts to hire better-prepared teachers who use more effective instructional strategies, cut class sizes, and provide teachers and students with more resources. All of these have the potential to increase students' opportunities to learn (Elliott, 1998).

---

*In this state, the scores of most special education students are now counted and included in the calculation of schools' grades. However, a debate over this requirement of the No Child Left Behind Act continues nationwide.

Finally, we recommend examining preservice teacher-education programs to determine the extent to which they include coursework in culturally responsive pedagogy and quality field experiences in the highest-need schools. We suggest that all states review their teacher certification/licensure requirements to make sure they include standards specific to teaching culturally and linguistically diverse students and that they require evidence from teacher-preparation programs indicating they are addressing diversity in significant ways (Miller, Strosnider, & Dooley, 2000).

District Level

Findings. At the district level, our findings point to systemic or "institutional" bias against the lowest-income and, in particular, Black student populations. While not necessarily evident in funding patterns per se, this bias seemed to be built into hiring practices that resulted in inadequate instruction for the very children who had the least preparation for schooling. As we have shown, and as others have also found, many schools serving students from racially, ethnically, economically, and linguistically diverse neighborhoods have less-qualified teachers, inadequate resources, and high turnover among administrators (Ansell & McCabe, 2003; Darling-Hammond, 1995; Krei, 1998; Oakes et al., 2002). Also, we noted a striking need for ongoing professional development for teachers in the highest-need schools.

Recommendations. We recommend that school districts reexamine how they allocate their resources and place priority on the hiring and retention of effective principals and teachers in the highest-need schools. Such a process of self-examination necessitates asking tough questions about who benefits from current policy and practice and who is being marginalized or disadvantaged (Townsend & Patton, 2000). Through these questions being asked, resources can be reallocated based on need and equity. Districts should develop a system of incentives and supports for teachers that will attract strong teachers to the highest-need areas, in order to provide more equitable distribution of quality instruction. Extremely weak instruction should not be tolerated and whatever supports or consequences are necessary should be readily available.

To provide sufficient professional development, we see promise in models that focus on collaboration between school districts and local universities, whether these partnerships are called "professional development schools," "partner schools," or by another name (Klingner, Ahwee, Garderen, & Hernandez, in press; Levine, 2002; Murrell, 2000). Strong partnerships have the potential to provide in-service teachers with the knowledge and skills to implement culturally responsive and effective instructional practices and to provide preservice teachers with real-life preparation in the schools most in need of their expertise and energy.

School and Classroom Levels

Findings. At the level of the individual school, a variety of detrimental school-based policies and practices worked against the success of the least prepared children. In low-income schools serving predominantly Black populations, commonly noted features included the assignment of weaker teachers to weak students, fragmented and discontinuous instruction, the retention of extremely weak teachers, and the inappropriately extensive use of out-of-school suspension, along with inadequate support to teachers in matters of discipline. In the schools serving midrange SES populations, more equitable opportunity to learn was accompanied by a raising of the bar in response to high local norms and to increasing statewide pressures to excel. This, in turn, resulted in increased pressure to enact the special education placement of children who probably would not have been referred in higher-poverty schools and who could have been adequately served in general-education classrooms. In the only school that served predominantly White, high-SES students, the busing of a lower-income African American population resulted in a discrepancy in levels of preparation for schooling and a clear overrepresentation of the latter group was evident in special education programs.

At the level of the classroom, the vast range of instructional quality was the variable of most concern. The inequity of this lay in the fact that the schools serving the neediest children included levels of teacher incompetence that were not evident in schools serving better-off children. When this disadvantage was compounded with poorly founded negative beliefs about families, individual children were at increased risk of inappropriate consequences and decisions. We conclude that, while we could not document a pattern of individual ethnic bias, the built-in bias of having poor teachers, and teachers who hold untested preconceptions about families, can create an accumulation of negativity that increases the likelihood of special education placement for poor and culturally/linguistically diverse children.

Recommendations. Our recommendations are primarily derived from what we witnessed in schools that seemed to run more smoothly and equitably than other schools. First, administrators need to take into account how decisions affect all students, including those who typically are marginalized. Effective school leaders must be able to see the "big picture" and ensure that the conglomeration of programs and policies they enact make sense when implemented simultaneously and enhance rather than fragment the curriculum. High priority should be given to quality instructional time in class without interruptions (Berliner & Casanova, 1989; Leonard, 2001). Teachers should be assigned to classrooms in equitable ways that ensure all students have access to the most effective teachers and stimulating instruction.

School leaders should consider alternatives to suspension and put into practice discipline policies that are proactive rather than strictly punitive, such as in-house counseling support for anger management and other emotional/behavioral needs, positive reinforcement systems and behavioral supports, and increased relationship building with students and their families (Townsend, 2002; Utley, Kozleski, Smith, & Draper, 2002). We also recommend implementing alternative programs (other than special education) that provide students with more intensive, early assistance within general education, such as by using Title I funds in creative ways (Borman, 2000).

Given the propensity we noted among teachers and administrators to blame families for students' difficulties and to speak in disparaging ways about them, we suggest providing professional development for school personnel in proactive collaborative models that focus on finding common ground upon which to build and include parents in assessment, placement, and policy-making decisions. Efforts should be made to restore the balance of power in parent-professional discourse (Kalyanpur & Harry, 1999). The emphasis should be on families' and communities' resources and abilities, or "funds of knowledge," that can promote student learning and enrich schools and classrooms (Moll, Amanti, Neff, & González, 1992; Nieto, 1999). Parent liaisons can serve as cultural intermediaries who assist faculty in understanding community and family strengths.

Referral Process

Findings. In the referral process, there was a good attempt, on paper, to protect against inappropriate placement. However, it was evident that even full compliance with the letter of the regulations was not always tantamount to equitable or appropriate decision making. In most cases the process was not carried out as intended. In practice only cursory attention was given to pre-referral strategies. The ecology of the classrooms from which students were referred was ignored. Most students were pushed toward testing, on the basis of an assumption that poor academic performance or behavioral difficulties had their origin within the child and indicated a need for special education. There was tremendous variation in the quality of what transpired during referral or placement meetings. These differences were influenced by the intentions, knowledge, skills, and commitment of CST or multidisciplinary team members.

Recommendations. The referral process needs to include greater account-ability for appropriate and adequate regular-education instruction prior to the decision to evaluate a child. We recommend that CSTs take seriously the district's current charge to develop specific instructional objectives and strategies for each child brought to the team. Participants should be knowledgeable about a wide range of pre-referral interventions and devote sufficient time at team meetings to selecting the best strategies for individual students based on data collected by the teacher and others prior to the meeting. Pre-referral strategies should be varied and significant, such as providing individual tutoring through an after-school program. Teams should develop specific instructional objectives for each child, specify who is responsible for addressing these objectives, and establish the time frame in which they are to be monitored (Klingner & Artiles, 2003).

Even in this school district where so many personnel are quite knowledgeable about second-language issues, we noted a lack of attention to these issues during the referral process. We suggest that someone who is an expert in second-language acquisition be present at all CST and IEP meetings when the referred student is an English-language learner and that the agenda include a discussion of recommendations from the bilingual assessor or other language-acquisition expert (Ortiz, 1997).

Of great concern was our finding that almost no attention was paid to the ecology of the classrooms from which children were referred. We believe it to be of paramount importance that the classroom context be considered when discussing students' behavior and learning at CST and IEP meetings (Harry et al., 2002). Observations should be required to take place in the classroom of the referring teacher as well as in different settings. These observations should be completed by someone other than the classroom teacher for the purpose of determining whether the child's difficulties are being exacerbated by the classroom he/she is in (for example, with instructional practices or disciplinary styles that are not responsive to cultural differences) and whether the child seems to be receiving an adequate "opportunity to learn."

Special Education Services

Findings. The quality of special education services is the final but not least important aspect of the entire process. As has long been observed by the courts, scholars, and practitioners alike, if special education services were of high quality and were fully focused on the return of students to the mainstream wherever possible, there would be little controversy over placement rates. As in the case of general-education instruction, we found great variability in the quality of these programs and, in the schools with the lowest-income students, inappropriately large classes. However, the quality of special education teachers, although exceedingly variable, seemed to be more equitably distributed across schools than was the quality of general-education teachers. Finally, a crucial concern was the unduly restrictive placement of students designated ED and MR. Until special education can develop the reputation of a being a service designed to remediate and integrate students with learning and behavioral difficulties, it will continue to be a source of stigma and controversy.

Recommendations. We recommend decreasing class size in special education classrooms, particularly in resource or pullout programs, so that it is more likely that instruction can be tailored to the needs of individual students (Vaughn, Moody, & Schumm, 1998). Further, there needs to be additional preservice and in-service instruction for special education teachers, particularly in the areas of differentiated instruction and functional behavioral supports (Utley et al., 2002). We also stress the need to increase opportunities for students in self-contained classrooms to be in inclusive settings for a greater portion of their school day, with support, as stipulated in IDEA.

IN CONCLUSION: ATTENDING TO SCHOOL-BASED RISK

Some may argue that disproportionately large percentages of culturally and linguistically diverse students in special education simply reflect disproportionately large problems experienced by this population. Rather than assuming that intrinsic, family, or community risk factors account for excessive special education placement of minorities, we call on the field to attend to and address the prevalence of *school-based risk* for these children. Recognizing that children begin their academic careers with differential preparation for schooling, we contend that schools play a tremendous role in further directing the outcomes of these children. Schools must be prepared to meet children at any point on the continuum of learning, and begin there.

To return to the premise stated in the introduction to this book: To conclude that the children we saw being placed in special education were sufficiently deficient in cognitive or social/behavioral skills to warrant special education placement would require consistent evidence of their failure to progress despite appropriate and adequate instruction in supportive educational environments. This was by no means the case. We found a great deal of evidence of inappropriate and inadequate instruction and school-based decision making that increased the likelihood of special education placement for some children. In many cases, there was simply no way of knowing how children would have fared in more effective educational circumstances or with intensive instructional supports in the regular classroom. In many cases, also, the lack of standard criteria for referral to special education allowed schools to respond inappropriately to the pressure of local norms and high-stakes testing. We conclude that it cannot be assumed that high special education placement rates reflect genuine learning and behavioral deficits.

We are confident in our finding that the overrepresentation of minorities in special education programs is caused by much more than the existence of intrinsic or family based deficits. Indeed, the perception that a child is disabled results from a complex weave of widely varying beliefs, policies, and practices at all levels—family and community, classroom, school, district, state and federal government, and society at large.

In framing the problem so broadly we run the risk of seeming to frustrate those who are anxious for a quick fix or a clearly identifiable scapegoat. We believe, however, that to frame the problem more narrowly, seeking a simple answer in micro-level interactions or in monolithic constructs, such as racial or class discrimination, is to miss the opportunity to view the big picture. The overrepresentation of minorities in special education is not a phenomenon that exists in a vacuum. Indeed, minorities are overrepresented in many of the society's most detrimental circumstances, such as the justice system and among the homeless, while being underserved by the health care system and underrepresented in the nation's most powerful institutions, such as the U.S. Senate and the leading television networks.

Sociologist William Julius Wilson (1998) posited that an understanding of the Black-White test score gap must go beyond the assumption that "collective outcomes" are the result of the "properties of individuals" (p. 508). Citing discriminatory patterns in disparate areas such as housing, employment, government taxation policies, and corporate decisions regarding the location of industries, Wilson argued for attention to the "impact of relational, organizational, and collective processes that embody the social structure of inequality" (p. 508).

Clearly, racism is integral to these processes. But in education, as elsewhere, there are other belief systems that intertwine with racism and intentionally or unintentionally perpetuate it. Most detrimental is the hegemony of the norm—the society's determination to sort children by their perceived failure to fit into a prescribed schedule of personal and academic development. *The "normative" schedule, however, is not a matter of intrinsic ability. Rather, it represents the normative pace of children who have been prepared for certain learning milestones.* That norm is then imposed upon all who enter the schoolhouse door, notwithstanding the fact that neither communities nor schoolhouses offer equal opportunities to attain the norm. Special education, built on the criterion of intrinsic deficit, comes to be seen as the place where children who fall outside the parameters of the norm "belong." School personnel, anxious to locate the "right placement" for struggling students, invoke this criterion, expressing the opinion that "maybe there's something else going on"—some deficit, some intrinsic misconnection, some missing piece.

We conclude that, with regard to the high-incidence disability categories, special education's lofty intentions have been subverted by the fixation on identifying the "something else" and locating the correct box with the correct deficit label. Fraught with ambiguity and contradiction, the search for a disability results in errors that have lasting, detrimental effects on children. It is true that some children benefit from special education services as currently constructed. However, children who "fall through the cracks" of the categorical system are left to flounder, while well-meaning teachers throw their hands up in frustration. Children who inappropriately receive a disability label are introduced, at best, to what Gergen (1994) described as "a potential lifetime of self-doubt" (p. 151). At worst, these children are relegated to school settings that further isolate them from the world of their "normal" peers while failing to remedy their perceived deficits.

Because of the nation's continuing social structure of inequality, children at the receiving end of these errors are disproportionately the children of minorities. These structural inequalities belie the nation's wealth and global status, as does the overrepresentation of minority students in categories of deficit. We contend that special education should be an addition to, rather than a replacement for general education. We recommend that special education relinquish its search for intrinsic deficit and, in Lisa Delpit's words in the preface to this book, "teach children what they need to know."

References

Algozzine, B., Christenson, S., & Ysseldyke, J. (1982). Probabilities associated with the referral to placement process. *Teacher Education and Special Education, 5,* 19–23.

Ansell, S. E., & McCabe, M. (2003). Off target. *Education Week, 22*(17), 57–58.

Anyon, J. (1981). Social class and school knowledge. *Curriculum Inquiry, 11,* 3–41.

Artiles, A. J. (2003). Special education's changing identity: Paradoxes and dilemmas in views of culture and space. *Harvard Educational Review, 73,* 164–202.

Artiles, A. J., Rueda, R., Salazar, J., & Higareda, I. (2002). English-language learner representation in special education in California urban school districts. In D. J. Losen & G. Orfield (Eds.), *Racial inequity in special education* (pp. 117–136). Cambridge, MA: Harvard Education Press.

Artiles, A. J., Trent, S. C., & Kuan, L. A. (1997). Learning disabilities research on ethnic minority students: An analysis of 22 years of students published in selected refereed journals. *Learning Disabilities Research and Practice, 12,* 82–91.

Ballenger, C. (1992). Because you like us: The language of control. *Harvard Educational Review, 62*(2), 199–208.

Becker, H. S. (1969). *Studies in the sociology of deviance.* New York: Free Press.

Berliner, D., & Casanova, U. (1989). Effective schools: Teachers make the difference. *Instructor, 99*(3), 14–15.

Blair, C., & Scott, K. G. (2000). Proportion of LD placements associated with low socioeconomic status: Evidence for a gradient? *The Journal of Special Education, 36,* 14–22.

Bogdan, R., & Knoll, J. (1988). The sociology of disability. In E. L. Meyen & T. M. Skrtic (Eds.), *Exceptional children and youth: An introduction* (3rd ed., pp. 449–547). Denver, CO: Love.

Bonilla-Silva, E. (1996). Rethinking racism: Toward a structural interpretation. *American Sociological Review, 62*(3), 465–481.

Borman, G. D. (2000). Title I: The evolving research base. *Journal of Education for Students Placed at Risk (JESPAR), 5,* 27–45.

Bowers, C. A. (1984). *The promise of theory: Education and the politics of cultural change.* New York: Longman.

Bowles, S., & Gintis, H. (1976). *Schooling in capitalist America.* New York: Basic Books.

Bourdieu, P. (1986). The forms of capital. In J. Richardson (Ed.), *Handbook of theory and research for the sociology of education* (pp. 241–258). Westport, CT: Greenwood.

Bradley, R., Danielson, L., & Hallahan, D. P. (Eds.). (2002). *Identification of learning disabilities: Research to practice.* Mahwah, NJ: Lawrence Erlbaum.

Brady, N. C., & Halle, J. W. (1997). Functional analysis of communicative disorders. *Focus on Autism and Other Developmental Disabilities, 12*(2), 95–104.

Brantlinger, E. (2001). Poverty, class, and disability: A historical, social, and political perspective. *Focus on Exceptional Children, 33*(7), 3–19.

Bridgeland, W. M., & Duane, E. A. (1987). Elementary school principals and their political settings. *Urban Review, 19,* 191–200.

Bronfenbrenner, U. (1977, July). Toward an experimental ecology of human development. *American Psychologist, 32*(5), 513–531.

Brophy, J. (1986). Teacher influences on student achievement. *American Psychologist, 41*(10), 1069–1077.

Brown v. Board of Education, 347 U.S. 483 (1954).

Cartledge, G., & Milburn, J. F. (1996). *Cultural diversity and social skill instruction: Understanding ethnic and gender differences.* Champaign, IL: Research Press.

Clark, K. B. (1965). *Dark ghetto: Dilemmas of social power.* New York: Harper & Row.

Clark, R. (1983). *Family life and school achievement: Why poor Black children succeed or fail.* Chicago: University of Chicago Press.

Cole, M. (1996). *Cultural psychology: A once and future discipline.* Cambridge, MA: Harvard University Press.

Collins, R., & Camblin, L. D. (1983). The politics and science of learning disability classification: Implications for Black children. *Contemporary Education, 54*(2), 113–118.

Cummins, J. (1984). *Bilingualism and special education: Issues in assessment and pedagogy.* San Diego, CA: College Hill.

Darling-Hammond, L. (1995). Inequality and access to knowledge. In J. A. Banks & C. A. Banks (Eds.), *The handbook of multicultural education* (pp. 465–483). New York: Macmillan.

Darling-Hammond, L., & Post, L. (2000). Inequality in teaching and schooling: supporting high-quality teaching and leadership in low-income schools. In R. D. Kahlenberg (Ed.), *A notion at risk: Preserving public education as an engine for social mobility* (pp. 127–168). New York: Century Foundation Press.

Delgado, R., & Stefancic, J. (2000). *Critical race theory: The cutting edge* (2nd ed.). Philadelphia: Temple University Press.

Delpit, L. (1988). The silenced dialogue: Power and pedagogy in educating other people's children. *Harvard Educational Review, 58*(3), 280–298.

Delpit, L. (1995). *Other people's children: Cultural conflict in the classroom.* New York: New Press.

Diana v. State Board of Education, Civil Action No. C-7037RFP (N.D. Cal. Jan. 7, 1970 and June 18, 1973).

Donovan, S., & Cross, C. (2002). *Minority students in special and gifted education.* Washington, DC: National Academy Press.

Dunn, L. M. (1968). Special education for the mildly retarded: Is much of it justifiable? *Exceptional Children 35*, 5–32.

Edmonds, R. R., Frederickson, J. R. (1978). *Search for effective schools: The identification and analysis of city schools that are instructionally effective for poor children.* Cambridge, MA: Harvard University Press.

Eitle, T. M. (2002). Special education or racial segregation: Understanding variation in the representation of Black students in Educable Mentally Handicapped programs. *Sociological Quarterly, 43*(4), 575–605.

Elliott, M. (1998). School finance and opportunities to learn: Does money well spent enhance students' achievement? *Sociology of Education, 71*, 223–245.

Essed, P. (1991). *Understanding everyday racism: An interdisciplinary theory.* London: Sage.

Fass, P. S. (1991). *Outside-in: Minorities and the transformation of American education.* New York: Oxford University Press.

Ferguson, R. (1991). Paying for public education: New evidence on how and why money matters. *Harvard Journal on Legislation, 28*, 465–498.

Ferrante, J., & Brown, P. (1998). Classifying people by race. In J. Ferrante and P. Brown (Eds.), *The social construction of race and ethnicity in the United States* (pp. 109–119). New York: Longman.

Ferri, B. A. (2004). Interrupting the discourse: A response to Reid and Valle. *Journal of Learning Disabilities, 37*(6), 509–515.

Ferri, B. A., & Connor, D. J. (2005). In the shadow of *Brown*: Special education and overrepresentation of students of color. *Remedial and Special Education, 26*(2), 93–100.

Figueroa, R. (1989). Psychological testing of linguistic-minority students: Knowledge gaps and regulations. *Exceptional Children, 56*(2), 145–152.

Fletcher, J. M., Francis, D. J., Shaywitz, S. E., Lyon, G. R., Foorman, B. R., Stuebing, K. K., & Shaywitz, B. A. (1998). Intelligent testing and the discrepancy model for children with learning disabilities. *Learning Disabilities Research and Practice, 4*(13), 186–203.

Fletcher, J. M., & Morris, R. D. (1986). Classification of disabled learners: Beyond exclusionary definitions. In S. J. Ceci (Ed.), *Handbook of cognitive, social, and neuro-psychological reports of learning disabilities* (pp. 55–80). Hillsdale, NJ: Lawrence Erlbaum.

Fordham, S. (1988). Racelessness as a factor in black students' school success: Pragmatic strategy or pyrrhic victory? *Harvard Educational Review, 58*, 54–84.

Gay, G. (2000). *Culturally responsive teaching: Theory, research, and practice.* New York: Teachers College Press.

Gerber, M., & Semmel, M. (1984). Teacher as imperfect test: Reconceptualizing the referral process. *Educational Psychologist, 19*, 137–148.

Gergen, K. J. (1994). *Realities and relationships: Soundings in social construction.* Cambridge, MA: Harvard University Press.

Gillborn, D., & Youdell, D. (2000). *Rationing education: Policy, practice, reform and equity.* Buckingham, UK: Open University Press.

Giroux, H. A., & McLaren, P. (1994). *Between borders: Pedagogy and the politics of cultural studies.* New York: Routledge.

Goffman, E. (1963). *Stigma: Notes on the management of spoiled identity.* New York: Simon & Schuster.

Gonzalez, V., Brusca-Vega, R., & Yawkey, T. (1997). *Assessment and instruction of culturally and linguistically diverse students with, or at-risk of learning problems.* Boston: Allyn & Bacon.

Gottlieb, J., Alter, M., Gottlieb, B. W., & Wishner, J. (1994). Special education in urban America: It's not justifiable for many. *Journal of Special Education, 27*(4), 453–465.

Gould, S. J. (1981). *The mismeasure of man.* New York: Norton.

Gramsci, A. (1971). *Selections from the prison notebooks.* (Q.Hoare & G.N. Smith, Eds.). New York: International. (Original work published 1929–1935)

Gresham, F. M. (1993). "What's wrong with this picture?" Response to Motta et al.'s review of human figure drawings. *School Psychology Quarterly, 8*(3), 182–186.

Hardy, L. (1999). Building blocks of reform. *American School Board Journal, 186*(2), 16–21.

Harry, B. (1992). *Cultural diversity, families, and the special education system: Communication and empowerment.* New York: Teachers College Press.

Harry, B., Allen, N., & McLaughlin, M. (1995). Communication versus compliance: African American parents' involvement in special education. *Exceptional Children, 61,* 364–377.

Harry, B., Kalyanpur, M., & Day, M. (1999). *Building cultural reciprocity with families: Case studies in special education.* Baltimore: Brookes.

Harry, B., Klingner, J., & Hart, J. (2005). African American families under fire: Ethnographic views of family strengths. *Remedial and Special Education, 26*(2), 101–112.

Harry, B., Klingner, J., Sturges, K., & Moore, R. (2002). Of rocks and soft places: Using qualitative methods to investigate disproportionality. In D. J. Losen & G. Orfield (Eds.), *Racial inequity in special education* (pp. 71–92). Boston: Harvard.

Harry, B., Sturges, K., & Klingner, J. (2005). Mapping the process: An exemplar of process and challenge in grounded theory analysis. *Educational Researcher, 34*(2), 3–13.

Hart, J. E. (2003). *African American learners and 6-hour emotional disturbance: Investigating the roles of context, perception, and worldview, in the over-representation phenomenon.* Unpublished doctoral dissertation, University of Miami.

Heller, K. A., Holtzman, W. H., & Messick, S. (1982). *Placing children in special education: A strategy for equity.* Washington, DC: National Academy Press.

Heubert, J. P., & Hauser, R. M. (Eds.). (1999). *High stakes: Testing for tracking, promotion, and graduation.* Washington, DC: National Academy Press.

Hill, R. B. (1971). *The strengths of Black families.* New York: Emerson Hall.

Hilliard, A. G., III (1997). *Annotated selected bibliography and index for teaching African-American learners: Culturally responsive pedagogy project.* Washington, DC: American Association of Colleges for Teacher Education.

Hilliard, A. G., III (2000). Excellence in education versus high-stakes standardized testing. *Journal of Teacher Education, 51,* 293–304.

Hosp, J. L., & Reschly, D. J. (2002). Regional differences in school psychology practice. *School Psychology Review, 31,* 11–29.

Irvine, J. J. (1990). *Black students and school failure: Policies, practices, and prescriptions.* New York: Praeger.

Jackson, S. A., Logsdon, D. M., & Taylor, N. E. (1983). Instructional leadership behaviors: Differentiating effective from ineffective low-income urban schools. *Urban Education, 18,* 59–70.

Jacobson, S. L. (1989). Change in entry-level salaries and its effect on recruitment. *Journal of Educational Finance, 14,* 449–465.

Jussim, L., Eccles, J., & Madon, S. (1996). Social perception, social stereotypes, and teacher expectations: Accuracy and the quest for the powerful self-fulfilling prophecy. In M. P. Zanna (Ed.), *Advances in experimental social psychology, 28,* 281–388. San Diego, CA: Academic Press.

Kalyanpur, M., & Harry, B. (1999). *Culture in special education: Building reciprocal family-professional relationships.* Baltimore: Brookes.

Kavale, K. (1990). The effectiveness of special education. In T. B. Gutkin & C. R. Reynolds (Eds.), *The handbook of school psychology* (pp. 868–898). New York: Wiley.

Kellam, S. G., Ling, X., Merisca, R., Brown, C. H., & Ialongo, N. (1998). The effect of the level of aggression in the first grade classroom on the course and malleability of aggressive behavior into middle school. *Development and Psychopathology, 10,* 165–185.

Keogh, B.K. (2000). Risk, families, and schools. *Focus on Exceptional Children, 33*(4), 1–10.

Keogh, B. K., & Speece, D. L. (1996). Learning disabilities within the context of schooling. In D. L. Speece & B. K. Keogh (Eds.), *Research on classroom ecologies: Implications of inclusion of children with learning disabilities* (pp. 1–14). Mahwah, NJ: Lawrence Erlbaum.

Klingner, J. K., Ahwee, S., Van Garderen, D., & Hernandez, C. (in press). Closing the gap: Enhancing student outcomes in an urban professional development school. *Teacher Education and Special Education.*

Klingner, J. K., & Artiles, A. (2003). When should bilingual students be in special education? *Educational Leadership, 61*(2), 66–71.

Klingner, J. K., Cramer, E., & Harry, B. (in press). Challenges in the implementation of Success for All by four urban schools. *Elementary School Journal.*

Knoff, H. M. (1993). The utility of human figure drawings in personality and intellectual assessment: Why ask why? *School Psychology Quarterly, 8*(3), 191–196.

Kohn, A. (2000). Burnt at the high stakes. *Journal of Teacher Education, 51,* 315–327.

Kozol, J. (1991). *Savage inequalities.* New York: Crown.

Krei, M. S. (1998). Intensifying the barriers: The problem of inequitable teacher in low-income urban schools. *Urban Education, 33,* 71–94.

Ladson-Billings, G. (1994). *The dream-keepers: Successful teachers of African American children.* San Francisco: Jossey-Bass.

Lareau, A. (1989). *Home advantage: Social class and parental intervention in elementary education.* Philadelphia: Falmer Press.

Lareau, A., & Horvat, E. M. (1999, January). Moments of social inclusion and exclusion: Race, class, and cultural capital in family-school relationships. *Sociology of Education, 72,* 37–53.

Larry P. v. Riles, 495 F. Supp. 926 (N. D. California 1979), *aff'd,* 793 F.2d 969 (9th Cir. 1984).

Lee, D. R. (1982). Exploring the construct of "opportunity to learn." *Integrated Education, 20*(1–2), 62–63.

Leonard, L. J. (2001). From indignation to indifference: Teacher concerns about externally imposed classroom interruptions. *Journal of Educational Research, 95,* 103–109.

Leone, P. E., Walter, M. B., & Wolford, B. I. (1990). Toward integrated responses to troubling behavior. In P. E. Leone (Ed.), *Understanding troubled and troubling youth* (pp. 290–298). Thousand Oaks, CA: Sage.

Levine, M. (2002). Why invest in professional development schools? *Educational Leadership, 59*(6), 65–69.

Lomax, R. G., West, M. M., & Harmon, M. C. (1995). The impact of mandated standardized testing on minority students. *Journal of Negro Education, 64,* 171–185.

MacMillan, D. L., Gresham, F. M., & Bocian, K. M. (1998). Discrepancy between definitions of learning disabilities and school practices: An empirical investigation. *Journal of Learning Disabilities, 31,* 314–326.

McIntosh, Peggy. (1989). White privilege: Unpacking the invisible knapsack. *Peace and Freedom, 49*(4), 10–12.

McNeil, L., & Valenzuela, A. (2000). The harmful impact of the TAAS system of testing in Texas: Beneath the accountability rhetoric. In G. Orfield & M. L. Kornhaber (Eds.), *Raising standards or raising barriers? Inequality and high-stakes testing in public education* (pp. 127–150). New York: Century Foundation Press.

Mehan, H. (1985). The structure of classroom discourse. In T. A. Van Dijk (Ed.), *Handbook of discourse analysis* (pp. 119–131). London: Academic Press.

Mehan, H., Hartwick, A., & Meihls, J. L. (1986). *Handicapping the handicapped: Decision making in students' educational careers.* Stanford, CA: Stanford University Press.

Mercer, J. R. (1973). *Labeling the mentally retarded.* Berkeley: University of California Press.

Merton, R. (1948). The self-fulfilling prophecy. *Antioch Review, 8,* 193–210.

Miller, M., Strosnider, R., & Dooley, E. (2000). States' requirements for teachers' preparation for diversity. *Multicultural Education, 8*(2), 15–18.

Moll, L. C., Amanti, C., Neff, D., & González, N. (1992). Funds of knowledge for teaching: Using a qualitative approach to connect homes and classrooms. *Theory into Practice, 31*(2), 132–141.

Montague, M., & Rinaldi, C. (2001). Classroom dynamics and children at risk: A follow up. *Learning Disabilities Quarterly, 24,* 73–84.

Motta, R. W., Little, S. G., & Tobin, M. I. (1993). The use and abuse of human figure drawings. *School Psychology Quarterly, 8*(3), 162–169.

Muller, E., & Markowitz, J. (2004). *Disability categories: State terminology, definitions, and eligibility criteria.* Alexandria, VA: National Association of State Directors of Special Education.

Murphy, J. (1988). Equity as student opportunity to learn. *Theory into Practice.* 27, 145–151.

Murrell, P., Jr. (2000). Community teachers: A conceptual framework for preparing exemplary urban teachers. *Journal of Negro Education, 69,* 338–348.

National Academy of Sciences (NAS). (2002). *Unequal treatment: Confronting racial and ethnic disparities in health care.* Washington, DC: National Academy of Sciences.

Nichols, P. L., & Chen, T.-C. (1981). *Minimal brain dysfunction.* Mahway, NJ: Lawrence Erlbaum Associates.

Nieto, S. (1999). *The light in their eyes.* New York: Teachers College Press.

Oakes, J. (1985). *Keeping track: How schools structure inequality.* New Haven, CT: Yale University Press.

Oakes, J., Franke, M. L., Quartz, K. H., & Rogers, J. (2002). Research for high-quality urban teaching: Defining it, developing it, assessing it. *Journal of Teacher Education, 53,* 228–234.

Ochoa, S. H., Rivera, B. D., & Powell, M. P. (1997). Factors used to comply with the exclusionary clause with bilingual and limited-English-proficient pupils: Initial guidelines. *Learning Disabilities Research and Practice, 12,* 161–167.

O'Connor, C. (1997). Dispositions toward (collective) struggle and educational resilience in the inner city: A case analysis of six African American high school students. *American Educational Research Journal, 34*(4), 593–629.

Ogbu, J. U. (1987). Variability in minority school performance: A problem in search of an explanation. *Anthropology and Education Quarterly, 18,* 312–334.

Ortiz, A. A. (1997). Learning disabilities occurring concomitantly with linguistic differences. *Journal of Learning Disabilities, 30,* 321–332.

Ortiz, A., & Yates, J. (2001). A framework for serving English-language learners with disabilities. *Journal of Special Education Leadership, 14*(2), 72–80.

Oswald, D. P., Coutinho, M. J., Best, A. M., & Singh, N. N. (1999). Ethnic representation in special education: The influence of school-related economic and demographic variables. *Journal of Special Education, 32,* 194–206.

Parrish, T. B., Hikido, C. S., & Fowler, W. J., Jr. (1998). *Inequalities in public school district revenues.* Washington, DC: National Center for Education Statistics, U.S. Department of Education.

Pflaum, S. W., & Abramson, T. (1990). Teacher assignment, hiring, and preparation: Minority teachers in New York City. *Urban Review, 22,* 17–31.

President's Commission on Excellence in Special Education. (2002). *A new era: Revitalizing special education for children and their families.* Jessup, MD: U.S. Department of Education.

Pugach, M. C. (1985). The limitations of federal special education policy: The role of classroom teachers in determining who is handicapped. *Journal of Special Education, 19*(1), 123–137.

Reid, K. R., & Valle, J. W. (2004). The discursive practice of learning disability:

Implications for instruction and parent-school relations. *Journal of Learning Disabilities, 37*(6), 466–481.

Reschly, D. J. (2000). Assessment and eligibility determination in the Individuals with Disabilities Education Act of 1997. In C. F. Telzrow and M. Tankersley (Eds.), *IDEA Amendments of 1997: Practice guidelines for school-based teams* (pp. 65–104). Bethesda, MD: National Association of School Psychologists.

Reschly, D. J., Kicklighter, R. H., & McGee, P. (1988). Recent placement litigation, Part I, regular education grouping: Comparison of Marshall (1984, 1985) and Hobson (1967, 1969). *School Psychology Review, 17,* 9–21.

Rogoff, B., & Chavajay, P. (1995). What's become of research on the cultural basis of cognitive development? *American Psychologist, 50*(10), 859–877.

Rosenblum, K. E., & Travis, T. C. (2000). *The meaning of difference: American constructions of race, sex and gender, social class, and sexual orientation.* New York: McGraw-Hill.

Rosenthal, R., & Jacobson, L. (1968). *Pygmalion in the classroom.* Austin, TX: Holt, Rhinehart & Winston.

Sacks, P. (2000). *Standardized minds: The high price of America's testing culture and what we can do to change it.* Cambridge, MA: Perseus Books.

Sadler, J. Z. (Ed.). (2002). *Descriptions and prescriptions: Values, mental disorders, and the DSMs.* Baltimore: Johns Hopkins University Press.

Sameroff, A. J., Seifer, R., Baldwin, A., & Baldwin, C. (1993). Stability of intelligence from preschool to adolescence: The influence of social and family risk factors. *Child Development, 64,* 80–97.

Scheurich, J. J. (1998). Highly successful and loving, public elementary schools populated by low-SES children of color: Core beliefs and cultural characteristics. *Urban Education, 33,* 451–491.

Schneider, B. L. (1985). Further evidence of school effects. *Journal of Educational Research, 78,* 351–356.

Schwartz, M. A., & Wiggins, O. P. (2002). The hegemony of the DSMs. In J. Z. Sadler (Ed.), *Descriptions and prescriptions: Values, mental disorders, and the DSMs* (pp. 199–209). Baltimore: Johns Hopkins University Press.

Skiba, R. J., & Peterson, R. L. (2000). School discipline at a crossroads: From zero tolerance to early response. *Exceptional Children, 66*(3), 335–346.

Skrtic, T. M. (1991). The special education paradox: Equity as the way to excellence. *Harvard Educational Review, 61*(2), 148–206.

Sleeter, C. (1986). Learning disabilities: The social construction of a special education category. *Exceptional Children, 53,* 46–54.

Spencer, M. B. (1995). Old issues and new theorizing about African American youth: A phenomenological variant of ecological systems theory. In R. L. Taylor (Ed.), *Black youth: Perspectives on their status in the United States* (pp. 37–70). Westport, CT: Praeger.

Spindler, G. D., & Spindler, L. S. (1990). *The American cultural dialogue and its transmission.* London: Falmer.

SRI International (1995). *National longitudinal transition study of students in special education.* Menlo Park, CA: SRI.

Stanovich, K. E. (1991). Word recognition: Changing perspectives. In R. Barr, M. L. Kamil, P. Mosenthal, & P. D. Person (Eds.), *Handbook of reading research* (pp. 418–452). Hillsdale, NJ: Erlbaum.

Steele, C. M. (1997). A threat in the air: How stereotypes shape intellectual identity and performance. *American Psychologist, 52,* 613–629.

Strauss, A., & Corbin, J. (1998). *Basics of qualitative research: Techniques and procedures for developing grounded theory* (2nd ed.). Thousand Oaks, CA: Sage.

Tatum, B. (1992). Talking about race, learning about racism: The applications of racial identity development theory. *Harvard Educational Review, 62,* 1–24.

Townsend, B. L. (2002). "Testing while Black": Standards-based school reform and African American learners. *Remedial and Special Education, 23,* 222–230.

Townsend, B. L., & Patton, J. M. (2000). Reflecting on ethics, power, and privilege. *Teacher Education and Special Education, 23,* 32–33.

Trueba, Henry, T. (1989). *Raising silent voices: Educating the linguistic minority for the 21st century.* New York: Newbury House.

Tyack, D. B. (1993). Constructing difference: Historical reflections on schooling and diversity. *Teachers College Record, 95*(1), 8–34.

U.S. Department of Education (2001). *The longitudinal evaluation of school change and performance in Title I schools: Final report.* Washington, DC: Planning and Evaluation Service, Author.

Utley, C. A., Kozleski, E. B., Smith, A., & Draper, I. (2002). Positive Behavioral Support: A proactive strategy for minimizing discipline and behavior problems in urban, multicultural youth. *Journal of Positive Behavior Supports, 4,* 196–207.

Valencia, R. R., & Villarreal, B. J. (2003). Improving students' reading performance via standards-based school reform: A critique. *Reading Teacher, 56,* 612–621.

Vaughn, S., & Fuchs, L. (2003). Redefining learning disabilities as inadequate response to instruction: The promise and potential problems. *Learning Disabilities: Research and Practice, 18,* 137–146.

Vaughn, S., Moody, S., & Schumm, J. S. (1998). Broken promises: Reading instruction in the resource room. *Exceptional Children, 64*(2), 211–226.

Weber, G. (1971). *Inner-city children can be taught to read: Four successful schools.* Washington, DC: Council for Basic Education.

Wilson, W. J. (1998). The role of the environment in the Black-White test score gap. In C. Jencks & M. Phillips (Eds.), *The Black-White test score gap* (pp. 501–510). Washington, DC: Brookings Institution Press.

Ysseldyke, J. (2001). Reflections on a research career: Generalizations from 25 years of research on assessment and instructional decision making. *Exceptional Children, 67*(3), 295–309.

Ysseldyke, J. E., Algozzine, B., & Thurlow, M. L. (1992). *Critical issues in special education* (2nd ed.). Boston: Houghton Mifflin.

Index

Abramson, T., 26
Accountability, 11, 12, 14, 108, 111, 176, 180
Achievement, 7, 16, 67, 94, 100, 108, 112, 117, 161
  and BD, 148, 155, 157
  and disabilities as points on continuum, 8–10, 14
  and EH, 148, 155, 157
  and EMR, 123, 124
  gap in, 24, 182
  influence of teachers on, 56–69
  and LD, 134, 135–44
  and "qualifying" for special education, 96, 106, 107, 108
Administrators, 68, 108, 112, 154
  beliefs of, 95, 102
  and bilingual issues, 116, 118
  and "culture of referral," 95
  and discipline, 33–35
  findings and recommendations concerning, 173, 177, 178
  lack of support for teachers by, 32, 33–35
  and "qualifying" for special education, 96, 108
  and school structure, 32, 33–35, 38, 39
  and teachers as initiators of referrals, 97–98
  turnover among, 38, 177
  See also Principals
Ahwee, S., 177
Algozzine, B., 4, 97
Allen, N., 87
Alter, M., 97
Alternative strategies, 102, 105, 113, 114, 179

Amanti, C., 179
Ansell, S. E., 26, 177
Anyon, J., 23
Artiles, A. J., 5, 17, 122, 180
Assessment, 15, 22, 24, 115, 131, 133–35, 158, 173, 179. See also Psychological evaluations; Testing; specific test or disability
Austin (student), 49, 137–39, 144, 145, 157, 160

Baldwin, A., 16, 86
Baldwin, C., 16, 86
Ballenger, C., 53
Bay Vista Elementary School, 61–63, 94
Becker, H. S., 13
Beecher Stowe Elementary School, 25, 33, 35
Behavior, 6, 31, 51, 102, 112, 122, 125
  acting out, 50, 101, 168, 170
  bias and, 45–48
  and classroom arrangements, 48–49
  and culture, 42, 48–49
  disabilities as metaphor for explaining, 7
  and EH, 158
  and EMR, 124, 125, 129, 130
  and family identity, 73, 82, 84, 85
  findings and recommendations concerning, 179, 180, 181
  functional assessment of, 158, 181
  and high-incidence disabilities, 8–10
  and LD, 132, 133, 135, 136, 137–38, 139, 145
  and learning opportunities, 56, 63–67, 68
  and "qualifying" for special education, 96, 106

Behavior (*continued*)
  and referrals, 96, 179
  and school structure, 27, 29
  and special education as exile or
    solution, 168, 169–70, 172
  and students' variable behavior across
    settings, 63–67
  and teachers as initiators of referrals, 98,
    100, 101–2
  See also Behavior Disorders (BD);
    Classroom management; Discipline
Behavior Disorders (BD), 13, 22, 135, 146–
  58, 174, 182. *See also* Behavior
Behavior modification programs, 6, 167–
  68
Berliner, D., 179
Best, A. M., 17, 49
Bias, 5, 15, 16, 17, 40–55, 92, 98, 174,
  177, 178. *See also* Discrimination;
  Racism
Bilingual assessors, 114, 115–16, 117–18,
  119, 180
Bilingual issues, 113–22, 127–29, 130,
  170, 175, 176, 180
Blair, C., 16, 86
Bocian, K. M., 4, 5, 17, 125
Bogdan, R., 13
Bonilla-Silva, E., 41, 88
Borman, G. D., 179
Bourdieu, P., 87
Bowers, C. A., 87
Bowles, S., 23
Bradley, R., 134
Brady, N. C., 158
Brantlinger, E., 23, 39
Bridgeland, W. M., 39
Bronfenbrenner, U., 103
Brophy, J., 67
Brown, C. H., 158
Brown, P., 13
Brusca-Vega, R., 117

Camblin, L. D., 4–5, 124
Cartledge, G., 53
Casanova, U., 179
Chavajay, P., 8
Chen, T.-C., 86
Christenson, S., 97
Clark, K. B., 41

Clark, R., 86
Class size, 16, 26, 106, 109, 112, 144, 157
  findings and recommendations
    concerning, 173, 176, 181
  and special education as exile or
    solution, 160, 161–63, 164–65, 172
Classroom management, 96, 102, 104,
  137
  and BD, 147, 149, 150, 158
  and cultural consonance and dissonance,
    50, 53–55
  and EH, 149, 150, 158
  and EMR, 125, 129
  and ethnicity, 49–53
  findings and recommendations
    concerning, 174
  and learning opportunities, 57–61, 62,
    68
  and school structure, 24, 27, 29, 31, 33
  and special education as exile or
    solution, 161, 163
  styles of, 50–53
  and teachers as initiators of referrals, 98,
    100
  See also Discipline
Classrooms
  arrangements in, 48–49
  ecology of, 103, 104, 147, 154, 157,
    168, 179, 180
  findings and recommendations
    concerning, 178–79, 180
  perceived bias in, 48–49
  quality of, 154
  and referrals, 48–49, 179, 180
  and students' variable behavior across
    settings, 63–67
  See also Class size; Classroom
    management
Clementina (student), 125–28, 130, 161
Cole, M., 8
Collins, R., 4–5, 124
Community involvement specialists (CIS),
  75–76, 119, 120–21
Connor, D. J., 10
Corbin, J., 19
Coutinhoe, M. J., 17, 49
Cramer, E., 177
Creekside Elementary School, 57–61, 62,
  63, 94

Cross, C., 2, 3–4, 5, 8–9, 14, 16, 17, 41, 56, 85–86, 125, 134, 176
CST (child study team), 21, 38, 102, 135, 152
  and bilingual issues, 114, 115, 116, 118, 119, 120, 122
  and cultural consonance and dissonance, 49–53
  and EMR, 127, 128, 129–30
  ethnicity of, 49–53
  and family identity, 74, 75–76, 77, 81, 89
  findings and recommendations concerning, 179, 180
  and identity construction, 92, 93, 96, 99–100, 101, 102, 104, 105
  and learning opportunities, 59, 67
  members of, 49–50
  and "qualifying" for special education, 104, 105
  See also Placement; Referrals
Culture, 5, 8, 9, 93, 111, 129
  and bias, 42–48
  and cultural consonance and dissonance, 40–55
  and cultural hegemony, 41, 42–45, 55
  and documenting behavior, 45–48
  and family identity, 70–90
  findings and recommendations concerning, 175, 176, 180
  as mediator of discriminatory practices, 42
  of parents, 87–88, 90
  and "qualifying" for special education, 105, 106–7
  and race, 45–48, 88–89
  and "risk," 85–89
  school, 23–24, 93
  of school district, 39
Culture of power, 45, 67
Culture of referral, 24, 95, 113, 144
Cummins, J., 114–15, 116
Curriculum, 36, 53–54, 157
  findings and recommendations concerning, 173, 178–79
  and high-stakes testing, 111
  and school structure, 23, 26, 36, 38
  and special education as exile or solution, 160, 167–68
  See also Success for All (SFA) curriculum

Danielson, L., 134
Darling-Hammond, L., 26, 41, 177
Day, M., 87
Deficits, 7, 11, 18
  assumption of, 15–16, 90, 158
  cognitive, 68, 142
  family-based, 90, 182
  findings and recommendations concerning, 182, 183
  interpretations of, 16
  intrinsic, 8–9, 13, 15–16, 72, 103, 134, 158, 173, 174–75, 182, 183
  and LD, 10, 134, 135, 142
  and paradox of IDEA, 13
  and process approach, 16
  and school-based risk, 182, 183
Delgado, R., 16, 41, 88
Delpit, Lisa D., 45, 90, 183
Desegregation, 11, 18, 29, 49
Developmental delay, 3, 112, 125–30
Diagnostic and Statistical Manual of Mental Disorders (DSM), 13–14
Diana v. State Board of Education (1970), 10
Differential Ability Scales (DAS), 106, 142
Disabilities, 7, 92, 113
  constructing, 8–10
  definitions and criteria of, 103, 107–8
  and ethnic disproportionality in special education programs, 10–12
  and guidelines for referrals, 95–96
  high-stakes testing as filter for, 107–10
  low-incidence, 3
  as points on continuum, 8–10, 14
  and "qualifying" for special education, 103, 107–8
  and race, 10–12
  reified views of, 8–10, 18
  as stigma, 12–13, 22
  See also High-incidence disabilities; *type of disability*
Discipline, 151, 152
  findings and recommendations concerning, 173, 174, 178, 179, 180
  and parents, 34, 35–36
  and school structure, 24, 26, 32, 33–36, 38
  and support for teachers, 32, 178
  and teachers as initiators of referrals, 97–98, 100

Discrimination, 15, 40–41, 42, 68, 86, 87, 182. *See also* Bias
Donovan, S., 2, 3–4, 5, 8–9, 14, 16, 17, 41, 56, 85–86, 125, 134, 176
Dooley, E., 177
Draper, I., 179, 181
Duane, E. A., 39
Dunn, L. M., 2, 10

"Early response" strategies, 158, 160, 179
Eccles, J., 42
ED. *See* Emotional Disturbance
Edith (student), 147, 154–56, 157, 161, 167–68, 169, 170
Edmonds, R. R., 39
Educable Mental Retardation (EMR)
    accuracy of judgments in diagnosing of, 3
    and bilingual issues, 127–29, 130
    characteristics of, 4
    and culture/bias, 49
    and delayed development, 125–30
    and EBD, 124
    and EH, 170
    and "falling between the cracks," 123, 124–25, 131
    as high-incidence disability, 2–3
    and identity construction, 96, 106–7
    and IQ, 3
    and LD, 123, 124–25, 128
    and learning opportunities, 129, 131
    outcomes of, 161
    placement patterns and rates for, 2–3, 4, 19, 20
    and "qualifying" for special education, 96, 106–7
    reduction in use of, 4
    and special education as exile or solution, 161, 162, 163, 164, 170, 172
    stigma of, 4, 130
    See also Mild Mental Retardation (MMR)
Education for All Handicapped Children Act (EHA), 12
EH. *See* Emotional Handicap
Eitle, T. M., 49
Elementary and Secondary Education Act (ESEA), 11
Elliott, M., 176

Emotional Disturbance (ED)
    accuracy of judgments in diagnosing of, 3
    and BD, 146, 148, 153, 154
    and constructing disabilities in schools, 8
    and ethnic disproportionality in special education programs, 3, 4, 5, 6, 19, 20, 21
    and family identity, 78, 79, 81, 83–85
    findings and recommendations concerning, 181
    as high-incidence disability, 3
    and identity construction, 96, 100, 105, 106
    increase in diagnosis of, 4
    and LD, 132, 133–34, 137–38, 145
    outcomes of programs of, 14, 161
    and pattern of ethnic disproportionality in special education, 3, 5, 6
    placement patterns and rates for, 19, 20, 21
    and "qualifying" for special education, 96, 105–6
    and research process, 20, 21
    and special education as exile or solution, 161, 168, 172
    stigma of, 135
    and teachers as initiators of referrals, 100
    variability in definitions and eligibility criteria for, 5
Emotional Handicap (EH), 49, 105
    and BD, 146–58
    efficacy of, 156
    and EH concept as untenable, 158
    and EMR, 170
    exiting programs of, 150, 157
    and identity construction, 95, 97, 105
    and LD, 133, 134, 135–36, 138, 139, 145, 156, 157
    outcomes of, 161
    and program quality, 167–68
    and restrictive settings, 157, 169–70, 172
    and special education as exile or solution, 160, 161, 162, 163, 169–70, 172
    stigma of, 157, 160
EMR. *See* Educable Mental Retardation
English-language learners (ELLs), 113–14, 116, 118, 122, 128–29, 176, 180

ESOL, 44, 46, 58–59, 100, 170
and bilingual issues, 113, 114, 116, 117, 118, 121
and EMR, 126, 127–28, 130, 131, 170
and LD, 135, 136, 142
and school structure, 30–31, 36, 37
Essed, P., 41
Exiting, from special education programs, 100, 150, 157, 160, 171

"Falling between the cracks," 14, 123, 124–25, 131, 132, 134, 183
Family/parents, 6, 16, 21, 51, 102
and BD, 147, 149, 151, 152, 153–54, 155, 156
and bilingual issues, 119–21
blaming, 68, 179
conclusions about, 89–90
conferences with, 74–75, 76, 77–79, 102
configuration of, 78, 85–86
and culture, 50, 87–88, 90
and discipline, 34, 35–36
as "doing the best they could," 89
educational level of, 68, 76, 78, 89
and EH, 149, 151, 152, 153–54, 155, 156
and EMR, 126, 127
and exiting from special education programs, 171
findings and recommendations concerning, 178, 179
identity construction of, 68, 70–90, 103–4, 112, 178
and LD, 132, 133, 134, 136, 144
and learning opportunities, 68, 69
and nature/nurture argument, 71, 72–73
and paradox of IDEA, 12, 14–15
participation of, 74–77
and placement, 91, 92, 93
and "qualifying" for special education, 103–4
relationship building with, 179
and school structure, 24, 34, 35–36, 39
social capital of, 90
stereotyping of, 73–74, 112, 156
and teachers as initiators of referrals, 98, 99, 101
translation services for, 119–20
Fass, P. S., 10

Federal level, findings and recommendations concerning, 174–75
Ferguson, R., 26
Ferrante, J., 13
Ferri, B. A., 5, 10
Figueroa, R., 117
Fletcher, J. M., 5
Foorman, B. R., 5
Fordham, S., 42, 45
Fowler, W. J. Jr., 176
Francis, D. J., 5
Franke, M. L., 26, 177
Frederickson, J. R., 39
Fuchs, L., 144, 175
Funding/resources, 12, 23, 26, 175–76, 177, 179

Gay, G., 42, 50, 53
Gerber, M., 97, 104
Gergen, K. J., 15, 124, 183
Germaine (student), 132–33, 135, 136, 144–45, 157, 160
Gillborn, D., 111
Gintis, H., 23
Giroux, H. A., 43, 55
Goffman, E., 7, 13
González, N., 179
Gonzalez, V., 117
Gottleib, B. W., 97
Gottlieb, J., 97
Gould, S. J., 10
Gramsci, A., 42
Green Acres School, 24, 25–26, 27, 29, 30, 37, 39, 94, 172
Gresham, F. M., 4, 5, 17, 105, 125

Hallahan, D. P., 134
Halle, J. W., 158
Hardy, L., 26
Harmon, M. C., 11
Harry, B., 8, 19, 22, 53, 76, 87, 103, 175, 179, 180
Hart, J., 21, 76, 133, 154, 156, 170
Hartwick, A., 9–10, 17, 91, 92, 104, 111, 112
Hauser, R. M., 176
Head Start, 12, 83, 89
Heller, Kirby A., 2, 15, 159, 173
Hernandez, C., 177
Heubert, J. P., 176

Higareda, I., 122
High-incidence disabilities, 3–10, 14, 133,
    153, 162, 175, 183. *See also specific
    disability*
High-stakes testing, 95, 100, 144, 162
    findings and recommendations
        concerning, 173, 175, 176, 182
    and identity construction, 107–11, 112
    impact of, 7, 11–12
    and "qualifying" for special education,
        96, 103–4, 107–11
    and school-based risk, 182
Hikido, C. S., 176
Hill, R. B., 86
Hilliard, A. G. III, 86, 176
Holtzman, Wayne H., 2, 15, 159, 173
Home Language program, 36, 37, 120–21
Horvat, E. M., 23–24, 55, 87–88
Hosp, J. L., 5, 146
Hyper feelings, 36–38

"I am special" to chaos (exemplar), 64–67
Ialongo, N., 158
IDEA. *See* Individuals with Disabilities
    Education Act
Identity construction, 7, 9, 17
    and "culture of referral," 95
    discourse of, 91–112
    family, 70–90
    and guidelines for referrals, 95–96
    and high-stakes testing, 107–11, 112
    and placement patterns, 93–95
    and "qualifying" for special education,
        103–11
    rational model of, 92–93
    and school district of hyphenated
        identities, 18–21
    and teachers as initiators of referrals,
        97–102
Individualization, 17, 92, 102, 106, 139,
    157, 158
    findings and recommendations
        concerning, 181
    and school structure, 37–38
    and special education as exile or
        solution, 160, 161–62, 163–65, 172
Individualized education plans (IEPs), 11,
    21, 78, 105, 112
    and BD, 149, 153, 154
    and EH, 149, 153, 154

findings and recommendations
    concerning, 180
and LD, 143, 170
and special education as exile or solution,
    159–60, 162, 163, 165, 170
Individuals with Disabilities Education Act
    (IDEA), 12–15, 134, 157, 172, 174–
    75, 181
Instruction, 15, 51, 94, 98, 100, 102
    and BD, 148, 151, 152, 156
    differentiated, 181
    and EH, 148, 151, 152, 156
    and EMR, 125, 129, 130, 131
    findings and recommendations
        concerning, 173, 174, 176, 177–78,
        179, 180, 181
    and high-stakes testing, 109
    and LD, 133, 143, 144
    and learning opportunities, 56, 57–58,
        59–60, 61, 62, 63, 66, 67, 68–69
    and "qualifying" for special education,
        104, 109
    and school-based risk, 181
    and school structure, 24, 27, 29, 30
    and special education as exile or
        solution, 159, 160, 161–62, 163–66,
        168, 169, 172
    undifferentiated, 163–65
    See also Individualization
IQ, 16, 93, 96, 106, 117
    bias in tests for, 5
    and EMR, 3, 123, 124, 125, 127
    findings and recommendations
        concerning, 175
    and LD, 5, 132, 134, 135, 136, 138
    and school-based risk, 16
Irvine, J. J., 41–42

Jacintha (parent), 80–83, 88, 89, 152
Jackson, S. A., 39
Jacobson, L., 42
Jacobson, S. L., 26
James (student), 125–26, 128–30, 131, 161
Jussim, L., 42

Kalyanpur, M., 8, 87, 179
Kanita (student), 88, 100, 104
    and BD, 147, 148–51, 154, 157
    and cultural capital in racialized society,
        88

and ED, 53, 100
and EH, 147, 148–51, 154, 157, 161,
    167, 169, 170
and family identity, 83–85, 86, 89
and gifted program, 134, 149, 151, 157,
    161
and LD, 134, 145
and special education as exile or
    solution, 161, 167, 168, 169, 170
Kauffman Assessment Battery for Children
    (KABC), 106
Kavale, K., 22
Kellam, S. G., 158
Keogh, B. K., 16, 25, 55, 67, 69, 70, 124, 158
Kicklighter, R. H., 3, 12
Kindergarten, 96, 99–100
King, Martin Luther Jr., 1, 43
Klingner, J., 19, 22, 53, 76, 103, 175, 177,
    180
Knoff, H. M., 5, 105
Knoll, J., 13
Kohn, A., 176
Kozleski, E. B., 179, 181
Kozol, Jonathan, 23
Krei, M. S., 26–27, 177
Kuan, L. A., 5

Labeling, 12–15
Ladson-Billings, G., 51
Language programs/skills, 18, 36, 37, 142,
    162. *See also* Bilingual issues
Lareau, A., 23–24, 55, 87–88
Larry P. v. Riles (1979/1984), 3, 4, 10,
    125, 171
LD. *See* Learning Disabilities
Leadership, 25–26, 33, 39, 179. *See also*
    Administrators; Principals
Learning Disabilities (LD)
    accuracy of judgments in diagnosing of,
        3, 4, 5
    and achievement, 135–44
    and BD, 135, 156, 157
    and bilingual issues, 117–18, 122
    as catchall category, 125, 139–41, 144
    and class size, 172
    constructing, 8, 132–45
    and cultural consonance and dissonance,
        49
    definition and criterion for, 4–5, 67,
        133–35

and ED, 132, 133–34, 137–38, 145
and EH, 133, 134, 135–36, 138, 139,
    145, 156, 157
and EMR, 123, 124–25, 128
and exiting from special education
    programs, 171
and falling between the cracks, 132, 134
and family identity, 78
findings and recommendations
    concerning, 173, 174, 175, 182
as high-incidence disability, 2–3, 8–10
and high-stakes testing, 144
and identity construction, 94, 95, 96,
    100, 106, 110, 112
increase in use of, 4, 125
and IQ, 5
and learning opportunities, 67
and MR, 4–5
need for reconceptualization of, 5
outcomes of programs of, 14, 160–61
and paradox of IDEA, 14
and placement, 93
placement patterns for, 2–5, 19, 94
and premise of project, 22
and process approach, 17
as protective strategy, 133, 135–36
and "qualifying" for special education,
    96, 106
as relative to peer group, 136–39
and restrictive settings, 170–71
and school-based risk, 17, 182
and slow starters, 142–44
and special education as exile or
    solution, 160–61, 162, 163, 166,
    170–71, 172
and teachers as initiators of referrals, 99,
    100
"true," 140–41, 144
Learning opportunities, 22, 24, 56–69,
    100, 136, 142, 154, 166
    and classroom management, 57–61, 62,
        68
    and EMR, 124, 129, 131
    findings and recommendations
        concerning, 173, 174, 176, 178, 180
Lee, D. R., 67
Leonard, L. J., 179
Leone, P. E., 146
Levine, M., 177
Ling, S., 158

Little, S. G., 5, 105
Logsdon, D. M., 39
Lomax, R. G., 11
Lyon, G. R., 5

MacMillan, D. L., 4, 5, 17, 125
Madon, S., 42
Mainstreaming, 6, 168–71, 180, 181
Markowitz, J., 2, 5
Mathematics, 6, 11, 37, 109, 175
    and LD, 132, 136, 137, 142, 143
    and special education as exile or
        solution, 162, 163, 164–65
Matthew (student), 6–8, 66, 161
    and BD, 96, 147–48, 149, 157
    and bias, 48, 49
    dream of, 1–2
    and ED, 2, 6, 145
    and EH, 138, 145, 147–48, 149, 157,
        168
    and LD, 6, 137, 138–39, 144, 145
McCabe, M., 26, 177
McGee, P., 3, 12
McIntosh, Peggy, 43
McLaren, P., 43, 55
McLaughlin, M., 87
McNeil, L., 11–12
Mehan, H., 9–10, 17, 91, 92, 104, 111,
    112
Meihlss, J. L., 9–10, 17, 91, 92, 104, 111,
    112
Mental Retardation (MR), 2–3, 4–5, 6, 17,
    125–30, 163, 169, 172, 181. See also
    Educable Mental Retardation
Mercedes (student), 123, 124, 128, 131
Mercer, J. R., 2, 10
Merisca, R., 158
Merton, R., 42
Messick, Samuel, 2, 15, 159, 173
Milburn, J. F., 53
Mild Mental Retardation (MMR), 2, 4, 8,
    95. See also Educable Mental
    Retardation
Miles (student), 78, 89, 142, 143–44, 160
Miller, M., 177
Moll, L. C., 179
Montague, M., 158
Moody, S., 181
Moore, R., 103, 175, 180
Morris, R. D., 5

Motta, R. W., 5, 105
Ms. E (teacher), 51–52, 53, 100
Ms. L (teacher), 64–67, 68, 143, 149
Ms. Q (teacher), 46–48, 99
Muller, E., 2, 5
Murphy, J., 67
Murrell, P. Jr., 177

National Academy of Sciences (NAS), 2,
    3, 4, 8–9, 14, 15, 16–17, 41, 85–86,
    134
National Longitudinal Transition Study of
    Students in Special Education, 14
Nature/nurture argument, 71, 72–73
Neff, D., 177
Nichols, P. L., 86
Nieto, S., 179
No Child Left Behind (NCLB) act, 11, 112,
    173, 176

Oakes, J., 23, 26, 115, 177
O'Connor, C., 45
Office for Civil Rights (OCR), 2, 3
Ogbu, J. U., 42, 45
Ortiz, A. A., 117, 180
Oswald, D. P., 17, 49
Other Health Impaired (OHI), 3, 105, 153

Parents. See Family/parents
Parrish, T. B., 176
Partnerships, school-university, 177–78
Passive style, 50, 51–53, 65–66, 100, 149
Patton, J. M., 177
Paul (student), 135–36, 144, 161, 166
Peers, 136–39, 155, 156
Peterson, R. L., 85, 158
Pflaum, S. W., 26
Placement, 9–10, 22, 24, 39, 91, 102, 136
    criteria for, 12–13, 17–18, 173–74,
        175
    findings and recommendations
        concerning, 173–74, 175, 179
    main premise of, 92
    and paradox of IDEA, 12–13
    patterns of, 2, 3, 93–95
    and process approach, 15, 17
    as ratification of actions taken earlier,
        91
    rational model of, 92–93
    and research process, 19–21

and restrictive settings, 169, 170
and school-based risk, 17
and special education as exile or
    solution, 169, 170
and teachers as initiators of referrals,
    97–102
Post, L., 41
Powell, M. P., 115
Pre-referral activities, 15, 52
President's Commission on Excellence in
    Special Education (2002), 134
Principals, 48, 96, 167
    assignment of, 25–26
    and assignment of teachers, 30, 31
    constraints on, 29–30, 32
    findings and recommendations
        concerning, 177
    and firing of teachers, 31–32
    and high-stakes testing, 108–9, 110
    hiring and retention of, 23, 25, 26, 38,
        177
    influence of, 26, 38, 39
    and "qualifying" for special education,
        108–9, 110
    and school structure, 23, 25–26, 29–30,
        31–32, 37, 38, 39
    and special education as exile or
        solution, 162, 163, 171, 172
    See also Administrators
Process approach, 15–18
Psychological evaluations, 21, 84–85, 92,
    103
Psychologists, 6, 96, 97, 102, 160
    and BD, 146, 147, 148, 151, 153, 155,
        156, 157
    and bilingual issues, 114, 115–17, 118,
        119
    and EH, 151, 153, 155, 156, 157
    and EMR, 123, 124, 127, 129
    and high-stakes testing, 110
    and identity construction, 105–7, 111
    and LD, 132, 133, 134, 135, 136, 142,
        143
    philosophies of, 103, 105–7
    and placement, 91, 95
    and "qualifying" for special education,
        103, 104–7, 110
Pugach, M. C., 97

Quartz, K. H., 26, 177

Race, 5, 7, 18, 50, 97
    and culture, 45–48, 88–89
    and disability as parallel or converging
        discourse, 10–12
    and family identity, 87, 88–89
    and stereotypes, 85
Racial inferiority, 10, 12
Racism, 4, 5, 13, 40, 68, 112
    and cultural consonance and dissonance, 41
    and family identity, 87, 88–89, 90
    findings and recommendations
        concerning, 174, 182
    institutional and individual, 41
    as internalized by victims, 41
    and process approach, 16, 17
    and school-based risk, 17, 182
    and self-fulfilling prophecy, 42
    as structural issue, 41–45
    and teachers, 41, 44
    See also Bias
Reading, 6, 11, 96, 114, 151, 156
    findings and recommendations
        concerning, 175
    and LD, 132–33, 135, 140, 143, 171
    and "qualifying" for special education,
        109, 110
    and special education as exile or solution,
        160, 162, 163, 166, 168, 171
    See also Success for All (SFA) curriculum
Referrals
    and BD, 156, 157
    and bilingual issues, 113–22
    criteria for, 174, 175, 182
    and cultural consonance and dissonance,
        49
    and EH, 156, 157
    and ethnicity, 49–53
    findings and recommendations
        concerning, 174, 175, 179–80, 182–
        83
    guidelines for, 95–96
    and high-stakes testing, 110
    and premise of project, 22
    racial bias in, 40
    and school-based risk, 182–83
    and school structure, 24, 27
    teachers as initiators of, 97–102, 110
    variable rates of, 118–19
    See also "Culture of referrals";
        Placement

Reid, K. R., 5
Reschly, D. J., 5, 22, 146
Restrictive settings, 92, 136, 153, 156, 157
   findings and recommendations concerning, 174, 181
   and special education as exile or solution, 160, 161, 162, 168–71, 172
Retention, 26, 101, 143, 160
Rewards and punishments, 12, 31, 62–63, 82
Rinaldi, C., 158
Risk, 2–3, 4, 12, 55, 69, 136
   family/home-based, 16, 70–71, 85–87, 89
   findings and recommendations concerning, 178, 181–83
   individual, 70–71
   and process approach, 16–17
   school-based, 16–17, 25, 38, 69, 70, 181–83
   and school structure, 25, 38
   and stereotypes and cultural capital, 85–89
Rivera, B. D., 115
Robert (student), 88, 170
   and BD, 147, 151–54, 156, 157, 158
   and ED, 100, 105
   and EH, 147, 151–54, 156, 157, 158, 168
   and family identity, 80–83, 86, 89
   IEP for, 105
   and "qualifying" for special education, 104, 105
   and referrals, 100
   and special education as exile or solution, 161, 168, 170
Roberts Apperception Test, 84, 105–6
Rogers, J., 26, 177
Rogoff, B., 8
Rosenblum, K. E., 13
Rosenthal, R., 42
Rueda, R., 122

Sacks, P., 11
Sadler, J. Z., 13–14
Salazar, J., 122
Sameroff, A. J., 16, 86

Scales of Independent Behavior, 128
Scheduling, 24, 26, 36–38
Scheurich, J. J., 39
Schneider, B. L., 26–27
School district, 18–21, 39, 95, 134, 146, 174, 177–78, 180
Schools
   adversarial climate between home and, 70–90
   beliefs about special education of, 118–19
   and cultural capital, 23–24
   culture of, 93
   findings and recommendations concerning, 173, 174, 178–79, 181–83
   and individual agency, 23–25, 38, 39
   leadership in, 25–26, 33, 39
   quality of, 24, 95, 113, 162
   and school-based risk, 16–17, 25, 38, 69, 70, 181–83
   social contexts of, 124
   state rankings of, 1, 7, 12, 24, 39, 108, 111, 139, 144, 162, 171, 173, 176, 178
   structure of, 23–39
   See also specific topic
Schumm, J. S., 181
Schwartz, M. A., 13
Scott, K. G., 16, 86
Seifer, R., 16, 86
Semmel, M., 97, 104
Serious Emotional Disturbance (SED), 133, 169
SES (socioeconomic status), 16, 18, 19, 41, 98, 106, 146, 148
   and family identity, 75, 87, 90
   findings and recommendations concerning, 178
   and identity construction, 93, 94, 95, 106
   and LD, 137, 140
   and learning opportunities, 56, 63, 68
   and placement patterns, 20, 93, 94–95
   and school structure, 23, 24, 27
   and special education as exile or solution, 162–63, 166, 172
   and stereotypes, 85
SFA. See Success for All (SFA) curriculum

Shaywitz, B. A., 5
Shaywitz, S. E., 5
Singh, N. N., 17, 49
Skiba, R. J., 85, 158
Skrtic, T. M., 11, 12, 107, 111
Sleeter, C., 5
Slow starters, 10, 142–44, 160
Smith, A., 179, 181
Smith, Mrs (Grandma S.), 83–85, 89
Social capital, 71, 87–88, 90, 106–7
Social structure, 41–45, 182, 183
Special education
    as alternative to school failure, 14
    benefits of, 22, 159–67, 183
    emergence of, 10–11
    as exile or solution, 95, 159–62
    exiting from, 100, 150, 157, 160, 171
    findings and recommendations
        concerning, 171–72, 173–83
    goals of, 111
    and ideal versus reality, 112, 159–67,
        172
    ineffectiveness of, 174
    need for reconceptualization of, 175
    as negative thing, 119, 169–70, 171
    as protective strategy, 14
    "qualifying" for, 103–11
    quality of, 100, 131, 173, 180–81
    as scapegoat, 100
    stigma attached to, 18, 175, 181
    as support rather than alternative, 17–18
Specific Learning Disability (SLD), 2–3. *See
    also* Learning Disabilities
Speece, D. L., 67, 124, 158
Spencer, M. B., 42
Spindler, G. D., 42
Spindler, L. S., 42
SRI International, 14
Standards, 11–12, 51, 98, 107, 111, 139,
    176. *See also* Accountability; High-
    stakes testing
Stanovich, K. E., 5
State
    findings and recommendations
        concerning, 173, 174, 175–76, 178
    ranking of schools by, 1, 7, 12, 24, 39,
        108, 111, 139, 144, 162, 171, 173,
        176, 178
Steele, C. M., 42

Stefancic, J., 16, 41, 88
Stereotypes, 13, 156
    and cultural consonance and dissonance,
        40, 42, 54–55
    and family identity, 70–90, 112
    power of, 89
    and "risk," 85–89
Strauss, A., 19
Strosnider, R., 177
Stuebing, K. K., 5
Sturges, K., 19, 22, 103, 175, 180
Success for All (SFA) curriculum, 109, 140
    and bias, 53–54
    and EMR, 128, 129
    and referrals, 96, 98, 101
    and schedduling and interruptions, 36,
        37, 38
    and special education as exile or
        solution, 162, 163, 166, 167
Sunnybrook School, 18, 48, 94–95. *See
    also* Matthew
Suspensions, 34, 35–36, 82, 158, 178, 179

Tatum, B., 41
Taylor, N. E., 39
Teachers
    assignment of, 30–31, 38, 178, 179
    autonomy of, 111
    beginning, 33
    behavior of, 27, 29
    beliefs of, 95, 102
    bias of, 40–55
    desegregation of, 29
    effectiveness of, 11, 57–67, 68, 142, 166,
        172, 179
    ethnicity of, 29, 49–53, 99–100, 139,
        143
    expectations of, 42
    findings and recommendations
        concerning, 176
    firing of, 31–32, 38
    hiring and retaining, 26–32, 38, 39, 60,
        176, 177, 178
    incentives for, 34, 176, 177
    influence on achievement of, 56–69
    informal diagnoses by, 103, 104–5
    as initiators of referrals, 97–102, 110
    as making a difference, 160, 161
    philosophies and personalities of, 53, 98

Teachers (*continued*)
  preparation and professional
    development of, 30, 33–34, 60, 90,
    176, 177–78, 179, 181
  professionalism of, 46–48
  qualifications of, 56, 177
  quality of, 16, 24, 26–32, 39, 55, 56, 57,
    68, 125, 160, 165–67, 172, 173,
    176, 177, 178, 180–81
  racism among, 41, 44
  relationship between students and, 62–63
  shortages of, 160, 167, 172
  substitute, 167
  support for, 32, 33–35, 178
  "surplused," 29
  turnover of, 25, 26–27
  See also specific topic
Teaching styles, 49–53
Testing, 5, 18, 61
  and BD, 146, 148, 158
  and bilingual issues, 114, 116, 117
  cultural and linguistic diversity in, 105
  and EH, 158
  and EMR, 127–28
  findings and recommendations
    concerning, 179
  and LD, 132, 137, 138, 144, 171
  and learning opportunities, 61, 67
  limitations of formal, 105
  and mental testing movement, 10, 11
  purpose of, 116
  and "qualifying" for special education,
    103, 105–6, 110
  and special education as exile or
    solution, 162, 171
  See also Assessment; High-stakes testing;
    Referrals; *specific test*
Thurlow, M. L., 4
Title I, 75, 76, 179
Tobin, M. I., 5, 105

Townsend, B. L., 176, 177, 179
Translation services, 119–20
Travis, T. C., 13
Trent, S. C., 5
Trueba, H. T., 117
Tutoring, 101, 102, 109, 113–14, 123,
  144, 180
Tyack, D., 10

U.S. Department of Education, 41
Utley, C. A., 179, 181

Valencia, R. R., 176
Valenzuela, A., 11–12
Valle, J. W., 5
Van Garderen, D., 177
Varying Exceptionalities (VE) classes, 162–
  63, 171, 172
Vaughn, S., 144, 175, 181
"Very Good, Mah Man!" (exemplar), 46–
  48
Villarreal, B. J., 176

Walter, M. B., 146
Weber, G., 39
Weschler Intelligence Scale for Children
  (WISC)-III, 84, 106, 127, 136, 150
West, M. M., 11
Wiggins, O. P., 13
Wilson, William Julius, 182
Wishner, J., 97
Wolford, B. I., 146
Woodcock-Johnson scales, 128, 136, 142
Writing, 6, 138, 140, 141, 142

Yawkey, T., 117
Youdell, D., 111
Ysseldyke, J., 4, 97

"Zero tolerance" policy, 80, 158

About the Authors

Beth Harry is a professor of special education in the Department of Teaching and Learning at the University of Miami. Her research focuses on the intersection of culture, family, and disability. In 2002 she served as a member of the National Academy of Sciences panel studying ethnic disproportionality in special education, and in 2003 she received a Fulbright award to study the education of minority children in Spain. She completed her secondary education at St. Andrew High School in Kingston, Jamaica, received her bachelor's and master's degrees at the University of Toronto, and received her PhD from Syracuse University. After teaching in general education in Canada and Trinidad, she entered the field of special education in response to the birth of her daughter, Melanie, who had cerebral palsy. Also in response to Melanie's needs, Beth founded the Immortelle Center for Special Education in Port of Spain, Trinidad.

Janette Klingner is an associate professor at the University of Colorado, Boulder. She was a bilingual special education teacher for 10 years before earning her PhD in reading and learning disabilities from the University of Miami. She is a co–principal investigator for The National Center for Culturally Responsive Educational Systems and an investigator for the Center on Personnel Studies in Special Education. Her research interests include disproportionate representation and reading comprehension strategy instruction for diverse populations. She is the chairperson of AERA's Special Education Research SIG, a co-editor of AERA's *Review of Educational Research*, and an incoming Associate Editor for the *Journal of Learning Disabilities*. In 2004 she won AERA's Early Career Award.